Mothering Across Cult...

Memoirs for Lupus

Mothering Across Cultures

Postcolonial Representations

Angelita Reyes

University of Minnesota Press

Minneapolis

London

Part of chapter 1 originally appeared as "Using History as Artifact to Situate *Beloved*'s Unknown Woman: Margaret Garner" in *Approaches to Teaching the Novels of Toni Morrison*, edited by Nellie Y. McKay (New York: Modern Language Association, 1997); reprinted by permission of the Modern Language Association. Part of chapter 5 originally appeared as "From a Lineage of Southern Women: She Has Left Us Empty and Full of Her" in *Unrelated Kin: Race and Gender in Women's Personal Narratives*, edited by Gwendolyn Etter-Lewis and Michèle Foster (New York: Routledge, 1995); reprinted by permission of Routledge and Taylor & Francis.

Lines from Lorna Goodison's poems "For My Mother (May I Inherit Half Her Strength)" and "Nanny" are reprinted by permission of the poet.

Lines from the poem "For strong women" from *The Moon Is Always Female* by Marge Piercy copyright 1980; used by permission of Alfred A. Knopf, a division of Random House.

Lines from the poem "Ethnic Monitoring or a Geography Lesson" by Makilo Zahno used by permission of the poet.

Lines from ¡*dundunbanza!* (WCD041) Sierra Maestra used by permission and courtesy of World Circuit Records, UK.

Every effort was made to obtain permission to reproduce copyrighted material. If any proper acknowledgment has not been made, we encourage copyright holders to notify us.

Published by the University of Minnesota Press
111 Third Avenue South, Suite 290
Minneapolis, MN 55401-2520
http://www.upress.umn.edu

Library of Congress Cataloging-in-Publication Data

Reyes, Angelita Dianne.
    Mothering across cultures : postcolonial representations / Angelita Reyes.
        p.   cm.
    Includes bibliographical references and index.
    ISBN 0-8166-2351-1 (alk. paper) — ISBN 0-8166-2353-8 (pbk. : alk. paper)
    1. Blacks in literature.   2. Slavery in literature.   3. Women in literature.   4. Literature, Modern—History and criticism.   I. Title.
PN56.3.B55 R49 2001
809'.933520396—dc21   2001003296

Printed in the United States of America on acid-free paper

The University of Minnesota is an equal-opportunity educator and employer.

12 11 10 09 08 07 06 05 04 03 02   10 9 8 7 6 5 4 3 2 1

In memory of my mother,
Bettie Shields Reyes

Contents

Acknowledgments

Alice Walker described how the spirit of her ancestors supported her own creative energy for writing about her mother's memories and stories. Because of those connections to the past she was able to "gather up the historical and psychological threads of the life [her] ancestors lived, and . . . felt joy and strength and [her] own continuity." Likewise, I have been honored to have the strength of my ancestors who constantly gathered around me during the challenges and continuity of this research, fieldwork, and writing. I felt their joy and presence that was, indeed, enabling for my continuity.

I cannot count the ways in which many people have contributed to the successful completion of this book. They come from diverse backgrounds, ethnicities, and cultures. For their time and enthusiasm I thank my research assistants, Catherine Linstead, Cheryl Ting, and Jennifer Horne. I give many thanks to Tom Washington, Klass van der Sanden, Jenneke Oosterhoff, and April Knutson for their assistance with translations. For his technical expertise I give a special thank you to Reed Munsen at the University of Minnesota. I am very grateful to my editor, Richard Morrison, and the production team at the University of Minnesota Press for their time and energy regarding this project.

I am deeply appreciative to my multicultural Nottingham family who welcomed me and made my stay very wonderful. I thank the community who shared their beliefs and energy with me that kept ideas running and working. I thank the Nottingham Business and Technology Group for allowing me the opportunity to explore the issues of diversity, gender, and history with them.

I would like to acknowledge the generous support of the National Endowment for the Humanities Summer Fellowship, which was the catalyst for my fieldwork on marronage in Jamaica in 1988. I was honored with welcome by my Jamaican family of colleagues at the University of the West Indies, Mona. I thank them all for their support during my intermittent field trips to Jamaica and for introducing me to new concepts and ideas; I am especially delighted to have had the hospitality of Betty Wilson, Carolyn Cooper, and Maureen Warner-Lewis. I take great pleasure in thanking the staff at The West India Collection at the University of the West Indies, Mona, the National Library of Jamaica, and the Jamaica Archives in Spanish Town; and to Mrs. Eppie D. Edwards a special thank you for your efficiency and support. I am especially grateful to the Maroons of Moore Town for welcoming me into their community and for allowing me to experience their culture firsthand and learn from it.

For my archival work in Guadeloupe I am indebted to the director, Monsieur Jean Paul Hervieu, at the Archives départementales de la Guadeloupe, for his interest in my work and for his kindness; and I thank Madame Hervieu for her gracious hospitality. I am especially indebted to Madame Hervieu for keeping company with my six-year-old daughter when I was doing tedious work in the archives—*mille fois merci.*

I wish to acknowledge the financial support of the Historical Society of Pennsylvania and the Library Company of Philadelphia for that most productive research summer of 1990 in Philadelphia. Many thank yous to the Chief of Reference, Phillip Lapsansky.

This work could not have been completed without the generous support of a sabbatical, international travel grants, and two Faculty Summer Research Fellowships from the University of Minnesota. I am appreciative to the Council for the International Exchange of Scholars and the Fulbright Program for the Fulbright year in 1996–97 to the Republic of Benin, which enabled me to make the "return" journey of the flying African.

I take great pleasure in thanking the staff of the following libraries for their assistance and interlibrary loan support: the Edinburgh University Library, and the Mitchell Library in Glasgow; the Rigsarkivet (Danish National Archives) in Copenhagen; Yale University Libraries; and the

Ohio Historical Society. I would like to thank Jay Semel, director of Iowa House (now the Obermann Center for Advanced Studies at the University of Iowa) for providing very pleasant research facilities. I am also appreciative to the women's studies department at the University of Iowa for my year as a Rockefeller Fellow.

To many colleagues and friends I pour libations; to Barbara Webb as I remember the enduring nights that we talked for hours about the aesthetic and production issues of this project. You gave no thought to the telephone distance. You were with us during our mother's passing and you have been with me during the creation of this book. I thank you for your intellectual and moral support when I couldn't see the light at the end of the tunnel.

To Angelo Costanzo, I am much indebted for your support through the years and for putting me on the trail of Mary Magdalene and the eighteenth-century African Moravians. And thank you Janis Mayes for your sister help.

To the late Professor Charlotte H. Bruner, Iowa State University: she always encouraged me and I shall never forget our many talks and conference get-togethers.

To my students in the Women's Personal Narratives course through the years—they were sharp and savvy and offered intellectual nourishment—I pour libations.

To colleagues and students in Viv' Jeudi, our monthly series at the University of Minnesota on francophone research and pedagogy, I thank you for the camaraderie and intellectual stimulation that added to this study.

I pour libations: to my kin and unrelated kin family in Honduras I deeply thank you for my Garífuna heritage; I thank you for the gifts of *punta,* and memory-telling. To my father, Raimundo Hill Reyes, I thank you for the gifts of culture, language, marronage memory and history, for bringing the world to me even before I left home.

I pour libations to the kin, who must take immeasurable credit in helping me to attain this goal: my sister, Bernice Reyes Akinbileje; my brothers, Glenn E. Reyes, Thurston Reyes, and Raimundo M. Reyes.

And to my beloved daughter Alexandria, whose childhood innocence, cheerfulness, and unabashed zest for life opened doors for me during my earlier field trips to Jamaica, Guadeloupe, and Scotland; whose charm and curiosity and flair for languages were gifts. Sharing adventures was delightful and made me happy that you came into my world. And another special thank you for your patience: when this project labored and needed to give birth, you were satisfied to eat "breakfast things for dinner" because I had no time to cook. I pour libations.

For his expressed pleasure in being with me and coming into my life, and for his patience when I had to be at the computer doing all-nighters that became the wee hours of too many mornings, I pour libations to my dear husband Hilaire Moussougan.

To my kin who have recently joined the ancestors: Paul Shields Jr., George Venable, and our Aunt Bert, Bethenia Venable Rogers; I thank you for what you left for me in memory-telling and perseverance.

And to my beloved mother, Bettie Shields Reyes: Thank you for enabling me, the first born. You had so much to give, and I am empty and full of you; and even though you are no longer physically with me, you continue to be spiritually with me. I'm giving back and fulfilling memories, a mi madre a quien amo con toda mi vida.

INTRODUCTION

I'm Not Mad, I'm Postcolonial, a Woman, and a Mother

et aucune race
ne possède de monopole de la beauté, de l'intelligence, de la force
et il est place pour tous au rendez-vous de la conquête
[and no race has a monopoly on beauty, on intelligence, on strength
and there is room for everyone at the convocation of victory]
—Aimé Césaire, *Cahier d'un retour au pays natal*

Is there a line between middle-east and far east?
And where's nearly east?
And can't someone be black, Asian *and* far eastern?
In my colonial style geography books
With whole areas coloured empire pink
There was a line.
—Kamila Zahno, "Ethnic Monitoring or a Geography Lesson"

The title of this introduction, "I'm Not Mad, I'm Postcolonial, a Woman, and a Mother," is, in part, inspired from a line in Elizabeth Barrett Browning's 1848 poem, "The Runaway Slave at Pilgrim's Point." After killing her baby girl (an issue of rape) the protagonist, a fugitive slave mother, exclaims, "I am not mad, I am black." She asserts that her racial heritage is not the reason or substitute for irrationality. To what extent should we have compassion for a slave mother who, out of desperation, commits infanticide and then suicide? Browning wrote the poem for the abolitionist cause in the United States. The murder of a child by its mother would appear to most generations of readers as fanatical and irrational.

For Browning, however, real history intersects with the literary imagination. Browning's paternal family owned and operated sugar plantations in the West Indies during the nineteenth-century era of slavery. From them she had heard about a fugitive slave incident similar to the one she depicts in the poem. Browning voices the fugitive mother's blackness, or her plight as a slave, in terms of mothering, bondage, and miscegenation.

The subject who declares that she is not mad asserts her identity as a *rational* woman caught in slavery and with the *human* consciousness of what freedom means. Freedom. Freedom at the eighteenth- and nineteenth-century crossroads of the momentous European and African encounter was weighed down with economic rewards that overshadowed the moral consciousness about slavery. In this present historical moment many of us continue to negotiate the aftermath of colonialism as we are affected by the reverberations of postcolonialisms. We're not mad, we're women who have shared certain kinds of histories connected to colonization. We are connected through transnational identities, ideas, and values that are fluid and that overlap with our transcultural alliances.

What do we mean when we talk about postcolonial conditions? Before attempting to answer, I would like to address some potential concerns. My use of *we* is deliberate; it's a signifier for solidarity among women of color who are the progeny of slavery and colonization.[1] I have met women from other ethnicities "of color" (especially in Europe) who question its usage. Doesn't it put us in opposition to "white" women? Why does color have to be the essential determinant of identity? These challenging questions are justified. This term isn't meant to subsume particular ethnic identities, and the term doesn't have to put us in opposition to white women in Europe or the Americas. I like the term "of color," because it creates possibilities for networking and solidarity. My use of the term "of color," to echo Jamaican writer Michelle Cliff, affirms those aspects of history and culture that we were taught to despise; the image of color connects us to our shared global histories.

There are numerous discussions regarding the idea and usage of the term "postcolonial." It is not my intention, nor is it necessary, to engage in or summarize those critical responses and debates. Decidedly, redefining who or what identities are, for example, as new nations, dethroned patriarchies, or emerged ethnic groups, is a profoundly complex and debatable process. There should be a term better than "postcolonial" that can describe the dynamics of this collective heritage stretching across many time frames, cultures, and geographical boundaries. Just as we realize there are diverse definitions and theories of and ways to practice feminism, we can discuss the reverberations of colonial history and insist on attributes that empower us even as we continue to search for worthy decolonizing descriptions.

To highlight the idea of a new global consciousness and to recognize that there could be unity within the diversity of the human family, the epigraphs to this introduction include an image from Aimé Césaire's famous *Cahier d'un retour au pays natal:* "et aucune race / ne possède de monopole de la beauté, de l'intelligence, de la force / et il est place pour tous au rendez-vous de la conquête." The belief in the oneness of humanity, the equality of men and women, and the idea of unity in diversity does not constitute merely the enunciation of an ideal theoretical position. Rather, believing means that we know that an organic change is very necessary in the structures of present-day societies.[2]

Human rights activist Kathy Lee dealt with some of the gender issues of postcoloniality in a keynote presentation, "Prelude to the Lesser Peace." Lee discussed how we all are a part of a global upheaval because all of humanity is *pregnant* with new perspectives about world peace, racial unity, equality among men and women, and so on. She emphasized that most of humanity doesn't know that it's *laboring* to give birth to something wonderful. This pregnancy began in the nineteenth century with such events as the abolition of slavery, new inventions in science and technology, and women's suffrage. Humanity continues the labor pains of this monumental pregnancy that *will* come to term. Kathy Lee concluded her gynocentric metaphor by saying, "I used to live in South Africa. When a woman was eight or nine months pregnant, they would say she is '*highly* pregnant'! Well, our world is highly pregnant with its urgent need to deliver what will be the era of a most great peace that can only be realized when we no longer have the injustices that are still among us. It's never easy to give up anything familiar, even if it doesn't suit you anymore; it's a painful loss. We feel the loss when we give up prejudices until we grieve, give it up, and take on new ideas which replace the old." The postcolonial consciousness began in the nineteenth century and its momentum will continue to reverberate until humanity gives birth to new ways of being with each other in the world.

During nineteenth-century European expansion, there was a popular expression, "the sun never sets on the British Empire." Indeed, it was a painful loss for the British to slowly forfeit their empire and adopt a different policy toward emerging nations. As I write here in Nottingham, England, I'm fascinated by the fact that at one time the British had colonies in all hemispheres of the globe. The diverse ethnic groups living here in Nottingham are the progeny of that colonization. I've developed a friendship with an Indian woman; despite our fluency in other languages, we both have English as our primary language. We are political "minorities" in our countries. Although we may not like the semantics of "minority," it's forced on us by the media and by usage. I'm a "minority" in the United States and she's a "black minority" in the United Kingdom. We're also mothers and are trying to bring about distinct transformations that will make a better world for our children. Carole Boyce Davies highlights the "politics of location and geography" in relation to women of color as "migrating subjects" (*Black Women, Writing and Identity* 20). No one identity label characterizes all of our qualities as individuals. Many of us have migrated socially, psychologically, and logistically; we have married interracially and interculturally; we're single mothers, married mothers, adoptive and adopted mothers, other mothers, lesbian mothers, and childless mothers. We're trying to transform the old societies and the old ways of thinking. We believe that, as women and mothers, we're the first educators of children.[3] As the first caregivers, we're also the first teachers. Therefore, it is important that *we* have the education, through formal and nonformal learning, and are responsible not only to ourselves, but to our families and to our communities.

Because we are first teachers, our male and female children learn from us. First teachers are not adequate if they are ignorant or illiterate. Our children are distinct products of our beliefs and the way we act. We also forge new pathways for the next generation. Just as, early in their development, children can learn prejudices from those who interact with them every day, they can instead learn tolerance and can grow to appreciate difference. Many of us live with the hope and anticipation for our progeny that there will be better words to describe people's differences in nonracist and nonethnocentric terms. Whiteness is erased by whites. Blackness, however, is racialized. Nonwhites in the United States are consistently marked by the larger society from the viewpoint of race.[4]

This is an exciting time and also a challenging historical moment. To be the progeny of any once-colonized people means to be a modern-day complexity of different histories in different places and cultures. Government systems that can no longer operate and modes of thought that have outlived their own times are being dismantled; global, political, and cultural forces are still in a volatile flux. And both women and men are caught up in these crises of cultural representation and transformation. Edward Said states that "representation has thus had to contend not only with the consciousness of linguistic forms and conventions, but also with the pressures of such transpersonal . . . and transcultural forces as class, the unconscious, gender, race, and structure" ("Representing the Colonized" 206). Indeed, both representation and transformation, in the context of our contemporary lives, have complex implications. And certainly, as women coming from histories of colonization, we do not exclude our male kin who have also been a part of those same histories. In explaining and practicing our feminisms, we understand the extent to which we can align with our men because of the very system of colonization that has constructed systems of both racism and sexism. It's not possible for us to deny the role that racism has played in our history even as we investigate "truths" that will transform old ideas about gender and class. We can acknowledge the importance of past male thinkers, statesmen, and public intellectuals, even if some of these figures may have been less than insightful about our gender issues; they nevertheless addressed ideologies of colonization that also affected women's lives. We believe that there is room for both women and men at the convocation of global feminisms.[5]

Representation and transformation. How do we get people to consider new avenues for exploration and investigation into culture and ideas? How can we effectively move people into new ways of seeing and categorizing the world around them? What should we call each other collectively? Colonial legacies have influenced contemporary transnational identities, which further complicate how others view us. How do our transcultural identities inform ethnicity, class, and gender in the context of national alliances? How should we deal with outdated legacies of colonialism that persist despite the influences of progressive thinking and ideas that are conveyed by global technology? How can knowledge about colonialism and slavery empower us? To what extent have the legacies of slavery informed our contemporary identities as women?

I am reminded of the time when I was conducting field research among the Maroons in Jamaica. I met a young doctor who, having recently graduated from medical school in England, was in Jamaica doing research on sickle cell anemia. She has a Persian first and surname and is surprised that the Jamaicans think that she is "white." Shahnazz (not her real name) was born in Iran, then her parents migrated to England when she was four years old. She had never returned to the place of her birth. Even though she is a *British* citizen, the English do not consider her to be "English." Shahnazz says that the English and Britishers (the nonwhites in England) see her as a "woman of color." The English assume that she is from somewhere else even though England has been the only home in her memory. She doesn't even have the chance to make an "ethnic choice" because she is always from "somewhere else." Likewise, a third-generation Caribbean woman, Beryl, who was born in England, tells me, "No matter how much of this country [England] is in us, they will never allow us to be English." I hear the anger in her voice. For Beryl, representation is a painful reminder of color prejudices and colonial signatures that, she believes, should remain in the past.

How can there *not* be a crisis when migrating subjects attempt to situate and transform identities that are all-encompassing? Does this mean sheer madness for the migrating subject? How do people like Shahnazz answer the compelling question "who are you?" when they migrate to new places? Coming to terms with his own representation (his father is Cameroonian and his mother is French), tennis star Yannick Noah says that when he is in France, he is black; when he is in Africa, he is white.

We may view postcoloniality as a dynamic decolonizing process of change and continuity, not as a conclusive event in history marked by geopolitical boundaries and national flags. How then do we begin to transform ways of thinking so that we are not categorized by phenotype and other superficial indicators? The personal and political chameleons with which Shahnazz, Beryl, and Yannick Noah have to contend are everyday reminders of the colonial conditions that are being challenged, transformed, and decolonized across cultures.

What Does This Awl Mean?

I believe that writing takes a lot of courage. Many women writers have the courage to create new ways of interpreting history and culture. My particular approach to writing about women writers focuses on theory, practice, and the application of autobiography and memory through personal scholarship. How can we "do" theory so that it becomes meaningful enough to put into practice?

In her book *What This Awl Means: A Feminist Archaeology at a Wahpeton Dakota Village,* Janet Spector discusses how she mapped out a particular feminist approach to understanding the memory of an archaeological dig that she conducted at a nineteenth-century Indian village site in Minnesota. The awl is a perforating tool used to make holes in leather for sewing. The title of Spector's book is meant to indicate how personal and cultural artifacts highlight the accomplishments of forgotten or unknown Dakota women in Minnesota history. Awls could be beautiful tools with carved handles made from antler, wood, or bone. Spector writes, "I turned my attention to an artifact . . . a small antler awl handle, delicately inscribed with a series of dots and lines. I felt certain that a Wahpeton woman had once used that tool at Little Rapids and that its inscriptions conveyed a great deal about her accomplishments to those who understood their meaning" (18). Although small and seemingly insignificant, the awl was an important tool that Indian people used long before their contact with Europeans. To whom could the particular awl have belonged? Spector imagines how

> Mazaokiyewin used the sharp-pointed awl for punching holes in pieces of leather before stitching them with deer sinew. . . . When [she] had completed more complicated work, such as sewing and decorating a buckskin dress or pipe bag, she formed diamond-shaped clusters of four small dots which symbolized the powers of the four directions that influenced her life in many ways. She liked to expose the handle of this small tool as she carried it in its beaded case so that others could see she was doing her best to ensure the well-being of their community. (24–25)

With her approach to bringing a human quality to archaeology, Spector places the awl that she finds into an autoethnographic context and traces a memory that could have been.

What does this all mean for New World women of African descent? Our awls—our personal and communal artifacts—have dynamic meanings that may shift as we migrate culturally, psychologically, or geographically. And certainly our awls are taken with us and represent change as well as continuity and diversity. Even though we migrate, we shouldn't lose the awls that could be our artifacts of empowerment. We can't afford to forget context, association, and meaning. Our personal and communal awls have sometimes been lost or forgotten. We can find them as "texts" and return them to a meaningful context. We may not be trained archaeologists, but many of us retrace history and cultural memories in order to move forward. One of the awls that represent our history is that of mothering. This metaphoric awl contains the idea that we want to celebrate our potential as mothers and celebrate the women who mothered around us. Many of us believe that we are "mothers" even if we never have biological children. We are what I am signifying: the mother-women.

What do I mean by "mother-women"? Kate Chopin used the term in her 1899 novel *The Awakening*. The central character, Edna Pontellier, lives in a society that sanctifies "women who idolized their children, worshipped their husbands, and esteemed it a holy privilege to efface themselves as individuals and grow wings as ministering angels" (19). In that context, the biological/reproduction premise foregrounds mothering. The woman who mothers in that way is a long-sufferer for her children and husband: she's the ubiquitous angel in the house. When I first read Chopin's novel, I was simultaneously amused by and attracted to her use of the image of certain women as unsullied angels. I began to think about a revised image of the concept, that of mothering-women. The women of my New World history could not be angels in the house; nor could their ancestral mothers have been allowed that privilege. Reality was considerably different across cultures in the Americas. The revised image contributes to defining our heritage and lineages as we transform the residue of colonialism into agencies of empowerment across our cultures and national alliances. Our lineage is transcultural and transnational. In this narrative, lineage is past, present, and future. The title of this book, *Mothering Across Cultures*, accentuates the importance of transformation and decolonizing the representation of mothering. The connections are what Chinosole calls the "matrilineal diaspora" through which poet Audre Lorde celebrated "the house of self." The attributes of the matrilineal diaspora enable "the capacity to survive and aspire, to be contrary and self-affirming across continents and generations" (Chinosole 379). The significance of the matrilineal diaspora is central to this present exploration because the idea also engages women-centered histories of Africa and the diversity of its diaspora, and the autobiographical and biographical experiences of memory and history.

Mothering is a term that conveys the intensity of caregiving on many levels. Feminist mothering reclaims the roles of women even as it is also a human attribute. Harriet G. Rosenberg highlights the cross-cultural caregiving role of mothering in such a way that "caregiving is explained as a quality of human, not female, nature.... The web of caregiving ... moves well beyond the limited confines of the nuclear family. It is based in kinship/community ideology. It is not sentimentalized as a form of self-sacrifice" (Rosenberg 48–49).[6] Mothering, therefore, in this present context is meant as a caring of the mind, body, intellect, and culture of ourselves and our extended kinship of community within the diversity of the matrilineal diaspora. Decidedly, there is the kind of mothering—historical, biological, or other—that devours and destroys. Contemporary black women writers across cultures deal with these issues of fear and the detriment and determent of mothering. Whereas there is fear, according to Adrienne Rich, "in becoming one's mother" (57), Jamaican poet, Lorna Goodison celebrates the potential journey in becoming her mother. In *Mother Imagery in the Novels of Afro-Caribbean Women*, Simone A. James Alexander succinctly puts it this way:

> Amid this fear, the daughter is faced with the task of finding self, of becoming and creating a space where she is at home with herself. The search for self is "complete" when one has a sense of "home," when one has made peace with the mother and the mother's land. (25)

I connect with Alexander, who further writes that "this acquisition of 'wholeness' is achieved only with the help and nurturing presence of a mother who is defined by her spiritual mooring" (25). Indeed, it is in the moorings of spirituality and spiritual consciousness that the writers and historical figures that I have selected here search for wholeness across historical time and cultures. Mothering-women in this sense represent the womanism of wholeness and the vast possibilities for the once-colonized to achieve victory through self-affirmation.

American feminists have challenged traditional interpretations of mothering. In many instances, mothering has been rejected because of its reliance on the model of the biological mother whose primary responsibility is to raise her own children and offer an idealized, unchanging model of motherhood for her husband. It has meant subordination to others. Indeed, like Edna Pontellier, the ideal mother in middle-class, Euro-American culture had to be a "ministering angel." In that model, the responsibility for mothering lies with the biological mother for whom the role is exclusively "natural" and a mission of moral imperatives that embrace unconditional love and unconditional doing for others. Carroll Smith-Rosenberg describes the role of the middle-class mother as the guardian of religion and a paragon of virtue and morality. She discusses at length how these attitudes and beliefs were nurtured and strengthened in nineteenth-century Victorian America:

> Such a mother had the task of guiding the more worldly and more frequently tempted male past the maelstroms of atheism and uncontrolled sexuality. Her sphere was the hearth and the nursery; within it she was to bestow care and love, peace and joy. The American girl was taught at home, at school and in the literature of the period, that aggression, independence, self-assertion and curiosity were male traits, inappropriate for the weaker sex and her limited sphere. Dependent throughout her life, she was to reward her male protectors with affection and submission.... She was ... to remain a child-woman, never developing the strengths and skills of adult autonomy. The stereotype of the middle class woman as emotional, pious, passive and nurturant was to become increasingly rigid throughout the nineteenth century. (652)

Affection and submission were played out in the "nondeviant" feminine role of women as wives and biological mothers. The characteristics of the proper "American girl" remind me of Sojourner Truth's famous "Ar'n't I a Woman?" speech of 1851. In her speech Truth, as a former slave woman, had to assert herself in a way that the "American girl" could not:

> Dat man ober dar say dat woman needs to be lifted ober ditches, and to have de best place every whar. Nobody eber helped me into carriages, or ober mud puddles, or gives me any best place and ar'n't I a woman? ... I have plowed, and planted, and gathered into barns, and no man could head me—and ar'n't I a woman? I could work as much and eat as much as a man (when I could get it), and bear de lash as well—and ar'n't I a woman? I have born thirteen chilern and seen em mos' all sold off into slavery, and when I cried out with a mother's grief, none but Jesus heard—and ar'n't I a woman?[7]

Sojourner Truth challenged gender attitudes stipulated by nineteenth-century Euro-American society. Ahead of her time, she interwove race, class, and gender while abolitionists and women's rights advocates still saw these categories as mutually exclusive. Repeating the question "ar'n't I a woman?" throughout the speech for a resounding rhetorical effect, Truth forced her audience to think about what she was saying. Truth knew that her experiences and physical attributes made her capacity for being a woman rather profound. She never had the luxury of being a member of the socially defined weaker sex, a definition that created and glorified the American girl-woman. She understood that although she too was a woman, her body had been savagely denied the luxury of weakness.

Among women of African descent in the Americas there has been considerable variation in the definitions of mothering. In New World African cultures there are many ideas and practices of mothering based on cultural perceptions about kinship. During the early centuries of conquest and bondage in the Americas, newly arrived African women had to adjust the way they constructed and practiced family unity under the harsh and traumatic conditions of slavery. At that time, women were on mutual nurturing grounds with men trying to sustain family unity. The people believed that women were the first teachers of the children, thus women needed to be responsible and prepared for the role. They had these memories not only from women who mothered and the male kin who helped to sustain them, but from their traditions: hope, endurance, and the spirituality of their ancestors. What kind of spirit did the ancestral mothers leave for us? How do we rediscover the past in order to come to terms with our present historical moment? How does the past construct our feminist destiny? When will colonization cease to influence the construction of gender, race, and class? I use the concept of mothering-women to discuss transcultural and transhistorical mothering themes in novels by Toni Morrison (United States), Jean Rhys (Dominica/England), Simone Schwarz-Bart (Guadeloupe), and Mariama Bâ (Senegal). My approach to cross-cultural representations of mothering emphasizes how mothering itself intersects the cultural milieu and conditions of history and memory within the matrilineal diaspora. Through their writing these authors share their personal and collective awls with the experiences of history, race, ethnicity, class, generation differences, and gender. I conclude the exploration with an autobiographical text that locates my own sites of memory and culture through the voice of the woman who mothered me.

The concept of mothering-women summons Sojourner Truth's legacy. The concept also encompasses Alice Walker's paradigm of womanism. Implicit in Walker's assertion of womanism is the presence of the woman and girl-child as potential "mother." Empowered girl-children grow into women who learn how to assert themselves, who become "committed to the survival and wholeness of entire people, male *and* female." Walker also redefines what it means to act "uppity." When the girl-child becomes a woman and acts up, she is her own agent in a society that often denies her potentiality. She is "[t]raditionally capable, as in: 'Mama, I'm walking to Canada and I'm taking you and a bunch of other slaves with me.' Reply: 'It wouldn't be the first time'" ("Definition of a Womanist" 370). Indeed, when the mother-woman acts uppity, it is not the first time. The phrase "walking to Canada" signifies the escape from slavery into freedom, facing difficulties and meeting challenges, and it pays tribute to women of color who participate in the process of social and political transformations *without* leaving the family behind.

Women, regardless of ethnic heritage or prescribed racial identifications, can become mother-women; in good health, we have the capability to walk to Canada.

As individuals creating pathways into the new millennium, we want to act responsibly for ourselves, our families, and our societies. Yet we are not superwomen. Like the collective voice of an oracle of infinite knowing, we perceive that, indeed, *as an individual I love myself because there is no time for the long-sufferer. I have the capacity for many different roles and alliances across cultures. I am the professional woman and the working-class woman. I am the woman who stays at home as a first teacher. If I have ever been depressed and in the attic, I have come out. I am not there. I am the woman who gives counsel, and who seeks it. I am the woman who empowers herself to move off welfare. I theorize agency because I am the agent of transformation. I lose my patience and become exceedingly tired and feel very unloved. I am also the compassionate woman who is able to regain patience and be loved as if I have never been hurt or belittled, dehumanized and left out of histories—or out of the boardroom. I am the woman who believes in freedom and in claiming my choices as if my forebears were never enslaved or colonized and always had a choice. I am the woman who dances like nobody is watching. Along with my sisters and mothers of the world, I contribute to the diversity of inclusive feminisms from grassroots theories to transforming practices.*

> Guided by my heritage of a love of beauty and a
> respect for strength—in search of my mother's garden,
> I found my own.
>
> —Alice Walker

> A mi madre a quien amo con toda mi vida
> [To my mother whom I love with all my life]

This project began to grow as an inquiry into the theme of mothering across cultures through literature and autobiographical memory. Many events have taken place in my life since I first began thinking about the cultures of mothering. My scholarly ideas have been unabashedly influenced and shaped by the personal and transnational dynamics of my life in Europe, Africa, Latin America, the Caribbean, and the United States. Before I could finish this project, my own beloved mother passed on. My mother provided me with stability, education, a belief in myself, and a foundation for the opportunities life could offer. To echo Jamaican poet Lorna Goodison, may I inherit half of my mother's strength. My incredible mother had so many dreams and ambitions; she was not able to fulfill all of the personal ones. She deferred her dreams and sacrificed her ambitions so that I could have the opportunities to "jump at the sun." Mothering is an enormous responsibility that women of African ancestry have not had time to challenge or reject in order to protest sexism in our communities or in our larger societies. Most of our mother-women wanted their daughters to jump at the sun—nothing should stop us from pursuing the gift of life. My grandmother from Belize, Apolonia Estrada Hill, used to say in her Garífuna accent: "Aim for da moon, daughta, 'cause if you miss, you still among da stars."

On the one hand, during the decades of the sixties and seventies, theories about black women and mothering were often viewed in romanticized terms. Filomina Chioma Steady wrote about the overall biological heritage of women in traditional African societies:

> No doubt the most important factor with regard to the woman in traditional society is her role as mother and the centrality of this role for society as a whole. Even in strictly patrilineal societies, women are important as wives and mothers since their reproductive capacity is crucial to the maintenance of the husband's lineage, and it is because of women that men can have a patrilineage at all.... For African women, the role of mother is often central and has intrinsic value. (*The Black Woman Cross-Culturally* 29)

Mothering extends beyond those sociological and biological paradigms or the need to satisfy men who must have children at any cost.

On the other hand, how do we balance the traditions we need to hold on to with those intrinsic ones that should be left behind? Another generation of women writers and thinkers of African descent do not view women as inert mother-vessels. Edwidge Danticat, Tina Asa McElroy, Toni Morrison, Simone Schwarz-Bart, and Alice Walker are among the contemporary writers who assert the diversity of women's mothering roles. Mothering may begin with a woman's relationship to a child, but it can no longer simply end at that relationship. I agree with Johnnetta B. Cole, who writes,

> Among the rules of patriarchy are that all women are to be mothers, a rule applied to Black women no less than to White women. This ideal persists despite the fact that not all women are biological mothers and many women do not wish to be. What is of particular interest with respect to Black women in America is that racism and poverty frequently bring about situations in which many Black children will have surrogate mothers. These are the women who care for our young and fill in for mothers who cannot be there.... Many young African-American girls have multiple models of "mother." (*Double Stitch* xv)

The concept of having other mothers in the community is not unique for African American girls.[8] Among Caribbean, Latin American, and African societies as well, women often perform similar roles. In these cultures there has always been the other mother. Edith Clark's *My Mother Who Fathered Me: A Study of the Family in Three Selected Communities in Jamaica* is among the early studies that highlighted the role of other mothers in the extended kinship family in Jamaica in particular, and by extension throughout the Caribbean. Among Jamaicans, certain women in the neighborhood "yards" may be significantly referred to as "me odder madda."[9] Among the Garífuna in Honduras, an older woman who has arrived at a certain age and may not have had her own children is often called *abuela* (grandmother) by members of her extended family and community in their respect for her role as one of the revered other mothers. This is a personal title that carries prestige.[10] In such a capacity the honored woman is known as the other mother, *macomère* or *comadre*—the role that also extends the definition of godmother.[11]

We continue to create "feminine feminisms" that celebrate the fluid and diversified roles of mothering that move beyond the biological foundations of mother and child. When new perspectives of mothering across cultures are formulated and historical perspectives revisited, mothering will not be the biological *right* of passage. We will continue to mother our minds and intellect, a concept that Ruth Perry and Martine Watson Brownley illuminate in their collection of essays, *Mothering the Mind.*

The mothering terrain is often ambivalent and may at times seem to be contradictory. The heroine of Alice Walker's novel *Possessing the Secret of Joy* sits quietly in her therapy session. The psychotherapist is somewhat annoyed because Tashi has not responded to therapy and he tells her: "Negro women . . . can never be analyzed effectively because they can never bring themselves to blame their mothers" (18). That fictional observation is a slice of reality; many psychologists and other medical therapists believe that, regardless of race, culture, and class, relationships between mothers and daughters should be problematic. The remark made by the psychotherapist is comic irony because his therapy cannot succeed unless the patient "blames" and "indicts" her mother for her mental illness and the disruptions in her adult life. Debunking Western stereotypes of motherhood, psychologist Shari L. Thurer challenges what numerous American psychologists advocate:

> Psychological theories, especially those which have trickled down to a general audience . . . have not been kind to mothers. If a mother is too involved with her children, whatever that means, she is considered overprotective, stifling, or intrusive. If she is not sufficiently involved with her children, whatever that means, she is rejecting, cold, and narcissistic. Some psychotherapists are so sure that bad mothering is the cause of all later idiosyncrasies that they tend to discover it in every patient they treat. (xxi)

Like the doctor in *Possessing the Secret of Joy,* if modern psychologists cannot find blame for the problem, many of them will invent the bad mother and irresponsible (biological) motherhood. Yet, despite any ambivalence about mothering that mother-women of African descent in the Americas may have presented to their daughters, the importance of extended mothering provided the entire family with a source of refuge when the larger society failed and dismissed them. Mother-women continue to have connective and collective identities. We must not blame the mothers, because if we blame them, we also blame ourselves.

Ideas on mothering and motherhood, such as those initially posited by Nancy Chodorow, privilege individualism, separation from the mother, and autonomy rather than bonding and identification. Feminist writers and thinkers discuss the ambivalence of mothering when they find it difficult to identify with mothering in feminist arenas. In her essay "The World and Our Mothers," Vivian Gornick writes that mother-daughter relationships are complex and difficult because "our necessity, it seems, is not so much to kill our fathers as it is to separate from our mothers, and it is the daughters who must do the separating" (52). Responding to Gornick's assertions, Donna Perry writes that "this may be true of the fiction [and reality] of white women, but several women of color have immortalized successful struggles between mothers and daughters in fiction and autobiography. . . . Whereas Gornick and others, following the lead of modern psychoanalysis, claim that our greatest source of tension and conflict resides in the family, black women writers (and many writers of color) recognize that these familial tensions cannot be seen apart from the broader reality of racism" ("Initiation" 252). New World African communities, although frequently the source of male authority, are often the only source for family support away from day-to-day racism. Deborah Gray White explains that black women could deal with life by "falling back upon their families, the black female community, and the positive female identity that family and community helped to forge" (163). Mothering and its relationship to the family were until recently labeled by some feminists as the source of women's oppression. Our extended kinships provide that sense of place to which women of color can turn for solace and emotional support, even if the communities are not perfect. We unabashedly claim the women who mother us.

> We hold these truths to be self-evident, that all words are created equally; but, they are endowed by their authors with certain inalienable rights.

In 1776 Thomas Jefferson, not yet president of the United States, wrote the preamble and the text for the American Declaration of Independence. The preamble was etched out for posterity. Actually, it reads like, in part, like this: "We hold these truths to be self-evident, that all men are created equal, that they are endowed by their Creator with certain unalienable rights, that among these are Life, Liberty, and the pursuit of Happiness." We know that when the Declaration was signed and accepted by the newly formed Congress, all *men* in the new nation were not *treated equally*—slavery was still legal and no women or black men had the same rights as white men. From his beautiful Monticello estate in Virginia, Jefferson enjoyed his life, liberty, wealth, and pursuit of happiness while his slaves labored to ensure these things for him.[12] Yet just as Jefferson and other "founding fathers" used documents to formulate and engrave their beliefs, the people they enslaved began to write about *their* liberty and *their* inalienable rights. Despite laws throughout the Americas that forbade slaves to be literate, some slaves did learn to read and write. We know that literacy is a powerful tool that can become a weapon for the oppressed. Writing about the Haitian resistance to slavery, Jean Fouchard succinctly puts it this way: "A l'esclave sorti du rang, le maître confiera une scie, un violon, un pinceau, une mandoline. ... Mais il demeurait interdit d'avoir un syllabaire" [For a slave rising up through the ranks, the master provided a saw, a violin, an artist's paint brush, a mandolin. ... But it would remain forbidden for him to have a spelling book] (23). From their masters, they learned that reading and writing were rites of passage into the consciousness called humanity. And particularly in the United States, the slave narrative was one of the ways in which they could assert their *human* right to pursue life, liberty, and happiness.

Most slave narratives written by men were occupied with obtaining freedom and the adventure of the escape. Jean Fagan Yellin maintains that narratives written by women concentrated on their roles as mothers and protectors of their children. For example, the theme of Frederick Douglass's well-known *Narrative of the Life of Frederick Douglass* is about his early life as a slave, his preparation for escape, and his flight to freedom. But in *Incidents in the Life of a Slave Girl*, Harriet Jacobs (Linda Brent) postpones her actual escape from the South for seven years because of her children. Her role as a mother at that time is more important than escape. Jacobs's *Incidents* is a full narrative of her life before her escape, while Douglass's *Narrative* is an account of incidents in his life before he escapes. Nevertheless, the grandmother in both narratives, to the extent that she is able, fulfills the role of mothering.

The capacity of the grandmother is cross-culturally prominent in autobiographies and novels such as Maya Angelou's *I Know Why the Caged Bird Sings,* Nafissatou Diallo's *De Tilène au Plateau: une enfance dakaroise* (*A Dakar Childhood*), Zora Neale Hurston's *Their Eyes Were Watching God,* Simone Schwarz-Bart's *Pluie et vent sur Télumée Miracle* (*The Bridge of Beyond*), and Toni Morrison's *Beloved.* The grandmother provides what Senegalese writer Ken Bugul refers to in her autobiography, *Le Baobab fou* (*The Abandoned Baobab: The Autobiography of a Senegalese Woman*), as one of the reassuring landmarks of her life and culture. Writing about the grandmother in the Jamaican context, Michelle Cliff asserts that the powerful aspect of the grandmother originates in Nanny, the African warrior and Maroon leader. At her most powerful, the grandmother is the source of knowledge, magic, ancestors, stories, healing practices, and food. She is an inheritor of African belief systems, African languages. She may be informed with *àshe,* the power to make things happen, the responsibility to mete justice. ("Clare Savage as a Crossroads Character" 267)

Grandmothers, older aunts, sisters, and neighbor women often fulfilled the mothering role in the community and out of necessity performed as mother-women. Trinidad author Dionne Brand's short story "Photograph" movingly characterizes the kind of relationship that grandmothers as other mothers could have with their grandchildren:

All of the words which we knew belonged to my grandmother. All of them, a voluptuous body of endearment, dependence, comfort and infinite knowing. We were all full of my grandmother, she had left us full and empty of her. We dreamed in my grandmother and we woke up in her, bleary-eyed and gesturing for her arm, her elbows, her smell. We jockeyed with each other, lied to each other, quarreled with each other and with her for the boon of lying close to her, sculpting ourselves around the roundness of her back. Braiding her hair and oiling her feet.... We anticipated where she would sit and got there before her.... She had left us empty and full of her. (180)

Memory of the grandmother is another awl that summons intimate experiences that have provided recognizable cross-cultural strengths.

Perhaps strength is not the most appropriate word here because it has been negatively used to stereotype black women in the United States. Certainly for some people strength in a black woman is a negative characteristic. Much of the early social science research on the black family claimed that the "strong black matriarch" was the cause of its "destruction." That research ignored how people of African descent created their own unique ways of maintaining family unity. In his infamous study of 1965, "The Negro Family: Case for National Action," Daniel Patrick Moynihan wrote: "In essence, the Negro community has been forced into a matriarchal structure which, because it is so far out of line with the rest of American society, seriously retards the progress of the group as a whole, and imposes a crushing burden on the Negro male and, in consequence, on a great many Negro women as well" (quoted in Rainwater and Yancey 75). According to Moynihan and others who supported his position, "power" within the black family was shaped by the mother, the so-called matriarch, the misnamed, the "called out of name." The image of the "matriarch" was incorrectly identified as the source of the black male's social and economic disenfranchisement. The meaning of matriarch should define economic and political power in the same way that the term "patriarch" is used. In the African American historical context, black women have not been matriarchs. In the historical aftermath of slavery, the name of the African American mother continued to be manipulated through the ideology of a supposed matriarchy. Moynihan didn't understand what constituted the inner reserves of women of African descent. He didn't know that being an empowered woman is not the same as being a matriarch. "Black mothers," Patricia Hill Collins tells us,

> have a distinctive relationship to White patriarchy, they may be less likely to socialize their daughters into their proscribed role as subordinates. Rather, a key part of Black girls' socialization involves incorporating the critical posture that allows Black women to cope with contradictions. . . . Black girls have long had to learn how to do domestic work while rejecting definitions of themselves as Mammies. At the same time they've had to take on strong roles in Black extended families without internalizing images of themselves as matriarchs. (53)

I heard the following story among a group of friends. It illustrates the kind of fortitude that resonates as part of our collective past—the matrilineal diaspora. Toward the end of Reconstruction in the American South some members of the Ku Klux Klan visited a very pregnant woman one night. She lay in her bed almost ready to deliver her baby, when several of the hooded men forced entry into her little house. The Klansmen surrounded her bed and demanded to know the whereabouts of her husband. Her husband had been stirring up trouble in town by organizing the small black population and demanding certain kinds of social and political rights. Now the Klan was after him. They told the woman that she either tell them where he had gone or they would kill her and the unborn baby. The woman sat up in her bed and said, "Go ahead and kill me; I'm not telling you where he went." After much threatening and verbal abuse, they decided to leave without carrying out their threat. The only explanation that the woman could give for not being murdered that night was that, indeed, God was on her side. She was ready to die for the cause of justice. Perhaps the Klansmen realized her inner reserves and knew that she meant what she had said to them. The woman gave birth to a healthy girl-child. The daughter of that girl-child is alive today. She continues to tell her grandmother's story in order that we may know about destiny, determination, and the inheritance of our inner reserves.

After listening to such narratives, we may realize how insufficiently schooled much of white America, the other America, is in our suffering. The other America doesn't know how determined many of us are to make a better world for the next generation waiting to be born. This kind of empowerment is an attribute; it's the lineage of strength that Adrienne Rich describes as

> a kind of strength which can only be one woman's gift to another, the bloodstream of our inheritance. Until a strong line of love, confirmation, and example stretches from mother to daughter, from woman to woman across the generations, women will still be wandering in the wilderness. (246)

> Expensively kept, economically unsound, a spurious and useless political asset in election campaigns, racism is as healthy today as it was during the Enlightenment.
> —Toni Morrison, *Playing in the Dark*

The Age of Enlightenment initiated a profound intellectual and scientific upheaval in Western thought; its radical ideals replaced the anthropocentric worldview of Aristotle and the Middle Ages. The Enlightenment era also idealized the meaning of freedom. The inalienable rights of man, however, continued to be promulgated against the backdrop of world slavery. These rights of *European men* created, enhanced, and maintained slavery. "The concept of freedom," Toni Morrison reminds us, "did not emerge in a vacuum. Nothing highlighted freedom—if it did not in fact create it—like slavery" (*Playing in the Dark* 38). Contemporary historians, creative writers, and culture critics are among those redefining the ages of exploration and Enlightenment in order to reassess history and various truths connected to history. Rereading evidence is a search for new truths that may uncover information on the past. In particular, the slave experience in the Americas is rediscovered with remarkable energy and with, it seems to me, unprecedented interest. Much of this focus is on women and in redefining cultural artifacts, our interconnected awls of the past.

My field research on gender and slavery began with an initiation project commemorating the five-hundredth anniversary of Columbus's "momentous voyage" to the Americas. At that time I was researching the evidence of unsung eighteenth-century women in Jamaica, the island that Columbus "discovered" in 1494 during his second trip to the Americas. I searched for their personal stories because they had been lost in conventional history. I was not so much interested in the institution of their slavery as I was in uncovering some evidence of their personal definition and life stories.

How do we look for evidence in history when that very evidence could have been purposely hidden or ignored by the conquerors of history? James Wilkinson discusses how the "remains of the past comprise what survives of everything that ever happened; evidence consists of those remains that historians use in making histories. . . . The expanded definition of evidence is . . . a response to an expanded definition of history itself. As long as history was primarily a diplomatic and political record of the 'kings and battles' variety, evidence was primarily the written word—specifically, words written by those at or near the summit of the political hierarchy, where decisions were made and literacy prevailed" (80–81). My interests would focus on eighteenth- and nineteenth-century women who were illiterate and not in the recorded hierarchy. I therefore had to look for sources where evidence was not necessarily written down. I had to uncover different artifacts because illiteracy often prevailed; I had to look for other signs and directions of communication from the past.

> Ah wanted to preach a great sermon about colored women sittin' on high, but they wasn't no pulpit for me. . . . Ah said Ah'd save de text for you.
> —Zora Neale Hurston, *Their Eyes Were Watching God*

When Toni Morrison's novel *Beloved* was first published, I was attracted to the fugitive slave story of Margaret Garner on which the novel is based. Who was Margaret Garner? I couldn't find anything about Garner in the secondary history books, but during the course of my background research on slavery, I found Samuel May's little book, *The Fugitive Slave Law and Its Victims*. May's compilation referred to the 1856 references on Margaret Garner. I'd found the source that would lead me to other sources that would result in chapter 1, "Taking Flight and Taking Foot: From Margaret Garner to *Beloved*."

References to the Garner fugitive slave incident since the publication of Morrison's *Beloved* are based on literary hearsay or secondary sources that merge facts with fiction and legend. In chapter 1, I present a comprehensive account of the evidence surrounding the Garner case using primary sources from 1856 to 1867. The Garner incident was reported and debated in most of the antislavery tracts and newspapers in the United States, the West Indies, England, and Scotland. Antislavery societies in Glasgow and Edinburgh used the Garner case to help further the cause of abolition in the United States. (By 1856 England had already abolished slavery in its colonies.) Abolitionists of the time claimed that Garner was heroic. Was Garner a heroic slave mother? What *human* right did she have to take her daughter's life?

I use Toni Morrison's *Beloved* as a point of departure for discussing how the literary imagination can intersect with historical anecdotes and circumstances. But evidence can also be elusive. Obviously, nineteenth-century women like Garner did not and could not leave any nicely written narratives or legal briefs about the remarkable events in their lives. Because they were illiterate many of them could not write their own stories into history. Would they have wanted to? Would they have thought of leaving evidence for us, their historical descendants? In slavery, survival and resistance often depended on *covering up* evidence. Deliberate amnesia was a survival tactic. The people may have needed secrecy in order to gain a measure of stability in their unstable world. Many of their secrets will never be known.

Morrison says she was inspired to write *Beloved* because she was fascinated by a mother's love that could express itself in murder. I was fascinated by evidence in its relationship to the slave mother who would take flight, murder, and attempt suicide. What is the implication for morality here? Garner was not the first slave mother to commit infanticide; why should her story have been such a sensational one in 1856? Slavery corrupted slave owners but it also corrupted the enslaved. *Beloved* asks us to think about the past and the present: wherein lies the healing for both peoples? Morrison says, "Usually a book on slavery is about slave masters, the institution—a predictable plot. When I say *Beloved* is not about slavery, I mean that the story is not slavery. The story is these people—these people who don't know they're in an era of historical interest. They just know they have to get through the day. . . . they are try-ing desperately to be parents, husbands, and a mother with children" ("Five Years of Terror" 75).

The majority of the slaves (especially women) in the Americas left no written records of their interior motivations. We have to go to different sites that contain artifacts that might uncover things we have not known about. The artifacts invite us to discover clues in letters, diaries, photo-graphs, newspapers, cemeteries, old maps, and quilts.[13] The artifacts pro-vide interpretations of primary source materials that shed new perspec-tives on the past. How did women of African ancestry in the United States and in the Caribbean try to gain some control of their lives dur-ing slavery and colonialism? Knowing the past helps us come to terms with the present and helps us secure new foundations for the future. Such would be my application of research and practice.

My investigation into the Garner case involved the subjects of infanti-cide and suicide. I began to speculate about the folk motif known as the flying African. Stories about Africans who could fly are told throughout the New World. These legends and folk tales are about African people, brought to the Americas in bondage, who could fly or walk on the ocean in their attempt to return to their homeland. Newly arrived Africans sought freedom through marronage (living as fugitive slaves) or the re-turn to the homeland through death. Did Margaret Garner know about the stories of flying Africans?

What did these stories actually mean? What was the cover-up that the Africans so successfully managed? Here, I speculate (from the evidence of oral history accounts) that "to fly" is a euphemism, a utilitarian cover-up for "taking foot" (escaping) and for suicide. Saying that the people could fly was a deliberate attempt to misrepresent or encode what they, the survivors, knew was really happening. What Morrison calls "dismem-ory" was a kind of psychological protection—today we would call it a "defense mechanism"; their dismemory was self-inflected amnesia. In many instances, immediate memories of the actual Middle Passage were deliberately displaced or dismemoried because of this collective survival amnesia. Those who were left behind, the community of kin who did not commit suicide, became the interpreters and the mythmakers. They used their imagination to transfer the meaning and reality of death into the image of the flying African. The survivors could perform necessary rituals in remembrance of the ones who had dared to commit suicide;

they would subvert the horror of suicide in order to preserve what they believed would be the victim's safe spiritual passage back to Africa. Because taking one's own life was forbidden in their ontological beliefs, many slaves needed to conduct cleansing rituals when suicide occurred. For my purposes, I do not concentrate on the documentation or demographics of suicide, but on the encoding of suicide among New World slaves. I speculate on how the belief in the myth of the flying African may have acted as an agency of psychological and spiritual preservation for the survivors.

"Taking Flight and Taking Foot" places *Beloved* in dialogue with traces of this Middle Passage history: the virtual reality of the flying African as suicide, and the attempt for reconciliation with that history. The impact of the taboo (suicide) over a period of time leaves the community with repetitive tales and fantastic stories because the original trauma of suicide has been forgotten. *Beloved* is a story about recovering slaves, but it is also about recovering slave owners. As a very American novel, *Beloved* is both the story of a quest and a plea for reconciliation and recovery.

In chapter 2, "Surrogate Mothering: Maroon Nanny, Jean Rhys, and Marronage," I focus on the figure of an eighteenth-century African Jamaican, fugitive slave woman, Maroon Nanny, as a point of departure for discussing Jean Rhys's *Wide Sargasso Sea*. In the archives in Spanish Town, Jamaica, there is a copy of the deed that granted land to Nanny during peace negotiations with the British in 1741. Throughout the Americas marronage occurred when runaway slaves formed hidden enclaves of community and survival. Through archival research and fieldwork in Jamaica, Guadeloupe, Scotland, and the United States I investigated primary sources from slave records, ship logs, judicial records, unpublished journals, letters, land deeds, and eighteenth- and nineteenth-century broadsides in search of a different story that could highlight the integrity of Maroon legacies.

How is Rhys connected to Nanny? Jean Rhys and Nanny are "unrelated kin."[14] Their gender-oriented heritage adds to the complexity of their historical kinship. They both struggled for that sense of place they could claim as home. Rhys was a fugitive not only from her homeland, Dominica, but also from her island heritage. I discuss Rhys's novel, *Wide Sargasso Sea*, as an autobiographical extension of her personal and literary consciousness through the tropes of marronage, surrogate mothering, and gender alienation. Rhys, who died in 1979, seems to have found her own cultural recovery, her own cultural healing in the writing of her most acclaimed novel. I have placed Rhys's history next to Nanny's history. Living two centuries apart, Nanny was black and Rhys was a white Creole. "White" and "Creole" are flotilla words: the fluidity is, depending on the historical moment and place, a reflection of class, gender, and this thing we call race—all aspects of socially constructed relativity in motion. Who is Creole? Who is white in the Caribbean? Echoing Rhys, I would say damn few. Who is white, but poor? Who remains black *despite* being upper-class and educated? Rhys felt that being a white Creole who had "coloured relatives" carried emotional and cultural ambivalence. Whiteness continues to have more levels of interpretation in the Caribbean and Latin America than it does in the United States. How are "black" and "white" defined in racial terms? *Le Code Noir* (the Black Code) established by France in 1685 affirmed the superior position of Europeans in the Caribbean and by extension in the rest of the Americas. Even though *Le Code* may have defined the division between slaves and masters, it could not maintain the "purity of whiteness" because of the paradoxical intimacy that was inevitable between masters and slaves.[15]

Throughout her autobiographical writings, Rhys expressed her uncertainties toward race and race relations in the Caribbean. In many of her novels and short stories there is an autobiographical dialogue with her characters about her own ambivalence about race, gender, and powerlessness. Rhys creates this autobiographical dialogue not only with the landscape of the Caribbean, but with the character Christophine Dubois in *Wide Sargasso Sea*. A figure of intrigue in the novel's counternarrative, Christophine Dubois, former slave and surrogate mother, is the antithesis of the Rhys heroine. Whereas the central character, Antoinette Cosway, is not able to challenge inherent colonial oppression, Christophine acts as her own agent. Many choices are made by others for Antoinette because of the society's patriarchal, slavery-haunted system of values. Christophine, on the other hand, strives to make her own choices, even if they are limited. My analysis of *Wide Sargasso Sea* focuses on the role of Christophine in the text and in the context of Nanny's Caribbean landscape. Christophine holds a key to gender empowerment. Despite her hesitations about making Christophine an "articulate" black woman, Rhys must have admired her creation of this character. Christophine is written out of the heroine's life, but in keeping with the trope of marronage, her symbolic presence remains.

Chapters 1 and 2 focus on paradigms of mothering-women in specific historical and cultural contexts related to New World slavery. I highlight particular cultural anecdotes that serve as sources of representation for Morrison and Rhys. In chapter 3, "Refusing to Live on Scent: Textures of Memory by Way of *Pluie et vent sur Télumée Miracle*," I begin with a reconstructed autobiography of a West Indian slave woman named Magdalena. The Watcher is a first-person narrator who witnesses Magdalena inscribe herself into history through writing. The narrative that Magdalena writes is not "told-to" but is written "by herself." Eighteenth-century African Moravian slave narratives and petitions would become the harbingers of the more well-known nineteenth-century slave narratives written in the United States. In actual fact, a woman named Mary Magdalene wrote an autobiographical petition in Creole Danish to the Queen of Denmark sometime in 1739. Magdalene, an African woman born in what is now the Republic of Benin, was sold into slavery when she was a young girl. She was taken to the island of St. Thomas in the West Indies and there became a Moravian among the missionaries of the United Brethren. My portrayal of Magdalene is in the form of an eighteenth-century Moravian journal entry with an excerpt from the Magdalene narrative that was published in *The Proceedings of the United Brethren for 1739*. Magdalene's narrative (the full text is given in Appendix B) shows how an African woman had to adapt to the adversities of living in the New World as a slave. Many of the African-born slaves assumed new religions as they realized the hopelessness of seeing their homelands again. In the eighteenth century, as new cultures were forming in the Americas, women of African descent began to make significant choices regarding their own lives, which were fraught with indignities. Considering the male model of heroism, their choices may not seem heroic or particularly militant. Nevertheless, these mother-women in the Caribbean found inspiration and negotiated degrees of freedom. Literacy began the foundation for what Farah Jasmine Griffin refers to as "textual healing," because literacy allowed bonded people to "write themselves into humanity."

The opening fictional "memoir" of chapter 3 links Magdalena's story and Simone Schwarz-Bart's storytelling. Historically we have moved from the raw materials of literacy to the empowerment of writing. The fiction of Magdalena and the fiction of Télumée create a liaison between history and the creative imagination, and between history and memory.

From the outset of this chapter I want to highlight different levels of Pierre Nora's concept of *lieux de mémoire* (sites of memory). Whose memory is it? Wherein lies the invention of the memoir as testimony and memory in its relationship to our perspectives on history? Schwarz-Bart writes *Pluie et vent sur Télumée Miracle* as an inspirational narrative arising out of the folkloric landscape of Guadeloupe. The women and men struggle through their lives as poverty-ridden peasants, but their perseverance and hope are distinct and their spirit for living is forceful. Suffering has to be transcended, hence they refuse to live off the scent of life.

The narrative structure evokes archival memory. Remembering a particular woman named Fanotte helped Schwarz-Bart to create a collage of women she had known in her personal life or read about in history: "Ce n'est pas seulement sa vie, mais aussi le symbole de toute une génération de femmes connues, ici, à qui je dois d'être antillaise, de me sentir comme je me sens. Télumée c'est, pour moi, une espèce de permanence de l'être antillais, de certaines valeurs." [It's not only her life, but it's also the symbol of a generation of women that I knew, who made me be Caribbean, who made me feel as I feel. Télumée is for me a kind of permanence of Caribbean being, a certain kind of valor] (Toumson 14). Fanotte was not someone in the distant Middle Passage past for Schwarz-Bart: "Je l'ai connue pendant mon enfance.... Elle racontait sa vie comme quelque chose de nostalgique, de perdu, qui disparaîtrait á tout jamais" [I knew her during my childhood.... She would tell her life story as something nostalgic, something lost, which had altogether disappeared] (15). Fanotte's stories are the *learnings* (lessons of experiences) from which Schwarz-Bart creates and accentuates passages of textual healing. Furthermore, similar to Paule Marshall, who pays homage to the mother-women of her life, whom she fondly calls the "kitchen bards," Schwarz-Bart's storytelling creates ancestral *lieux de mémoire*.

In *A Room of One's Own,* Virginia Woolf was not impressed by women writers who "think back through [their] mothers" (79). There are those women who don't want to think back through their matrilineal past. And there are others who unabashedly remember the mothers. Chinosole's identification of the matrilineal diaspora embraces "that woman-centered power traced through [the] mother [and] sustained by loving women" (385). The loving women enabled themselves and the generations that would follow. The narratives of mothers—figurative, autobi-

ographical, or biographical—are central to our moving beyond the medi-
ocrity of survival. Elderly women of color often say to one another: "I
did the best that I could do for my children, in order to give them motherwit for life." We want to think back through the mothers because they
did the best they could do. We remember how much our mother-women
worked and provided nurturing grounds for us to move on. Alice Walker
writes about her "mothers' gardens" and describes southern women as
the "crazy saints" who could not realize their full potential as creators.
In writing back through her own cultural matrilineage, Schwarz-Bart
negotiates the tensions among memory, life-story, and colonial history.
The people who are still connected to that history must come to terms
with economic exploitation in its new forms: poverty inflicted on them
by the descendants of the slave owners and gender-oriented misery im-
posed on them by the men in and out of their lives. The Lougandor
mother-women struggle against the "rain and wind" of colonialism in
Guadeloupe. For them it is empowering to be able to think back through
the heritage and ancestral lineage of their mothers.

In chapter 4, "Crossing Bridges and Memory-Telling: *Une si longue
lettre*," I build cultural and historical bridges to an African text. Literacy
as empowerment in Magdalene's world is a foundation for the writing
of slave narratives as well as for the memories of Africa. What are the
recognizable transformations when we cross bridges to Africa? Whereas
in the previous chapter the eighteenth century is the setting for the
opening memoir, chapter 4 opens with what Pierre Nora calls a "real
environment of memory that lingers" on the island of Gorée. Gorée, off
the coast of Senegal, is history, place, and memory. If to some people
the island is a monument to slavery, how do we disengage it from the
wounding of the memory? Gorée may have a history to pass on, to echo
Toni Morrison in *Beloved*. Through memory-telling, however, we know
the past in order to empower ourselves for the future. I use Gorée as a
site of memory in order to situate Mariama Bâ's *mémoire* (the letter),
which tells us that we have to selectively and effectively disengage from
the past.

Mariama Bâ's novel, *Une si longue lettre*, is an epistolary narrative in
the first person. Remembering the words of Zora Neale Hurston, it's
one of the texts from on high. *Lettre* is about a Senegalese widow's emotional and spiritual redemption after the death of her estranged husband. What Eldred Jones wrote at the time of its publication in 1980 is

still relevant: "Mariama Bâ's first novel offers a testimony of the female condition in Africa while at the same time giving that testimony true imaginative depth. The distinguishing feature of this novel is the poise of its narrative style which reveals a maturity of vision and feeling. *Lettre* deals with the theme of women's emancipation in West Africa. But to say that it explores only the subject of emancipation is an oversimplification" (10). The novel is an excellent exploration of the complexities of mothering in a modern African nation. In this chapter I focus on a close reading of the text as representation. "No literature," writes Michelle Cliff, "can be understood as discrete from the culture from which it arises. Black women's literature embraces everything: it is visual, sonic, multilingual, percussive, explosive, Hollideist, Jamisonian, Hurstonian, Ida B. Wellesian, Hamerian, Bambaran—you get the drift. It should be read, or attempted, from the inside out, not from the outside in" ("Women Warriors" 20).

The central character of Bâ's novel, Ramatoulaye, finds herself in the difficult position of the contemporary non-Western woman caught up in a modern transitional society. She needs to express herself as a progressive woman who can oppose certain patriarchal traditions that would be detrimental to her and the progress of the next generation of women. How are the old ways modified? How do we embrace tradition as we disengage from those activities and values that no longer work for us? Her worldview becomes all-encompassing: she moves from a heightened awareness of herself, of the family, and of the nation. Ramatoulaye eventually sees herself connected to the larger domain of global feminisms. She is an educated, middle-aged widow and mother. Through the letter of memory-telling, Bâ allows Ramatoulaye to transform herself spiritually and emotionally. What kind of importance does the letter bring to memory-telling? Ramatoulaye reminds herself, "Le mot bonheur recouvre bien quelque chose, n'est-ce pas? J'irai à sa recherche. Tant pis pour moi, si j'ai encore à t'écrire une si longue lettre. . . ." (131) [The word "happiness" does indeed have meaning, doesn't it? I shall go out in search of it. Too bad for me if once again I have to write you so long a letter. . . ." (89)]. Through memory-telling the letter is written, and it becomes an artifact (or awl) in the milieu of Ramatoulaye's own foundation for healing.

Chapter 5 is the conclusion that explores autobiographical memory through my own mother's autobiographical narratives. The title "From

a Lineage of Southern Women: She Has Left Us Empty and Full of Her"
is inspired from Dionne Brand's short story "Photograph." My mother,
indeed, left me empty and full of her. When this project was near completion my beloved mother passed on. Johnnetta B. Cole states: "Because
of the countless ways in which individual mothers and daughters are
different, is it any wonder that Black mother-daughter relationships are
presented in all their various forms and stages of development? Mothers and daughters can be competitors or conspirators. Their relationship can be synergistic or parasitic; they can be adversaries or the closest
of friends and allies" (xiv). I was not only the daughter in our relationship, we were sister-friends. Many times when people saw my mother
and me laughing, teasing, and joking with each other, they said that we
acted more like sisters than like mother and daughter. A few days after
she died I started writing about her. I needed to write out the memories
of her in order to deal with my love and my loss, my emptiness and my
fullness. The memories would fill spaces of sorrow and upheaval. Writing memory helped to heal the wound of loss.

I believe my mother could have been one of Alice Walker's crazy
saints because, although she had wanted to write, she didn't—at least
not for a publisher's audience. Her writing was only the stuff of letters
and the wisdom of orality. But her writing and memory-telling were my
nurturing ground. She provided the sermon, the words and guidance
my siblings and I needed as touchstones. She provided the sermon; her
relentless work and energy enabled me to learn how to write the text.
I've tried to gather the legacies of some of her cultural awls into meaning.

My mother's memory-telling often held thousands of years in one
moment. I still hear my mother's speech patterns, feel her fears of the
outside world; I listen to her spirituality, and see her humbleness even
when she had validity for self-promotion in front of others. She lived in
the house of the matrilineal diaspora. I'd like to connect back, rather
than cast off, and pay homage to her inheritance of purpose, endurance,
and prosperity. Many of us are involved in collecting oral history and
connecting to the past through genealogical searches—in order to move
forward. Our sense of unrelated kinship arises out of the importance
we give to our learning stories, what Maxine Hong Kingston calls "talking story." My mother often told the story of how she had to fight on her
way to school. She did not articulate this little story as an episode of
gender, race, and class in a small East Coast town during the forties. In

order to attain that weapon of freedom, education, she simply had to fight certain white boys who didn't want black youth attending *their* high school. She would hide rocks in her lunch pail every day, because she never knew exactly when the boys would ambush her and her little brother on the road. How could anyone have wanted to harm that beautiful, soft-spoken schoolgirl who was to become my mother? Whenever I heard that story as a child I would feel sad and wonder what it was like to have to grow up in that social climate.

In her novel *The Autobiography of My Mother,* Jamaica Kincaid uses a sepia picture to reconstruct and parallel the narrator's memory of her deceased mother. As the story unfolds, the fragmented photo becomes a fully reconstructed picture. The title seems contradictory: how can it be *her* autobiography? We want to know whose story it is, the daughter's or the mother's? Are author, narrator, and protagonist one and the same? In order to come to terms with herself, the daughter-narrator must redefine her own memory of her mother and make it "an account of my mother's life," as it is also an account of her life. Is the daughter becoming her mother, as in Kincaid's previous novel, *Annie John*? In this novel, mother and daughter have the same name and the story belongs to both Annie Johns despite the antagonism between them. Near the end of the novel the narrator says, "She was my mother, Annie; I was her daughter, Annie" (105). Similarly, my memory/testimony takes the form of a shape-shifter—the text becomes someone else's memory—it's not my mother's autobiography, but rather an autobiography of my mother. Rememorying reveals how central the "politics of memory" is to configuring identity and values through oral and written narratives. In women's personal narratives, the autobiographical "I" may also be the autobiographical "we." Women's memories are both distant and belonging because they can represent those montages of public and personal awls.

CHAPTER ONE

Taking Flight and Taking Foot:
From Margaret Garner to *Beloved*

Everything I tells you am the truth, but they's plenty I can't tell you.
—Cato, Slave in Alabama, *Lay My Burden Down*

In the realm of the spirit, seek clarity; in the material world, seek utility.
—Gottfried Wilhelm Leibniz, *Theodicy*

The year is 1803. A group of African slaves has arrived on the shores of Georgia. Some are from Ouida and Abomey, but the majority are Igbo. They were shipmates during the horrendous voyage, despite their different languages and ancestors. For many weeks they had shared the same nightmares and the same unheard-of suffering. They don't know where they are—this place is as frightening as the black hull of stench that they were coming from. The noise and the strange languages of the men who have captured them increase as they disembark from the *Esperance*, the vessel that brought them here. A few days ago, they were given lemons and oil and were douched down and allowed to go up on deck. Men and woman, along with unborn children waiting inside of the beautiful women who had been victims of *la pariade*—the sexual merriment the crew had with the women just after they spotted land a few days ago— they look at their new surroundings as they hobble off the ship in chains. The morning sun is bright and the earth under their feet feels strange. They don't like it here; the salt air smells of more misery and calamity. One of the women, a technician of the unseen in her village, has brought her powers with her and she is able to see down through the passages of time. The future is her domain. She wants to tell her shipmates what is in store for them and their progeny. She sees how they will change and how some of them will hardly be able to recognize the children that the women will be forced to have with their captors. She wants to tell them that there are many terrible events that await them through many movements of time before the progeny will be able to overcome their oppression. She sees these things through the moments, year by year and century by century. The panoramic view is indelible. She is a woman of ancient science. The future is her domain. And she makes a decision. *We cannot stay here.* Her eyes lock into each set of eyes, and she speaks with her third eye and the spiritual language of return. She communes and consults like the technician that she is. Her shipmates become contumacious, and with one gesture of the seer's arm, they move in the opposite direction. Along with the defiant Igbos, they all agree to take foot back to their villages by walking into the ocean. Their captors are taken by surprise and can't stop the stepping Africans. In fact, the captors are frightened by the sudden tenacity, and the captors are weak in front of the Africans' moment of fortitude and resolution. The Africans leave but not without calamity and efforts to recapture them. And some were recaptured, and they became a part of the panoramic view that the woman saw. Their descendants tell the story of what happened:

> That happened in 1803. We still tell the story of the Georgia Igbos and, they say that if you sit near the mouth of Dunbar Creek on certain nights and listen closely, you'll hear the sound of the Ibos' rattling chains, along with the sounds of bare feet slapping against the dark waters. And, if you're not too frightened already, you may also want to keep an ear out for their solemn, defiant refrain as it drifts like a whisper through the marsh: "The water brought us the water will take us away."[1]

The story of the defiant African slaves at Dunbar Creek is also adapted by Paule Marshall in her novel *Praisesong for the Widow* and dramatized in Julie Dash's film *Daughters of the Dust.* In Marshall's novel, a little girl, Avey Johnson, does not believe her aunt Cuney's story about the "stepping Ibos": How is it possible for people to walk on the ocean without drowning?

> "Did it say Jesus drowned when he went walking on the water in that Sunday School book your momma always sends with you?"
> "No ma'am."

"I din' think so. You got any more questions?"
She had shaken her head "no." (40)

By comparing what the Igbos did to the phenomenon of Jesus walking on water, Marshall constructs an identifiable religious touchstone upon which Avey Johnson can accept the story—yes, the kidnapped Africans walked back to their homeland. Similarly, in Dany Bébel-Gisler's *Léonora: L'histoire enfouie de la Guadeloupe,* a ninety-eighty-year-old peasant woman, Anmann, recites a lament in Creole about African slaves who decided to return to Africa with the help of a shaman's magic. In part, she sings:

> Yo alé anhòo pon Boukan la
>   moun té ka pwan piwòg pou
>   alé Lapwent.
> "Apa èvè pyé annou nou ké alé asi lanmé."
> Afriken la té sav zafè a-i.
> Lè yo rivé anba pon la, i fè sòsyé
> a-i èvè zé la.
> On batiman parèt, flap!
> Yo pati, yo alé an Afrik.
>
> [They went to Moko Bridge, at
>   La Boucan, where the boats
>   leave for La Pointe.
> "We cannot walk across the sea
>   on our feet."
> But the African knew how.
> They went under the bridge. He
>   used his magic to break the two eggs.
> A large ship appeared
> They left and returned Africa.][2]

Versions of the walking-on-water motif are also among oral narratives collected by the federal Works Progress Administration (WPA) during the 1930s and 1940s in the southern United States. During that time WPA workers interviewed African Americans who were either direct descendants of slaves or who had been born into slavery about their cultural beliefs and practices and about their communal memories of Africa. Former slaves in Georgia retold the famous story of the group of Igbos who, disembarking on the shores of the new land, decided to rebel, and these old time stories continue to resonate: "The water will bring you back to us! The water will bring you back to us! / The water brought us the water will take us away" (Dominey 5). The story has become a legend of heroism and mysticism. Throughout the area of the Georgia and South Carolina Sea Islands, there are many legendary locations claimed for the "Ibo Landing." The actual incident took place in May 1803 along the shores of Dunbar Creek in Georgia.[3] Some people say the incident never happened. Whether it is based on fact or fiction, the story of the "steppin' Ibos" continues to be told among African Americans as truth. In 1938, Floyd White of St. Simons Island, Georgia, asked a WPA interviewer, "Heahd bout duh Ibo's Landing?" The interviewer replied that he had not, and Mr. White began to explain,

> Das duh place weah dey bring duh Ibos obuh in a slabe ship an wen dey git yuh, dey ain lak it an so dey all staht singin an dey mahch right down in duh ribbuh tuh mahch back tuh Africa, but dey ain able tuh git deah. Dey gits drown. (*Drums and Shadows* 175)

Floyd White describes a ritual process in which the Africans followed their leader to their deaths at a point on Dunbar Creek that later came to be known as "Ebo Landing" (*Drum and Shadows* 143). White, however, denies the legend its full import of mysticism because he states that "dey gits drown."

In contrast to Floyd White's interpretation, both Paule Marshall and Anmann (the Guadeloupean elder) maintain the legend's mysticism by insisting that the Africans did not perish. They are among the New World descendants who "know" that the Africans could, indeed, fly. Wendy Walters writes about "truths" that "demonstrate the struggle involved in revising hegemonic versions of history. As versions of superlative heroic resistance to the condition of enslavement, these stories cut across a recorded history which would deny such heroism. But the verbal emphases also indicate a reaction to a linear Western scientific mode of inquiry which would deny that people could fly" (Walters 9). How can familiar myths offer new interpretations about the past? Myths are parts of our worldview and they attempt to define truths as they enable us to understand the conflict and worldview of the past. At the intersection of oral history and the creative imagination, the legend that began at Dunbar Creek maintains that the Igbos did not drown. To claim otherwise would mean that the slaves failed to return to Africa. To acknowledge that the Africans, in fact, perished (as Mr. White said they did) makes the event less mystical and not at all empowering. A feat that sounds wonderfully magical and successful (to walk on water) is impossible at the levels of logical understanding and acceptance. On the other hand, to insist that the slaves did not drown and *could not* drown is to recognize the empowerment of believing *in mythic truth:* The Africans *did* accomplish their mission, or as they would say in the Caribbean during slavery times, "take foot dem"—they returned to Africa. And many of them knew that they could take spiritual flight from slavery.

Along with the idea of taking foot and returning to Africa by stepping across the ocean is the well-known legend about the "flying Africans," the people who could fly back to Africa. The legend of the flying African has not only drawn the attention of folklorists and anthropologists but has also fascinated writers and literary critics. Some literary works that use the motif depict slaves who escape from a plantation where they are empowered by a spiritual leader or sorcerer to fly away. In Julius Lester's recreated tale "People Who Could Fly," a shaman helps his people, who are working in the field, take flight back to Africa through the power of the word: "He uttered the strange word, and all of the Africans dropped their hoes, stretched out their arms, and flew away, back to their home, back to Africa" (152). In Virginia Hamilton's version of the story, the shaman, Toby, whispers the magic words as "[h]e raised his arms, holding them.... '*Kum...yali, kum buba tambe,*' and more magic words, said so quickly, they sounded like whispers and sighs." A slave woman hears his chant, which empowers her to ascend to the sky with her "child held now tightly in her arms. Then she felt the magic, the African mystery" (169).

The mystery of the flying African has usually been explained in romantic terms as the symbolic flight from slavery to political freedom. Could the motif have functioned with a more hidden meaning? Historian Michael Craton asserts that, in many areas, we only have snippets of information left to us from the most intimate realities of the slaves' lives.[4] Those of us who are interested in evidence and truth (and truth is not necessarily synonymous with documented facts) to reconstruct the slaves' own perspectives have to rely on pieces of information and intangible artifacts that remain accessible.

As listeners and readers of the folk stories of the flying African, we are expected to suspend our disbelief and accept the stories that empowered flight. Some contemporary readers have even addressed the actual implications of such a human impossibility. Within the multifaceted implications of the New World African legend, the act of flying is a clandestine and liberating agent. The question, of course, is not whether the early African slaves, who after all were human, could fly; the question becomes an investigation into how the depiction of flight goes beyond the slaves using magical images to indicate political freedom and liberation. Was the image of flying a cover-up, a euphemism for something else during slavery? What was the legend's function before it became a myth? Cannot at least some of this African mystery be uncovered through the deduction or logical speculation? To hide certain truths from the slave owners, could not the slaves have protected themselves by willfully losing and forgetting parts of their collective memory?

Plausible answers to these questions lie not in literary analyses of the flying African motif but within the snippets of covert cultural and ontological information that the slaves themselves left behind. This is not to say that previous explorations that have only emphasized the symbolic characteristic of the flying African motif would be invalidated; rather, by looking in nonliterary directions, by looking at "peculiar" incidents that are often only footnoted in primary and secondary sources, we can be privy to evidence that offers different perspectives on slaves' lives. With these perspectives we can return to the literary context, discovering how that once-hidden reality is recreated through folkloric intersections of history and the creative imagination.

> Dundunbanza ¿quièn te mandó?
> Dundunbanza ¡Embrómate ahora![5]

Many African peoples who were brought to the Americas in slavery believed that to take one's own life was both daring and an ontological abomination. Although they were diverse in their tribal backgrounds, they had similar ontological beliefs. One of their central tenets regarding life was that it was sacred and that individuals did not have the authority to commit suicide. We are familiar with an example of this belief in Chinua Achebe's novel *Things Fall Apart*. Because Okonkwo, an Igbo, has committed suicide, he cannot be buried by his own people, and his body is left to rot on the tree until strangers (the European administrators) come to claim it. It was a common practice among many West African peoples to not touch the corpse of a suicide victim. How could such a practice be revised in the New World where suicide would occur because of atrocities that the people had never known before? How could

What did suicide, caused by slavery, mean as an ontological act? Why do twentieth-century survivors of slavery insist they had witnessed and knew people who had witnessed Africans who could fly? How does a folk story also function as myth—a sacred truth—effectively producing and maintaining hidden *oral* transcripts of the people?

Emotional and psychological defense mechanisms enabled the early generations of African-born slaves to survive the memory of the dehumanizing effects of the Atlantic Middle Passage. Deliberate amnesia was one kind of defense. Few slave suicides were recorded. Most suicides among slaves throughout the Americas were not documented, officially recognized, or counted. When it did occur, suicide by hanging, drowning, swallowing the tongue (suffocation) and any other means may well have been dismissed or denied. The community of fellow slaves who did not escape or commit suicide would attempt to hide from the masters the truth of what really happened. They were the ones to explain the event as magical or supernatural. Monica Schuler maintains that the flying African not only implied suicide but also sudden and inexplicable disappearances of slaves by taking foot and taking flight (94). The motif of the flying Africans can be found in diverse communities of the Americas: in the United States, and throughout the Caribbean and Latin America. It would continuously regenerate its roots in the folklore and mysticism of cultures in the New World African diaspora.

Infinities of Conscious Pain: Salt and Suicide

Comparative folklore in the African diaspora indicates that the flying African was not a gender specific motif; it was applied to women and men alike. The interesting characteristic surrounding the motif, however, was that only New World Africans who abstained from eating salt had the ability to fly. For example, in Surinam, it is said that the main reason that "it would be mostly us men who would fly back" is because "our wives and children were forced to eat food in the houses where they worked," so they could not follow a salt-free diet (Breinburg 38). The ability to fly is inevitably connected to the early generations of African arrivants who had control over what they ate: "It was a long time ago, many years before Emancipation, that word had gone round that those of us who could stop eating salt would be able to fly back to Africa. So we all went on a salt-free diet" (Breinburg 38). Further north, an "old time" Jamaican had this to say to Monica Schuler:

The African [who] don't eat salt, they say they [be]come like a witch . . .
those Africans who don't eat salt—and they interpret all things. And
why you hear they say they fly away [it is because] they couldn't stand
the work when the taskmaster them flog them; and they get up and they
just sing their language, and they clapping their hands—so—and they
just stretch out, and them gone—so—right back. And they never come
back. (93)

In her novel *Abeng,* Jamaican writer Michelle Cliff creates her version of
the flying Africans:

Before the slaves came to Jamaica, the old women and men believed,
before they had to eat salt during their sweated labor in the cane fields,
Africans could fly. They were the only people on this earth to whom God
had given this power. Those who refused to become slaves and did not
eat salt flew back to Africa; those . . . who were slaves and ate salt to
replenish their sweat, had lost the power, because the salt made them
heavy, weighted down. (63)

There are various reasons given for why salt inhibited the slaves' ability to fly back to Africa. A prevalent argument is that, "for newly arrived
slaves to the New World, salt was one of the foods of the oppressors. . . .
To eat the food [with salt] would be a betrayal to their native culture"
("Possess Your Bird of Passage" 1). Some speculate that the African arrivants associated salt with European oppression.[9] To not eat salt may
have been a symbol of rejecting the brutality of slavery, but this reasoning assumes that the Africans were not accustomed to salt as an everyday food additive and preservative. Salt, on the contrary, was a major staple, and it tasted good. Salt avoidance is intimately connected to African
ethnographic, ontological, and historical texts and artifacts.[10] In regions
of West Africa, salt was a major trading commodity and was widely used
for exchange and consumption along the precolonial Saharan trade
routes. Even south of the Sahara, salt was a common gift for events such
as marriages, births, puberty rites, or warfare resolutions. Aside from
being exported to inland traders and caravans from the northern Sahara, salt was often exchanged for its weight in gold.[11] Such were the
prevailing socioeconomic factors that operated in much of precolonial
Africa.

The African arrivants forged new cultures throughout the Americas
despite slavery and colonization. During that long historical moment,
however, many of them still had the vibrant memory of Old World be-

liefs and practices. Slaves who came from central Africa (among them, the Bakongo) believed that eating salt would convert them to European Christianity and deprive them of their African mystic abilities. Moreover, "unwilling converts, forced to take salt in the baptismal ceremony or in salted foods, must have despaired that they would ever return to Africa" (Karasch 256). Catholic priests knew about salt avoidance among the New World Africans, and, instead of sprinkling salted baptismal water on the foreheads of the converted, they would have the slaves "eat the salt of God" (ibid.)!

In the context of ethnographic culinary practices related to divination and mysticism, certain foods are often avoided. Among numerous traditional African peoples, it was prohibited to eat food seasoned with salt (and other spices) in preparation for and during sacred ceremonies and rites-of-life passages. It was also believed that avoiding the use of salt further enabled the power of mysticism and divination. Having the discipline to refrain from salt manipulated psychic powers that helped to separate mystics and healers from the rest of the community. The Buganda of East Africa had specific prohibitions against the use of salt with the treatment of traditional medicine. Sir Apolo Kaggwa described one of the circumstances like this: "The reason why that drug killed the king was that he did not observe the conditions which had been given to him. He had been warned not to eat salt" (Kaggwa 181). Commenting on the salt taboo among non-Western cultures, Gabriella Eichinger Ferro-Luzzi maintains that "Even without sharing the extreme yogic view that austerities may lead to supernatural power, human beings, independently of culture, hold the deep conviction that success must be merited, that a sacrifice must receive its reward, with or without divine intervention . . . that there is a sort of balance in life in which a loss on one side will bring a gain on the other" (413). Furthermore, there was a widespread belief that salt could ward off evil. An instance of this was witnessed among the Wolof of Senegal. In a nineteenth-century description of the traditional beliefs among the Wolof, one European wrote, "When at night they hear the cry of some birds, owls or others, they take fright and cry out all together, *ckorom le nô doundé* (we live on salt), because they say, the sorcerers do not like souls that are salty" (Boilat 39).

Biocultural characteristics are associated with the avoidance of salt in the context of enabling psychic empowerment. What the ancients could observe, if not "scientifically" articulate, was that, because of its mineral properties, the overuse of salt could bloat the body, cause sweating, dehydration, and excess weight. For them these functions thwarted magico-religious empowerment. The Dogon believed that acute "sweating" robbed the strength of divination, and because "saliva is the life-force," strength would be broken by such an "evacuation of water" (Griaule 118–19). Thus in preparing the body and mind for healing and divination rites, salt was one of the substances that would not be consumed by shamans or diviners. For biocultural (cultural interpretations regarding the scientific relationship of salt to the body) and psychological (those connected to believing in the power of the interpretations) reasons, salt abstinence was found to be advantageous and powerful. In some cases salt was a sacred taboo. By avoiding salt, "exceptional persons" could attain special powers that would set them apart. Among the Bakongo, for example, these exceptional individuals could cross oceans and fly. (MacGaffey 50–56).

Another belief prevalent among African cultures regarding food and its ontological connection was that certain well-prepared foods caused "excessive heat" that prevented the "repairing" of the mind and body. Thus in divination and ritual performances, this physiological and psychological "heat" had to be avoided. One of the ways to avoid it was by not consuming spices and salt. Eating desirable, spiced foods would have been considered impure and a stimulus connected to passion and sexual pleasure. Any consumed food had to be bland. Thus, "abstinence from salt in its quality of a desirable item means a sacrifice, appropriate during periods of penitence like mourning" (Eichinger Ferro-Luzzi 413). Because of suffering and being taken away from their homeland, the New World Africans would have seen their bondage, indeed, as a period of mourning. Their reward for the sacrifice of salt abstinence would be the ability "to fly" or the "cleansing" of suicide. Superior spiritual strength was rewarded, and it justified empowerment. Africans who adapted to abstinence for the new conditions under slavery demonstrated that it would be one way to "keep the sacred, sacred" (Eichinger Ferro-Luzzi 413). The central tenet, avoid salt in order to return, would grow out of complex intersections of psychological and cosmological beliefs.

The unwilling immigrants of the Middle Passage, therefore, had inherited beliefs about salt avoidance: "The distasteful, salty and death-laden Middle Passage could have logically enforced the relationship between salt, death, and the spirit world," (McDaniel 80). After the "vibrant memory" of Africa folded into folkloric memory, the subsequent descendants of the arrivants would pass on stories of the flying Africans and continue the obsession with salt. How did some of them connect to the metaphor and reality of salt? In writing about Caribbean Canadian women's experiences as immigrants (contemporary arrivants), Meredith M. Gadsby uses the metaphor "sucking salt" to indicate not only "the act of overcoming hardship" but also "a strategy for preparing oneself for impending hardship" (153). Whereas some of the first arrivants may have had the ability to take flight because they did not eat salt, the survivors who were left behind had to suck the salt in order to "persevere and fight" (Gadsby 154).

The African arrivants inherited a cultural imprint of salt avoidance and its relationship to empowerment. Legends would be retold in honor of the ancestors, the old parents, who move further back into time and memory and who come forward because of memory. As the descendants pour libations in their memory, they weave stories of the flying Africans. When the Big Drum ceremony takes place among modern-day Carriacouns in the West Indies,

> The parents' plate must contain food from which salt has been withheld. . . . The widespread lore involving salt carried a great depth of meaning with variegated practices distributed throughout the Caribbean and West Africa. (McDaniel 79)

The cultural imprint intrigued not only the slave owners of the period, but also these descendants of the Africans who would not forget that their ancestors had the gift of flight. In this sense, the link between language (the speech of mythmaking) and its function (to protect the "pact" of suicide) is constructed and mediated by cultural ideologies of the community's responsibility to the individual and the individual's responsibility to the community. Neither is mutually exclusive of the other.[12]

Because the majority of Africans who were brought to the Americas as slaves believed that individuals did not have the cosmological right to self-chosen death, the rite of suicide had to be spiritually negotiated. The souls of suicides would wander in agitated and mournful oblivion if some kind of cleansing was not done. The spirit could be repaired by the community of kin left behind through ritual dance, songs, and chants and by evoking the power of speech through mythmaking. Suicides were invariably characterized and empowered by the spirit of remembering and resisting. In the milieu of New World slavery, suicide was not a reaction to despondency but rather an audacious act of resistance and spiritual redemption. Yet the spirit of the disappeared had to be reconstituted. Therefore, as defenses against slavery, suicide and suicide/murder meant something different for the captives. For example, in 1802 on the Caribbean island of Guadeloupe, a slave rebellion, led by Louis Delgrès, came to its end when a group of slaves blew themselves up at Matouba; they refused to be captured and killed by the French. Throughout history there are incidents of collective suicides committed for spiritual reasons arising out of warfare and rebellion.[13]

Stories of the flying African as a utilitarian cover-up for suicide operated in the context of a succinct network of characteristics that existed during New World slavery. In Western European theology (as defined by St. Augustine), Christians do not tolerate suicide. In his *Summa Theologica*, St. Thomas Aquinas who "reiterated the arguments of Aristotle (suicide is an act of cowardly aggression against the state) and Augustine (who unequivocally condemns suicide), added that suicide violates man's instinct to self-preservation and prevents him from fulfilling his obligations to himself, society, and God" (Sullivan II xv). During the European Renaissance, suicide was often treated with sympathy, understanding, and tolerance. John Donne's ideas and arguments on the defense of *felo de se* ("he who commits felony by murdering himself") were put forth in his famous *Biathanatos* (1608). Émile Durkheim's study *Suicide* (1897) places the act of self-chosen death in a sociological context; his ideas are based on "the conception that there is an essential distinction between the explanation of variations in suicide rates, and the aetiology of any given individual case of suicide" (Giddens x). Ancient Greek and Roman philosophy expressed attitudes that certain kinds of self-homicide were dignified and necessary. "In the Roman world the image of noble self-killing banishes hanging to the margin. Women, slaves and inferior people are expected to use that infamous means. . . . The method of self-killing was very important for the quality of the death thus obtained" (van Hoof 78).

One well-known form of suicide in a non-Western setting is Japanese *hara-kiri*. Originating in feudal Japan and Samurai culture, *hara-kiri* or *seppuku* (self-disembowelment) is ritual suicide associated with militarism and dignified death. One of the most publicized self-chosen deaths in the twentieth century was that of the Japanese author Yukio Mishima. He performed *hara-kiri* in 1970. Other types of suicide in Japan are usually "characterized by a goal-means discrepancy and an alienated conception of self, together with a self-destructive response to the definition" (Iga and Tatai 261–62).

In the United States there is much publicity surrounding medically assisted suicides connected to legal issues of euthanasia. Suicide is widespread among American youth and people who are clinically depressed. Publicized mass suicides have taken place among religious cults in the United States, Canada, France, Guyana, and Uganda. Terminal illnesses, clinical depression, extreme religious principles, and neurotic social dysfunction are not the motivating forces that, I maintain, characterize suicide in the historical context of the flying African. On the contrary, in the New World beginnings of slavery and resistance, the taking of one's own life, or collective suicide, as in the case of what happened at Matouba, was an active agency of spiritual resistance. Suicide in this context was not a response to clinical depression; it was a unique response of resistance for salvation. The desire to return to Africa, marronage, and death evolved out of the slaves' collective pain and ontological beliefs. Suicide was transformed into a paradoxical act of faith, hope, reconciliation, and ultimate defiance. Death was not unbearable. These ancestors conveyed another truth to us, "[t]hat suffering, pain, and persecution are only unbearable to those who had no purpose in life, no hope for the future" (Sears 28). As real people who once lived, the flying Africans had distinct reasons for dying, because they saw as their purpose the return to the homeland.

Can the suicides of the flying Africans be seen as exemplary deeds arising out of personal motivations? Discussing the parameters of Greco-Roman attitudes toward suicide, Anton J. L. van Hooff states that, "Self-killing is the most individual death, but it is always connected with the surrounding world. This world is very small if personal reasons like despair, grief and pain are involved. Much wider is the circle when suicide is placed in the perspective of the community: to sacrifice oneself for the well-being of the whole was always held as an exemplary deed" (182–83). When the suicide of the flying African is placed in the wider circle, it is clear that the well-being of the larger community (of slaves) was jeopardized. How was New World suicide viewed among the early generations of Africans? It is possible to get some understanding of the New

World slaves' beliefs regarding suicide by gleaning some of the African sources for their religious beliefs and folk practices. Their cosmological beliefs were rooted in ancient foundations that deemed suicide an irrational act against the creator. This is not to say that all ethnic groups in Africa had the same worldview regarding life and death. Suffice it to say that, among the ancient African people, there was a generally intense appreciation for affirming life; hence suicide, which was a display of arrogance, effrontery, and lack of respect for parents, ancestors, and progeny, did not frequently occur. In all probability the resistance suicide of the flying Africans was simultaneously sacred, communal, and covertly political—none of these being exclusive of the others. According to John S. Mbiti, "because traditional religions permeate all the departments of [African] life, there is no formal distinction between the sacred and the secular, between the religious and the non-religious, between the spiritual and the material areas of life" (2). When suicide took place, however, the temporal space would be repaired through ritual performances and mythmaking. According to Paul and Laura Bohannan, among the Tiv of Nigeria, for example, if suicide occurred, "everybody in the compound must be repaired. The place in which the suicide occurs becomes a 'bad and dangerous place....' The corpse of a suicide must not be seen, touched or even approached by women" ("The Place of Swende" 405). By using the word "repaired," the informant understood that the surviving kinfolk needed to undergo symbolic rituals that would counteract the forbidden action. The Tiv also believed that suicide was worse than committing murder. And likewise, suicide was almost unheard of among the Kanuri, Hausa, and Azande.[14]

If the return to the African homeland had to be accomplished through death, then so be it. Writing about the escalation of suicide and collective suicide in Cuba in 1840, María Poumier Taquechel informs us that,

Africano también era el gusto por el ahogo en ríos, lagos, o mar; esta técnica procedía de la creencia en un regreso inmediato del cuerpo hasta la tierra originaria; de la misma confianza en los medios naturales de viaje a Africa partían aquellos cimarrones que se ponían en marcha hacia el este, sin asentarse en ningún escondite para preservarse de los rancheadores. (77)

[Many Africans also preferred drowning in rivers, lakes, or the sea; this method arose out of their belief that the body therefore would immediately return to its original homeland; and this same belief in the natural journey to Africa would cause some maroons to set out in an eastward direction without taking refuge in any potential hiding place that might protect them from the slave hunters].

"I have long felt," Maureen Warner-Lewis tells us, "that the well-established folk belief in flying back to Guinea was a euphemism for suicide" (153). She affirms:

> Home—the site of the buried navel-string—is of such pivotal importance to the African psyche that African cultures have generally found ritual methods of returning to its psychic centre the spirit of the man who dies far from home. And since the African lived in a highly spiritual world, death was the surest way to return to Guinea [Africa], there to reunite with the ancestral spirits of the clan. So much so, indeed, that spiritual flight was not the prerogative of all. (28)

From a Eurocentric perspective that does not factor in African ontological considerations, Taquechel argues that, among Cuban slaves, the propensity for committing suicide in the 1840s could mainly be attributed to a lack of adequate Christian indoctrination (79). Such a conclusion assumes that Christianity would overrule an African worldview, and its teachings would prevent attempts to escape or commit suicide. Suicide is not a definitive "sin," but rather it is posthumously and paradoxically honored and moderated by the myth of the flying African.

Those who were left behind, the community of kin, became, of course, the interpreters and the mythmakers of memory. They performed the necessary rituals to remember and to subvert any knowledge of the utilitarian reality of suicide. Flying African stories encode these acts of suicide. In Cuba, where many such suicides took place, "la técnica más frecuente fue la del ahorcamiento; era también típica de los suicidios colectivos; en este sentido, tiene la mayor carga de significación cultural, aparece verdaderamente como el cumplimiento de un rito para la comunidad esclava" [The most frequently used method was hanging; it was also the most common form of group suicide. In this regard, death by hanging has the most cultural significance; it truly appears like the fulfillment of a rite of passage for the slave community] (Taquechel 76). The slaves claimed spatial harmony and may have wanted to separate themselves as much as they could from the painful injustices and violence inflicted upon them. One way in which they sustained themselves was through the psychological and spiritual acceptance that, yes, the people could fly! In this sense of "[t]he legend of the Flying Africans, in all its variations, is ultimately about this ability to transcend one's condition" (Walters 15). Flight, as Toni Morrison writes, was one of their gifts.

Cosmological perspectives toward suicide were transformed in the New World because of slavery. Suicide remained forbidden, but when it did occur, it would signify as a source of power, defilement, and "regeneration" by the survivors. In contrast, when suicide was documented by the slave masters, it was often presented as a reaction to despair and nostalgia. For African-born slaves the "text" of suicide was redemption and evoked an inversion of sacred beliefs. Throughout the Americas, records that slave owners kept indicate some African people were more prone to suicide than others. "More than any of other nations," writes Lorna McDaniel, "The Igbo were widely described as diffident, despondent, and suicidal. Their behaviour may have been misrepresented in historical documents, and the 'fixed melancholy' perceived in them may have reflected a final, audacious political stance of resistance rather than the despondency of dependency" (168).

In the process of Americanization and creolization, many hidden transcripts of the slaves' interior motivations remained hidden, but the signifiers for collective motivations would exist in the foundations of Negro spirituals, *voudun, candomblé,* and other forms of New World African religiosity and sacred performance arts that the descendants of the flying Africans created. What once had been the longing for an African homeland becomes the lamenting for a Christian heaven or a mythic remembrance of the "nation" spirit. The flying Africans, as legend and myth, therefore, underwent transformation as "a vision of the legend as process, rather than product, [that] allows us to contrast the ways in which creative artists make use of their culture's collective memories with the way that a social scientific discourse may view those memories as static elements which are quick to disappear" (Walters 15). In this transforming process, flying no longer existed in the collective memory as a hidden transcript for suicide. The motif of the flying African became lyrical and literary; it was enacted and performed through dance, music, and drama.

The kind of suicide that I am attempting to put into perspective, that of the hidden transcript of the flying Africans, is exemplified in the film *La Última Cena (The Last Supper)* (1976), directed by Tomás Gutiérrez Alea. The film depicts how suicide could have been enacted in the nineteenth-century context of slavery. The hidden transcript is uncovered. *La Última Cena* is based on an actual slave rebellion that took place in Cuba in 1790. After I saw the film, I sought archival information about this peculiar Cuban uprising.

The rebellion was prompted when the Count de Casa Bayona, in all his wealth accumulated from sugar and slavery, decided to imitate Christ by washing the feet of twelve of his slaves and serving them an elaborate dinner at his table. The slaves weren't as ignorant, ingratiating, or stupid as the Count thought they were. Here is Manuel Moreno Fraginals's penetrating observation about the rebellion that came to be known as the "last supper":

> Pero he aquí que estos esclavos, cuyos conocimientos teológicos no eran muy profundos, en vez de comportarse como los apóstoles, lo que hicieron después fue sublevarse valiéndose del prestigio que adquirieron frente a los demás miembros de la dotación y terminaron quemando el ingenio. (117)

> [But among these slaves their knowledge of theology was not very profound and instead of behaving like the apostles, they took advantage of the prestige they had acquired in the eyes of their fellow slaves to incite a rebellion and burn down the sugar mill.]

The twelve slaves were hunted and captured by the *rancheadores* and the infamous Cuban dogs and decapitated during the week of Palm Sunday and Easter.[15]

A pivotal scene in *La Última Cena* shows how one of the *cimarrones* (fugitive slaves), rather than letting the *rancheadores* kill him, decides to take his life by jumping off a cliff. Before he jumps, he performs a ritual dance and incantation in which he flaps his arms as imaginary wings and chants "in tongue." He then confidently jumps to his death as if in flight. This particular rebel decides that, because he has to die, he will not let the *rancheadores* kill him. The camera closes in on him as he looks at the cliff and then looks back and hears the dogs bringing the slave catchers nearer. If he lets them kill him, he becomes another victim. By choosing to commit suicide, he is spiritually empowered to return to the homeland. The *rancheadores* will not have the satisfaction of mutilating and then killing him. At that last moment, he assures his safe passage to Guinea through ritual suicide—he jumps from the cliff and takes flight. This scene reminds the viewer of an earlier scene where, during the Count's infamous dinner, one of the slaves (whose right ear has been cut off as punishment for trying to escape) proclaims his fierce determination to take flight with the help of the owl, *sunsundamba*. (The English subtitle translates this word generically as "bird.") *Sunsundamba* is an omen of fear, the unknown, and marronage. The film ends with a tableau of an eagle's flight dissolved with that of the slave who had his ear cut off, once more a Maroon escaping into the hinterland of the island.

The artistic consciousness of the flying African motif is also expressed in the Cuban slave narrative *The Autobiography of a Runaway Slave (Biografía de un cimarrón)*. In 1963 anthropologist Miguel Barnet met and interviewed Esteban Montejo, a Cuban who, at 103 years of age, was reported to be the last surviving former Maroon slave in the Americas. *The Autobiography* is the story of Montejo's life as a slave and as a freed person after slavery. In the as-told-to narrative, Esteban Montejo speaks about the power of the *sunsundamba*. He says that, "The barn owl sang a sad song, but it was a witch. When I saw an owl in my path [as a Maroon during slavery] especially when she went back and forth, I wouldn't go on because by doing that she was giving warning that there was an enemy or death itself nearby. The owl is wise and strange" (54). The owl has ancient symbolic properties: it has the ability to see at night, and its nocturnal life is highly stratified; its silent flight is uncanny; it can turn its head to see 360° around; and its talons aim to kill when necessary. These properties are connected to the success of taking flight. Montejo also vividly and unapologetically claims witness to the flying African:

> There are popoe [sic] who say that when a black dies he goes back to Africa. That's a lie. How would they go back to Africa? The ones who went back were alive, the ones who flew a lot—a tribe of wild men the Spanish refused to bring here anymore because it wasn't good business. But the dead don't fly!... What happened to the blacks, which is the same today as it was yesterday, is that the spirit went out of the body and set to wandering around in the ocean or in space. (120–21)

Significantly, Montejo brings up the topic of suicide: "What I do think is a fiction, because I never seen it ever, is that the blacks committed suicide" (42). And in the next instance he begins to talk about flying:

> Before, when there were Indians in Cuba, suicide did exist. They didn't want to be Christians, and they hung themselves from the trees. But the blacks didn't do that because they went flying, flying in the sky, and headed off for their homeland. The Musundi Congo were the ones who

flew the most. They disappeared through witchcraft.... There are some
who say that the blacks threw themselves into the rivers, but that's a lie.
The truth is that they tied a doodad they called a *prenda* around their
waist. That's where the power was. I know that like the palm of my hand,
and it's a fact. (43)

Montejo juxtaposes his *disbelief* in the possibility that African slaves
committed suicide with his *belief* in their ability to fly back to Africa instead! Yet he explains the tension between not believing the possible
(that slaves had committed suicide) and believing the improbable (that
they had the ability to fly) through his faith in *brujo* (obeah). The *prenda*
that slaves tied around their waists was a power source for flight and
faith. But is Montejo also covering up suicide by saying that "the blacks
didn't do that"? By focusing our attention on the Indians who did commit suicide, is he deliberately adding twentieth-century credence to the
hidden transcript of the flying African? Only Montejo would have known
the truth of the motivation behind the rhetorical strategy he uses with
his European interviewer.

I've come full circle by returning to symbols for suicide (and attempted
suicide) in the peculiar world of slavery. Gaston Bachelard's notion that
"all really inhabited space bears the essence of the notion of home" is
most appropriate here for connecting the early slaves' yearning for the
Africa they once knew to the healing of the cosmic journey and spiritual life that they believed would continue after physical death. Some
slaves were psychologically incapacitated from unsuccessful attempts at
running away. Others were spiritually empowered by their determination to escape. In this sense, lucrative relationships between the traumatic
events of slavery and the slaves' worldview could be sustained through
utilitarian perceptions of flight. Suicide in such a context was no longer
a cosmological "crime" but a material resolution that was repaired and
made sacred by the community. The community then established an illusion (the motif) for the unspeakable thing unspoken. Admiration and
awe are juxtaposed with horror when witnessing personal autonomy
manifested in the taking of life.

Suicide in the context of New World slavery is not a pathological occurrence. When it did occur, there was an ontological need to create a
space for cosmic harmony out of the chaos that it caused. Suicide, sui-
cide/kinship homicide, or sudden disappearance are assumed into the
captive community and transformed into illusions of flying through

rituals and mythmaking—an appropriation of Leibniz's utilitarian reality that is part of the epigraph to this chapter. And certainly, women were very much involved in taking flight and taking foot—even if it meant killing their children and attempting to commit suicide rather than surrendering to slavery.

> "You should have seen my little girl that—that . . . that died; that was the bird."
>
> —Margaret Garner

The opening scene of Toni Morrison's novel, *Song of Solomon*, begins with the insurance man, Mr. Robert Smith, preparing to leap from the roof of Mercy Hospital on blue silk wings: "I will take off from Mercy and fly away on my own wings. Please forgive me. I loved you all" (*Song of Solomon* 3). Morrison undoubtedly connects the flying African motif to suicide in a contemporary setting.[16] Everyone knows "that only birds and airplanes could fly" (*Song of Solomon* 9). From the outset, however, Morrison juxtaposes demystifying Mr. Smith's attempts at flight (he's really committing suicide) with the mystification of the refrain, "O Sugarman done fly away / Sugarman done gone / Sugarman cut across the sky / Sugarman gone home"—a refrain that will have profound meaning as the narrative unfolds. In this novel, Morrison simultaneously reconfigures and revitalizes the flying African motif. Like a classical hero, Milkman Dead embarks on a journey that enables him to soul-search and find his ancestral legacy in archaeological sites that are both genealogical and spiritual. The often-quoted ending of the novel, "For now, he knew what Shalimar knew: If you surrendered to the air, you could *ride* it," is life affirming. Witnessing suicide, however, is painful for the kinfolk who are left behind. Morrison aptly shows how flight can be a heroic moment but also arrogant and selfish, because individual flight violates the interrelated and interdependent sense of community. Milkman's significant leap, while the hills echo his voice around him—"Tar tar tar, said the hills . . . life life life life"—foreshadows Morrison's next novel, *Tar Baby*. While Milkman is able to resolve the ancestral riddle of Shalimar/Sugarman, Jadine Childs takes flight from the ancestral properties on an airplane bound for France, not Africa. She thinks that she might be able to deal with the haunting of the ancestral mother-women when "She would go back to Paris and begin at Go. Let loose the dogs, tangle with the woman in yellow—with her and with all the night women who had *looked* at her" (290). In much of her writing, Morrison connects both male and female modalities to the significance of flight, discovery, and recovery.

Toni Morrison affirms, "Any model of criticism or evaluation of Black literature that excludes males from it is as hampered as any model of criticism of Black literature that excludes women from it" ("Rootedness" 344). Morrison and other cross-cultural writers such as Paule Marshall, Maryse Condé, Simone Schwarz-Bart, and Mariama Bâ inscribe in their literary paradigms what I refer to as gender warmth. Their writing foregrounds cultural and historical artifacts that highlight the passions and struggles of black women and men trying to maintain kinfolk and the extended community. Gender warmth empowers women and men to bond with each other through the sentiments of reciprocity—they become helpmates of each other. Gender warmth signifies the complementary essence of spirit. Paule Marshall's central theme in *Daughters,* for example, addresses how at one time in New World black communities, men and women could unabashedly assist and sustain each other through gender-oriented differences that were assets rather than obstacles. Marshall imagines how the people had *worked together;* men did not treat women as pliable possessions. Gender identities were grounded in the life forces of the entire community. It was a time when, despite the hardships and trauma of slavery, reconstruction, and colonization, women and men unabashedly complemented and supported each other like two wings of a bird; if one of the wings was broken, the bird could not fly. Although separate entities like the wings, women and men could complement each other in unity and mutuality. Slavery, however, had systematically caused so much separation and dismantling, along with the dismemberment of the people's sustaining values. Long-lasting effects resulted from that great dismemberment and dismantling. In diverse ways, contemporary black women writers show how the people can reconstitute sustaining values through gender warmth. They accentuate unity through new kinds of multiple roles and ambitions that are inclusive.[17] Morrison states that the central female character in *Song of Solomon,* Pilate, is "[t]he best of that which is female and the best of that which is male, and that balance is disturbed if it is not nurtured, and if it is not counted on and if it is not reproduced. That is the disability we must be on guard against for the future—the female who reproduces the female who reproduces the female" ("Rootedness" 344). Through inclusiveness and attention to men in the community, gender warmth enables bonding, wholeness, and empowering reciprocity.

While *Song of Solomon* and *Tar Baby* repeat, preserve, and revitalize flight motifs, *Beloved* recreates the people in slavery and shows how taking flight and taking foot are profoundly a part of the most intimate experiences of slavery. *Beloved* is based on a nineteenth-century incident involving a fugitive slave woman in Ohio named Margaret Garner, who murdered her three-year-old daughter rather than allow her to be returned to slavery.[18] Amid the gunfire of the slave catchers, Garner also tried to kill her other children before she attempted suicide. Morrison's depiction of the Garner story in *Beloved* constructs meaning out of Emancipation-era consciousness in and across historical time and place; it is not only about slavery but also about the inner lives of the once-enslaved people. While *Beloved* brings Margaret Garner back into memory and knowledge, a rereading and reconstruction of the Garner infanticide challenges previously conceived and simplified images about nineteenth-century African American mother-women in slavery.

Of the Garner incident, Morrison says, "the [newspaper] clipping about Margaret Garner stuck in my head. I had to deal with this nurturing instinct that expressed itself in murder" (Clemons 75). Although Morrison acknowledges that documented historical evidence concerning the Garner case inspired the writing of *Beloved,* she is less concerned with recording this evidence in the novel. That is to say, Morrison deals more with constructing meaning out of the evidence and with creating the interior motivations of women like Margaret Garner who were enslaved and ultimately silenced in history. Through her portrayal of the complex human emotions of trauma, defensive pride, and community rejection, Morrison reasons that it is only through confronting suffering and then burying it that these people can heal themselves. They are in recovery along with the *recovering* slave owners. Amy Denver, the "whitegirl" who helps Sethe in childbirth while she is a fugitive from the Sweet Home plantation (whose slave owners are named Garner) says, "Anything dead coming back to life hurts. . . . More it hurt more better it is. Can't nothing heal without pain, you know" (*Beloved* 35, 78).

The Garner fugitive slave case, however, presents more than a story about a bonded mother's flight and resistance. Garner was a fair-complexioned slave woman, but her actions did not follow the conventional nineteenth-century image of the tragic mulatta.[19] While social and literary stereotypes of miscegenation involved both men and women, the situation of the mulatta presented a more sexually motivated dilemma than that of the male counterpart. Garner's fugitive status affirmed her communal sense of selfhood. That is to say, the attempt to take foot with her children, in-laws, husband, and other slaves, challenged popular nineteenth-century image of the mulatta's tragic, solitary womanhood without kin. Many mulattos formed and found bonding within the black kinship community. Another exception to the tragic mulatta stereotype is seen in Ellen and William Craft's account of their escape from slavery in 1848. Because she was able to pass for white, the Crafts disguised Ellen as a sickly southern gentleman traveling with his slave valet (the dark-complexioned William Craft) and escaped from Georgia. The Crafts later lived and traveled in Scotland and England as abolitionists. They were often described in the typical race and class superiority of the era: "Ellen is a gentle, refined-looking young creature of twenty-four years, as fair as most of her British sisters, and in mental qualifications their equal too. William is very dark, but of a reflective, intelligent countenance, and of manly and dignified deportment" (Orr 175). The enslaved mulatta who takes foot with her black mate and who does not succumb to escaping from blackness (by passing for white) is another testimony to gender warmth.

Certain truths surface from what Toni Morrison refers to as the "archaeological site" ("The Site of Memory" 114–15). This archaeological sense of place addresses what the memory and its image are really about. "Collecting" memory out of an African New World ethos is often arduous and becomes just that, an archaeological process. One returns to the (personal or communal) site searching for sustainable information from Middle Passage beginnings, digging for what was written out of history or suppressed even by the people themselves. Morrison says, "The exercise is also critical for any person who is black, or who belongs to any marginalized category, for, historically, we were seldom invited to participate in the discourse even when we were its topic" ("The Site of Memory" 110–11). Furthermore, Morrison points out that often the truth is veiled, as, for example, in early slave narratives, where many "proceedings were too terrible to relate." Truth turns into erasures because of race and gender subjectivity. In discussing the memory process, Morrison uses the image of the river that is engineered and straightened out to make room for modern development. "Occasionally," she says, "the river floods these places. 'Floods' is the word they use, but in fact it is not flooding; it is remembering. Remembering where it used to be. All water has a perfect memory and is forever trying to get back to where it was" ("The Site of Memory" 119). Morrison connects to a personal archaeological locale (for example, the images and feelings of her childhood home, Lorain, Ohio) and then places that site within the larger context of the events that significantly influenced the history of New World people of African descent.

With these multiple references to the flying African that is a signifier for taking flight and taking foot, I return to the image and remembering of Margaret Garner's archaeological site.

> I fall, I swoon! I look at the sky.
> The clouds are breaking on my brain;
> I am floated along, as if I should die
> Of liberty's exquisite pain
> In the name of the white child waiting for me
> In the death-dark where we may kiss and agree,
> White men I leave you all curse-free
> In my broken heart's disdain!
> —Elizabeth Barrett Browning,
>   "The Runaway Slave at Pilgrim's Point"

On the night of January 27, 1856, a group of seventeen slaves, consisting of men, women, and children, fled from the border of Kentucky into Ohio.[20] The fugitive group had taken advantage of the unusually cold winter and were able to cross the frozen Ohio River on a horse-drawn sleigh. They drove fast and hard in order to reach the outskirts of Cincinnati just before dawn. When they reached the city, they realized that such a large group of black people traveling together would cause suspicion, so they decided to break up into two groups. One group of nine quickly established contact with the local Quakers and continued to flee through the Underground Railroad to Canada. The other eight, the Garner family, got "turned around" in the city and had to ask directions to Mr. Joe Kite's house (a free colored man), which, of course, aroused suspicion.

The family consisted of four adults and four children whose ages ranged from about thirteen months to ten years. They were the four Garner children (Mary, Silla, Thomas, and Samuel); an elderly man, Simon Garner; Mary Garner, wife of Simon; Simon Jr., Margaret Garner's husband; and Margaret Garner. Silla was the baby whom Margaret Garner had on her lap during the court hearings. From primary and secondary accounts, it may seem that it was Silla who was killed. Silla and the other children were wounded. The sons, Thomas and Samuel, were approximately eight and ten years old. There were also different reports regarding their ages. Mary, the daughter whom Margaret killed, could have been the ten-year-old, or she could have been the three-year-old. However, from the emotive descriptions of the murder scene, it appears that the murdered child was probably a "knee baby" and therefore less than five years old. Regardless of ages, they were all apprehended under the Fugitive Slave law.

The infamous Fugitive Slave Act of 1850 stated that any slave who escaped from slavery could be seized by a white person in any state of the Union and returned to slavery as legal property of the owner.

> The claimant of any fugitive slave, or his attorney "may pursue and reclaim such fugitive person," either by procuring a warrant from some Judge or Commissioner, "or by seizing and arresting such fugitive, where the same can be done without process" to take such fugitive before such Judge or Commissioner. (May 3–4)

Thus by the time the family had stopped for shelter at Mr. Kite's, slave catchers were already in pursuit and soon found them. They surrounded the house and demanded that the slaves give themselves up. Accordingly,

> young Simon [Margaret's husband] fired from the window with a revolver, the ball from which struck the finger of one of the deputized marshals.... Upon this the door was burst in, when Simon fired three more shots at the party.... [A] deed of horror had been consummated, for weltering in its blood, the throat being cut from ear to ear and the head almost severed from the body, upon the floor lay one of the children of the younger couple, a girl three years old, while in a back room, crouched beneath the bed, two more of the children ... were moaning, the one having received two gashes in its throat, the other a cut upon the head. (*Cincinnati Commercial* 29 January 1856)

Levi Coffin, one of the principle abolitionists involved with the Ohio Underground Railroad gives a contemporary version of the infanticide in his autobiography, *Reminiscences:*

> The fugitives were determined to fight, and to die, rather than to be taken back to slavery. Margaret, the mother of the four children, declared that she would kill herself and her children before she would

return to bondage. The [slaves] were armed and fought bravely. The pursuers . . . battered down the door with some timber and then rushed in. At this moment, Margaret Garner, seeing that their hopes of freedom were vain, seized a butcher knife that lay on the table, and with one stroke cut the throat of her little daughter, whom she probably loved the best. She then attempted to take the life of the other children and to kill herself, but she was overpowered. (559–60)

From this description, we might envision Garner as a middle-aged woman who had, from many years of suffering and from having many of her children sold away, the paradoxical strength to love a child so much and to hate slavery even more that she could kill her child out of love. That image, however, does not match reality. Margaret Garner was only twenty-one years old and was pregnant at the time of her flight. In an interview, Margaret Garner said that, on her next birthday in June, she would be twenty-two years old. During the court hearings, Mary Garner, the mother-in-law, testified that Margaret Garner said to her, "Mother, help me to kill them. They will not go back to Kentucky." The elderly woman refused and hid under a bed.

In the style and custom of the period, Garner is described as

about five feet three inches in height, and rather stoutly than delicately made. She is a mulatto, showing from one-fourth to one-third white blood. Her forehead is high, and has a protuberance—not so large of course, but something like that which made Daniel Webster's so striking. Her eyebrows are delicate lines finely arched, and her eyes, though not remarkably large, are bright and intelligent. The African appears in the lower part of her face, in the broad nose and thick lips. Her ear is small, her wrist and hand large, and she wears a plain gold or brass ring. . . . Her eyes during the trial were generally cast down. She would look up occasionally for an instant with a timid, apprehensive glance. . . . [H]er general expression was one of extreme sadness. (*Cincinnati Commercial* January 30, 1856.)

The *Chicago Tribune* gave a different account of Garner: "The awful despair which must have overcome the mother, who is a rather amiable and intelligent looking female, before she was capable of committing such a deed, may be dimly imagined, but those of us who have 'free souls' cannot realize it. As the news of the tragedy spread over the city, it caused an universal shudder of horror and not here alone, but throughout the civilized world the sickening sensation will be felt. And this is not an item merely for the newspapers of today, but one of those facts of dark and startling significance which are for all time" (*Chicago Tribune* January 31, 1856).

The well-known governor of Ohio, S. P. Chase (who was later accused by abolitionists as being responsible for Garner's extradition to Kentucky) wrote that Garner was "naturally of a violent temper" (Shuckers 172). What gave Chase this impression of Garner's character is not clear. In fact, when asked during the hearing if she were not "excited to almost madness when she committed the act," Garner replied, "No . . . I was as cool as I am now; and would much rather kill them at once, and thus end their sufferings, than have them taken back to slavery, and be murdered by piecemeal" (*National Anti-Slavery Standard* March 15, 1856). As late as 1864, eight years after the incident, S. P. Chase was still defending his actions and involvement with the Garner case. In a letter, he claims that "in fact, I went beyond my duty in seeking to rescue Margaret after she had been taken back to slavery under the order of Judge Leavitt. She was not a *fugitive* from the justice of Ohio. . . . [M]y sympathy with Margaret Garner was, I think, quite as profound as that of Mr. Wendell Phillips, or any of those who join him in his misrepresenting me" (S. P. Chase to E. L. Pierce, January 24, 1864).

Most of the newspaper and abolitionists' accounts did not include the murdered girl's name. Garner's daughter was referred to as "it" or "the child." She remained essentially nameless. The focus was on Margaret Garner, and the killing was written about as a sensational crime of slavery. Contemporary reports frequently stated that Garner was a "mulatto" and that "the murdered child was almost white, and was a little girl of rare beauty." That Mary was "white" has explicit meanings found in legacies concerning black women and slavery. When complimented about the attractiveness of the surviving baby, Garner replied, "You should have seen my little girl that—that—(she did not like to say, was killed)—that died; that was the bird." The reporter noted, as the quote suggests, that it was difficult for Garner to articulate what she had done. I gleaned from the newspaper articles that, throughout the legal hearings, Garner remained calm and resigned to her fate—that she would be returned to slavery despite the resistance she and her family had made. Nevertheless, "they [the four Garner adults] declared they would go dancing to the gallows, rather than be sent back into slavery" (Coffin 561; May 55).

A glimpse of Garner's fortitude is further revealed during one of the court hearings. When asked from where she had received the scar that covered the length of her face, Garner responded, "White man struck me." Garner does not give any reason for the physical assault. She is not allowed to speak for herself in court. And even if she were able to speak, considering the social era, would she have been explicit about the sexual abuse she endured? Yet the implication of that abrupt response cannot be overestimated. Margaret Garner's scars, or what Hortense Spillers would call the "hieroglyphics of her flesh," are both hidden and revealed. The scar is a sign for physical brutality, the captive woman's plight, and her resistance. Spillers talks about the distinction between the "body" and the "flesh" of the captive woman:

> before the "body" there is the "flesh," that zero degree of social concep-
> tualization that does not escape concealment under the brush of
> discourse, or the reflexes of iconography. Even though the European
> hegemonies stole bodies . . . we regard this human and social irrepara-
> bility as high crimes against the flesh, as the person of African females
> and African males registered the wounding. (67)

Despite the wounding, Garner could still struggle against her circumstances, and her determination bears witness to the rebel spirit of women of color who found ways to affirm selfhood and kinship. On that January night in 1856, a young and pregnant slave/woman/mother not only sought freedom by fleeing with her husband, in-laws, children, and other slaves, but, when cornered by the slave catchers, she challenged them. By killing her daughter and attempting to kill the other three children and herself, Garner was no longer the powerless bonded woman. In those last moments before capture, she assumed the ability to choose death over enslavement. That consensus was paradoxical empowerment, determination, and sorrow.

Legal power, however, remained with the federal law and the slaveholders. The state of Ohio attempted to charge Garner with homicide and the two Garner men as accomplices. If they were to have been tried for homicide, then they could have remained in Ohio. To prevent this, Archibald Gaines, one of the slave owners who had pursued the fugitives into Cincinnati, evoked the Fugitive Slave law. Because the Garners were fugitives from Kentucky, Gaines was able to override the attempted homicide charge and claim ownership over the Garners and their surviv-

ing children. Julius Yanuck explains, in his comprehensive analysis of the
legal aspects of the Garner infanticide,

> Although the legal action to obtain a certificate [warrant] took place in a
> free state, no law of the free state could serve to emancipate the fugitive,
> and the law of the slave state determined the outcome of the hearing. (48)

Thus the family was the owner's legal property under the rights of the
Fugitive Slave law and could be extradited to Kentucky.

Local black and "yellow hued" (mulatta) women were involved as
much as they were allowed to be in their support of the Garner fugitives. In one account, the free blacks in Cincinnati were told to leave the
case alone "if they knew what was good for them." Cincinnati's free colored citizens tried to help the Garners, but they were kept out of the
court hearings and excluded from the proceedings. "The negroes, in this
fugitive slave matter, are acting very injudiciously, and if a riot is not
gotten up it will not be their fault. They had better for their own sake,
keep quiet, and such we have reason to know, is the counsel of their *true*
[sic] friends. Inasmuch as they are not citizens of the United States, they
ought to and must give precedence to those that are" (*Cincinnati Daily
Enquirer* February 2, 1856). In another report, the *Daily Enquirer* states:

> When the fugitives were taken to the omnibus, a large crowd was
> waiting, among which there was a plentiful sprinkling of sable and
> yellow hues. There was considerable excitement principally caused as
> the day previous, by a crowd of dark-hued damsels, who followed the
> vehicle, waving their handkerchiefs and uttering cries of encouragement.
> The snow fell fast, but it did not damp their ardor, for they continued to
> accompany the prisoners until they reached the Jail still cheering and
> waving their handkerchiefs, while the stout body-guard of the Marshal
> formed a phalanx behind and about the omnibus, sufficient to keep
> down any rebellion of turbulent uprising. (February 1, 1856)

Despite the efforts of local abolitionists, local colored citizens, the
American Anti-Slavery Society, and despite the national and international attention from the antislavery societies in Scotland and England,
after six weeks of complicated court proceedings, the slave family was
surrendered. They were actually kidnapped from the jail in Ohio and
taken back to Kentucky and into slavery. Garner's owner decided to sell
them because of the publicity. The boat sending some of the Garners
further south had a collision, and Margaret Garner fell or jumped into

the Ohio River with one of her children. Although Garner was rescued, her little girl, Silla, drowned. The dailies report that Garner welcomed the death because another one of her children had escaped slavery. As far as history and oral accounts reveal, Garner remained enslaved and died of tuberculosis in 1861. Garner's husband survived her.

It seems that the footnotes to Garner's story keep coming back into history. In 1862 *The Pacific Appeal,* a weekly newspaper based in San Francisco "devoted to the interests of people of color," provided some closure on what happened to the rest of the Garner family. It seems that the fugitive slave case was still in public memory: "The public will remember vividly the case of Margaret Garner, her husband, Robert Garner, and their family, who were arrested a few years ago, under the Fugitive Slave Law." According to the article, Robert Garner, "being under the Emancipation Law, [was] a free man writing from the U. S. gunboat Benton" in Washington, D.C. The article also stated that Margaret Garner's two sons (who had been with their mother during the attempted escape) were still living, although Robert Garner's mother (who had also been involved in the case) was still a slave in Kentucky.[21]

According to Yanuck, the Margaret Garner infanticide and attempted suicide case was considered one of the most sensational of all cases arising out of the 1850 Fugitive Slave law in that "the way Margaret Garner's little girl died embarrassed the South and disturbed the North more than a hundred arguments of antislavery philosophers" (47). Margaret Garner dared to take flight. The abolitionists gained additional momentum in bringing to the international forefront the condition of slaves in the United States. Contemporary newspapers in the United States and in Scotland echoed the sentiments that "the abolitionists love her [Margaret Garner] so well that they would rather have her hung for murder than return her to her master." During this period of anti- and proslavery debate, nineteenth-century American consciousness recognized that murdering one's children as an answer to slavery certainly was not a solution that either argument, proslavery or abolitionist, condoned. Of course, the irony rests in the fact that, legally, slaves were not considered full citizens with human rights and human obligations to other slaves. Despite the legal status of "property persona," the moral issues were real for everyone, captives and oppressors. And so the abolitionists had a field day because of the sensationalism.

Three years after her death, Garner's name was still heard in antislavery talk. The internationally known abolitionist Sarah Remond referred to Margaret Garner in a speech delivered in Warrington, England:

> the slaveholder found her; as he appeared at the door she snatched up a knife and slew her first-born child. . . . Above all the sufferers in America, American women who were slaves lived in the most pitiable condition. They could not protect themselves from the licentiousness which met them on every hand—they could not protect their honour from the tyrant. There were slaveholders everywhere in that country. There were no morals there; no genuine regard for womanhood or manhood. . . . And Margaret Garner would rather that her children should suffer death than be left in the hands of such beings. (Ripley 437–38)

Remond traveled extensively in England and Scotland speaking about slavery and its particular brutality toward women. She was involved with such groups as the London Anti-Slavery Society, the Glasgow Emancipation Society, and the Edinburgh Ladies Emancipation Society. She spoke to crowds of people who were eager to become involved in the antislavery movement. Remond unabashedly told audiences that "women are sold into slavery with cheeks like the lily and the rose, as well as those that might compare with the wing of the raven. They are exposed for sale, and subjected to the most shameful indignities. The more Anglo-Saxon blood that mingles with the blood of the slave, the more gold is poured out when the auctioneer has a woman for sale, because they are sold to be concubines for white Americans" (Ripley 438). In his discussion of the origins of the tragic mulatto stereotype, Sterling A. Brown writes that "pro-slavery apologists had almost entirely omitted . . . mention of concubinage. If anti-slavery authors, in accordance with Victorian gentility, were wary of illustrating the practice, they made great use nevertheless of the offspring of illicit unions" (193).

Sarah Remond was ahead of her time in recognizing that slavery held different meanings for men and women because of prescribed sex and gender roles. These roles were not at all androgynous. Slave women were often forced into unwanted sexual relationships with their overseers or owners. There were no laws to protect them from any sexual exploitation. An example is seen in the story of Celia, a nineteen-year-old slave woman who was hanged in 1855 for the murder of her owner. He had habitually raped her for five years. Eugene D. Genovese points out that "[slave] women paid a higher price than the white women or the men . . . for it was they who suffered the violence and the attendant degradation of being held responsible for their own victimization" (428).

The Garner infanticide was also a case of paradox: by taking flight, Margaret Garner was bonding herself to her daughter and family and resisting slavery as a mother-woman. The question remains: did she have the human right to take her daughter's life? Specifically addressing the forced sex that captive women in the Americas had to deal with, Deborah Gray White contends that "the choice put before many slave women was between miscegenation and the worst experiences that slavery had to offer. Not surprisingly, many chose the former, though they were hardly naïve" (34). Also discussing the issues of race and gender that operated during slavery, Angela Davis writes,

> in confronting the black woman as adversary in a sexual contest, the
> master would be subjecting her to the most elemental form of terrorism
> distinctively suited for the female: rape. . . . In its political contours,
> the rape of the black woman was not exclusively an attack upon her.
> Indirectly, its target was also the slave community as a whole. . . . [T]he
> master would not only assert his sovereignty over a critically important
> figure of the slave community, he would also be aiming a blow against
> the black man. (13)

Gerda Lerner explains that "the impact on the conquered of the rape of conquered women was twofold: it dishonored the women and by implication served as a symbolic castration of their men" (176).

Furthermore, as Sarah Remond acknowledged, the subject of colorism often influenced the social construction of the female slave. I will not deal fully here with the implications of colorism because I do so in my discussion of Jean Rhys and the complex manifestations of color prejudice in the West Indies. Depicting mulattas as favored was a comfortable image for whites but a less than accurate representation of the reality.[22] Garner's surviving daughter, Silla, was "rosy-complexioned." Garner knew that her beautiful fair-complexioned daughter could very well become another fancy girl (prostitute) and hence, another victim of the slave master's sexual aggressions.[23] And so, she wanted to protect the girl-child whom she loved.

Indeed, the accounts of the Garner case (including some of the articles by the white abolitionists) contain encoded values about mulatta slaves as well as the white community's shock that Garner would murder her daughter who was not only very beautiful, but who was also "white." Moreover, Garner defied the legal construction of patriarchy by destroying the owner's property through murder. The beautiful girl-child, whose phenotype resembled that of the slave owner, would have been a double economic asset. Because of their biological kinship to white slave owners, fair-complexioned slave women were often in positions as house servants (not that they always had better treatment) or as fancy girls. White women, who detested the infidelity of their men but could not do anything about it, often took out their anger and jealousies on the slave women who frequently looked like members of their own families. Although Garner was not explicit about the violence she experienced (she only mentions that she was struck by a "white man"), her case pointed to female victimization and to the sexual exploitation of black women that produced white phenotypes among their offspring. Rereading the infanticide in this context, we can see how her daughter's appearance revealed miscegenation, or worse, that Garner probably had been sexually abused by her white owners.

Yet social and literary stereotypes of the frail, resentful, and doomed mulatta served, in part, to maintain racial superiority among white Americans. Fair-complexioned slave women supposedly despised their dark-colored family and community. The stereotype was that they yearned for financially secure white men who could provide economic, if not legal, escape from oppression. However, because of the racial "taint" in their lineage (the failure to completely escape from being black), fair-skinned women would be depicted and stereotyped as "tragic" figures. The color flaw was the cause for suicide (note the narcissistic cause of suicide in this context) or death from an incurable disease—and in the nineteenth century, gender-specific illnesses were popular. The contrived image focused on the perceived romantic and tragic fate of "colored" women. The focus exemplified mixed-race women whose fair complexions enabled them "to escape" their blackness and, hence, social inferiority.[24]

The color stereotypes, however, became a kind of ruse to which some writers, both black and white, fell prey to in the late nineteenth- and early twentieth-centuries. Eugene D. Genovese analyzes how, in the United States, it was not until after the Civil War that divisions and attitudes between blacks and mulattos manifested recognizable *intraracial* color prejudice. Genovese states that "Little is known about the attitude of the black and mulatto slaves toward each other, but that little suggests

more fraternity than hostility. The widespread idea that the blacks en-
vied the mulattos and that the mulattos looked down on the blacks
came largely from postbellum sources" (429). It may be true that we do
not have a lot of information about personal relationships between blacks
and mulattos, but certainly archival material in the form of runaway
advertisements, foreign antislavery weeklies, letters, photographs, and
assorted reports from local antislavery societies provide evidence about
mulatto slaves who resisted slavery with the rest of the captive community, regularly in the United States and periodically in the Caribbean.

Harriet Jacobs' autobiography *Incidents in the Life of a Slave Girl:
Written by Herself* (1861) is one among many stories that challenge mulatta
stereotypes. Jacobs (who wrote under the pseudonym "Linda Brent")
sees herself as part of a distinct black community despite being belea-
guered by gender, bondage, miscegenation, and color. Furthermore,
throughout the narrative, Jacobs unquestionably embraces her immediate family and reaches out to her extended black community. "[She]
presents herself not as a cast-off love-sick mistress but as an outraged
loving mother; and in doing so she counters a . . . racial and sexual stereotype" (Yellin 274). Jacobs's recognition and representation of an enslaved
woman's selfhood places her in the forefront of a nineteenth-century
consciousness that embraced kinship and black womanhood. There were
mixed-race women who overtly and covertly resisted their enslavement,
and they were not psychologically attached to the master. Some of them
may have been physically and sexually subdued but not reduced into
tragic figures.

Despite being reduced by her chattel status, her race, and her sex,
Margaret Garner was not a tragic mulatta. Her story can be placed and
celebrated next to those witnesses to slavery who were also the victims.
Angela Davis observes that, "with the sole exceptions of Harriet Tub-
man and Sojourner Truth, black women of the slave era remained more
or less enshrouded in unrevealed history" (9). But Garner's fortitude
would be remembered among the folk, and her spirit would be recreated by the imagination of writers and poets.

Although Margaret Garner's name may not be in most history books,
during the time of the incident, her name was internationally propa-
gated by secular and religious abolitionists in the United States, the Caribbean, and Europe. Garner was referred to as "a noble woman indeed,
whose heroic spirit and daring have won the willing, or extorted the un-

willing, admiration of hundreds of thousands" and as a woman who was "most tender and affectionate, and all her passion was that of a mother's *fondest love*" (May 60, 61). Mary Livermore, a New England schoolteacher and editor of a suffrage newspaper, dedicated a poem to Garner entitled, "The Slave Tragedy at Cincinnati," in which the theme is that of a heroic woman whose love for her children was beyond doubt.

Another well-known white abolitionist and woman suffrage advocate, Lucy Stone Blackwell, became involved in the case and testified on Garner's behalf. (Keep in mind that, because she was a slave, Garner could not speak to defend herself.) While Garner was held in prison, Blackwell visited her and, at the close of one of the legal sessions, said,

> I thought the spirit she [Margaret Garner] manifested was the same with that of our ancestors to whom we had erected the monument at Bunker Hill—the spirit that would rather let us all go back to God than back to slavery. The faded faces of the negro children tell too plainly to what degradation female slaves must submit. Rather than give her little daughter to that life, she killed it. If in her deep maternal love she felt the impulse to send her child back to God, to save it from coming woe, who shall say she had no right to do so? (Coffin 565)

Both Blackwell and Livermore viewed Garner as the heroic mother. Undoubtedly, Garner's actions defied conventional forms of resistance, although she was not the first slave woman to commit infanticide. At one point during the Garner hearings, Lucy Stone Blackwell was asked if she would take one of the Garner children into her home. She did not accept. It is interesting to note her reasoning. She wrote to her spouse Henry B. Blackwell that "I received a letter yesterday from Mr. Jolliff [the Cincinnati lawyer and abolitionist who frequently assisted fugitive slaves and was involved in the Garner hearings] asking me to accept the guardianship... of one of the wounded little ones. I ... hoped they would all get their freedom, in which case, *such [sic]* a mother, was all the guardian they needed, but that I was willing to aid in any way I could, tho' such guardianship needed to be there, and now—my arrangements would keep me for some time absent" (Wheeler 155).

Although the Livermore's and Blackwell's pleas were well-intentioned, their sense of heroism operated from their privileged perspectives. Did Margaret Garner consider herself heroic? Garner sought to save her children, especially her daughters, from bondage and probable sexual abuse. However, as a fugitive mulatta, Garner demonstrated that she identified with the rest of her family and community of slaves. She took foot with them and eventually committed infanticide and attempted suicide. That her daughters were "white" underscores the implications of sexual relationships that Garner in all probability endured with her white slave owner. Does Garner's perceived heroism emphasize the killing of her child more than her efforts to *nurture* her children and seek an identity as a mother-woman outside of slavery? To echo Toni Morrison, we can only speculate about Garner's motivations that were expressed in a journey that ended in death and attempted suicide.

Deborah Gray White posits that "history is supposed to give people a sense of identity, a feeling for who they were, who they are, and how far they have come. It should act as a springboard for the future. One hopes that it will do this for black women" (167). Decidedly, the Margaret Garner incident can serve as an extended paradigm for historical revisions that are necessary regarding race and gender during the eve of Emancipation. How does Toni Morrison transpose these expansive ideas of taking flight and foot and resistance in her award-winning novel about compassion and reconciliation, *Beloved*?

> And it shall come to pass that in the place where it was said unto them, Ye are not my people; there shall they be called the children of the living God.
> —Romans 9:26

Morrison underscores that, although people cannot live in the past, they need to know their history. Similar to the historical consciousness of many women writers of African ancestry, Morrison consistently demonstrates commitment for the spiritual, mythic, and cultural properties of African people in the New World. What is seen or spoken is often an illusion. She often places emphasis on what is not spoken and what is not seen in order to convey certain realities in the people's lives.

In *Beloved* Morrison is more explicit than in her four previous novels about Middle Passage history and its connections to gender and race. Slavery, its memories, and the wanton post-Emancipation era provide the setting for *Beloved*. Morrison turns Margaret Garner into Sethe, the central character, and Garner's murdered daughter, Mary, becomes Beloved, the baby girl who initially returns in the form of a "hant" (a mischievous and cantankerous spirit) to haunt her mother. As an avenging hant, Beloved is the mother's reminder of slavery and its aftermath in that her presence connects to specific incidents that Sethe and the once-enslaved women and men like her want to forget. When she physically returns from the other side, Beloved brings a sense of otherworldliness with her: she is "born" out of a body of water, speaks like a child who is learning language, and does not have lines in her hands:

> A fully dressed woman walked out of the water. She barely gained the dry land of the stream before she sat down and leaned against a mulberry tree. . . . Everything hurt but her lungs most of all. Sopping wet and breathing shallow she spent those hours trying to negotiate the weight of her eyelids. . . . She had new skin, lineless and smooth, including the knuckles of her hands. (50)

Beloved's postnatal link to the spirit world (death) and to the Atlantic crossing of slavery makes her a kind of spiritual magus who must deal with her slave mother's fragmented consciousness.

When Beloved's spirit materializes into the physical being of a child-woman, she evokes both Sethe's guilt (the aftermath of the murder) and enables her psycho-spiritual recovery. From this perspective of guilt and redemption, Morrison reveals in *Beloved*, to borrow Mircea Eliade's term, a historical "structure of reality." For as Deborah Horvitz observes, "the powerful corporeal ghost who creates matrilineal connection between Africa and America, Beloved stands for every African woman whose story will never be told. She is the haunting symbol of the many Beloveds— generations of mothers and daughters—hunted down and stolen from Africa; as such, she is, unlike mortals, invulnerable to barriers of time, space, and place" (157). Thus the central characters in *Beloved* show us Margaret Garner's possible motivation, pain, and spiritual awakening. Garner herself never voiced her full story. We have only those historical awls that reflect Garner's own reality and interior motivations.

While *Beloved* itself is rooted in the particular story of Sethe and her family/community, it suggests personal reasons (as opposed to institutional reasons) that underlie the Garner murder: the pain of enslaved mothers loving their children (often with love that was "too thick"), their parents, and their sexual partners. The novel also explores reasons for the ubiquitous love/hate relationships that existed between white owners and female slaves. Morrison's approach to the Garner case generates plausible reasons for the choices slave mothers made. She consciously represents the spirit of women whose ancestors were forced to the Americas. Morrison tells us that "usually a book on slavery is about slave masters, the institution—a very predictable plot. When I say *Beloved* is not about slavery, I mean that the story is not slavery. The story is these people—these people who don't know they're in an era of historical interest. They just know they have to get through the day. I deal with five years of terror in a pathological society. . . . [T]hese people are living in that situation, and they survive it—and they are trying desperately to be parents, husbands and a mother with children" (Horn 75). The fact that Sethe obtains her freedom and then attains her redemption at the end of the ordeal (when Beloved, who becomes a demon of destruction, is exorcised by the mother-women of the black community) indicates that she will find that spatial harmony in the material world that eluded so many of her ancestors. Margaret Garner did not achieve her freedom. However, her flight certainly added to the sacrifices that enabled others to continue the struggle for ending slavery.

"This is not a story to pass on." Is it a story to pass *on*, as in to tell to others? Or is it a story to *pass* on, as in to forfeit the chance to hear the story? Which does Morrison mean? Do we pass *on* Middle Passage stories and forgotten lore as we make sure to *pass* on the Middle Passage because of (African American) pain and (European American) guilt? One critic asks, "Shouldn't parts of African American history be left behind and safely buried? *Beloved* is the kind of story that some black mothers, as well as white ones, would like never to be told" (Baker-Fletcher 632). Morrison's rhetorical strategy consistently says one thing in order to mean something different. It is her way of signifying meaning as she refers to syncopated possibilities of meaning in the African American ethos. Note how the refrain "this is not a story to pass on" does not enter the narrative until *after* the hidden story has been told and *retold* to Denver, Beloved, and Paul D. They have all taken flight and have become birds of passage. Baby Suggs, Sethe's mother-in-law, knows what happened and consequently decides that there is nothing else left but reconciliation because the past has been too full of hate. Certainly, *Beloved* consciously captures Middle Passage "proceedings too terrible to relate" in that it explores the reasons why a people might want to "forget" the story or at best communicate through euphemism and suppressed emotions (Clemons 74). In other words, the people are not only silenced by their owners, but they also silence themselves: the paradox of conscious amnesia.

Sethe suppresses what an older woman had told her about the violence and sexual abuse that the women experienced:

> She was remembering something she had forgotten she knew.... What Nan told her she had forgotten, along with the language she told it in.... [S]he was picking meaning out of a code she no longer understood. (61, 62)

In other moments, the old people attempt to force their children to remember. The grandmothers who experienced the crossing remember how the women were raped en masse aboard the slave ship just before the ship docked into the country that would hold them in bondage. Soon after arriving, the women had to deal with miscegenation as they traveled the third phase of the journey in the New World:

> "Telling you. I am telling you, small girl Sethe," and she did that. She told Sethe that her mother and Nan were together from the sea. Both were taken up many times by the crew. "She threw them all away but you. The one from the crew she threw away on the island. The others from more whites she also threw away. Without names, she threw them. You she gave the name of the black man. She put her arms around him. The others she did not put her arms around. *Never. Never.*" (62, emphasis mine)

Here Morrison constructs and mediates genealogical memories of the sexual exploitation of African women that was an integral part of the Atlantic crossing. The ritual mass rape aboard ship was labeled *la pariade*. One slaver wrote in his log book that "the sight of land is commonly the signal for merriment for a well-behaved cargo is invariably released from shackles, and allowed free intercourse between the sexes.... [T]he women, who are generally without garments, appear in costume from the wardrobe of tars, petty officers, mates, and even captains" (Cowley 232). Atlantic slavers frequently wrote in their journals about how the crew would use the African women for "merriment" when "all the sexes would mingle." Many women were pregnant, had given birth, or had killed the unnamed New World babies "without skin" (meaning "mulatto") by the time they reached the plantations.

Nineteenth-century abolitionists and slave owners alike recognized that murdering one's children could not be the vehicle for abolition. Likewise, the community of characters in *Beloved* tells us that they might be able to understand Sethe's reasoning about the crime: "She ain't crazy.

She love those children. She was trying to outhurt the hurter" (273). Morrison, however, explores how Sethe hurts as "thickly" as she loves her children. For Margaret Garner, the daughter Mary was the beloved "bird." Garner also reasoned that the murder would save her daughter from a life that would be far worse: enslavement. But how is this kind of crime forgiven in such an inhumane society? What constitutes justifying a murder that arises out of the paradox of love (for a child) and hate (for a way of life)? How can there be reconciliation among the progeny— the descendants of these mothers and masters—of this dehumanizing epoch in history? Can love and human compassion overrule? Of her exploration of such questions in *Beloved* Morrison says,

> What emerged was a series of real-life stories which for me said something very special about black women. The desperate need to nurture one's children is what informs everything about them.... That nurturing quality is so magnificent and so tender and so fierce. I was interested in the excesses of a violent system that would produce this all-consuming effort to love something well. You can't live in this world without loving anything—you just can't do it. (Smith, "PW Interviews" 51)

The fierceness and tenderness that produce an all-consuming effort bring to mind the sentiments that Marge Piercy expresses in her poem, "For strong women": "A strong woman is strong / in words, in action, in connection, in feeling / she is not strong as a stone but as a wolf / suckling her young." In exploring plausible answers to questions history did not and perhaps could not answer, Morrison moves the Garner case beyond the act of due process (the murder and futile legal efforts to keep Garner in Ohio rather than return her to slavery) and into the process of personal and communal reconciliation between black women and men and between slavery's black and white progeny.

We often reach out for redemption by examining and praising heroic deeds. When nineteenth-century abolitionists referred to Garner as heroic, they oversimplified Garner's private emotions and her determination to be the custodian of her children. Morrison explores a plausible private figure behind the public Garner as an individual rather than as a subject of historical and institutional (i.e. slavery) facts. "This woman was interesting to me because her story said so much about parenting and being a woman. This is not Medea who kills her children because she's mad at some dude, and she's going to get back at him. Here is something that is *huge* and *very* intimate. I imagined what would those circumstances be if this child could come back and say, 'How do you know death is better for me, since you've never done it?'" (Smith, "PW Interviews" 51).

Sethe serves her time in prison for the murder of her daughter, but the emotional and psychological trial continues long after; it is not until she confronts the past and its dehumanizing experiences through her renewed mother-daughter relationship with Beloved that she comes to terms with the business of living for the present and future. Until Beloved enters Sethe's household bringing new life as well as destruction (she blames Sethe and tries to emotionally destroy her), Sethe's "future was a matter of keeping the past at bay. The 'better life' she *believed* she and Denver were living was simply not that other one" (42, my emphasis). Beloved is both life and death—the Middle Passage's corruption and the people's survival. Therefore Sethe becomes whole again—she is rebirthed as a mother-woman—after Beloved forces her to reason with the past and to "dismember" her life.

There is reverence and honor for "those African women who did not survive the Middle Passage—those who were chewed up, spit out, and swallowed by the sea—those whose bodies and stories were never recovered. Morrison, speaking of the women whose stories are lost, says they are 'disremembered,' meaning not only that they are forgotten, but also that they are dismembered, cut up and off, and not re-membered" (Horvitz 165). The redemption from suffering and blame—the emotional new life—enables Sethe to regain the stature of courage. She was able to take foot. Therefore Sethe is not as much a heroine in the traditional sense of doing and achieving as she is in her ability to forgive and heal herself. This is the aftermath of her flight. She triumphs when she begins to recover from that collective pain. From this perspective, Morrison's use of flight actually makes its full circle of return: the Atlantic journey, slavery, infanticide, and the journey of healing together. Paul D tells her, "Sethe...me and you, we got more yesterday than anybody. We need some kind of tomorrow....You your best thing, Sethe. You are" (273). Indeed, because Sethe's heroism goes beyond the murder and "trying to outhurt the hurter," Paul D "wants to put his story next to hers" (273). Seth is inseparable from the community. She is not alone. Morrison's imagery thus moves beyond the point at which the Margaret Garners of the New World are disremembered from history and oral remembrance. In their efforts to understand the reasons why, Sethe, Paul

D, and slavery's other victims come to terms with the psycho-spiritual flight negotiating their lives after Emancipation. Morrison succeeds in creating the interior motivations of women and men who are legally allowed for the first time in their lives an attempt at human dignity.

Progeny

Sixty million and more. Toni Morrison remarked to an interviewer that he had not asked her about the meaning of "sixty million and more" to whom *Beloved* is dedicated (Clemons 75). Morrison explains that it is the best estimation of the number of Africans who died in captivity before reaching the New World and during the actual middle crossing. She states that "one account describes the Congo as so clogged with bodies that the boat couldn't pass. . . . They packed eight hundred into a ship if they'd promised to deliver four hundred. They assumed that half would die. And half did" (ibid.). Sixty million and more, therefore, is another Middle Passage metaphor that appropriates the dialectical relationship between the people's hidden transcript and its historical construction. On the one hand, the child-woman named Beloved is a hant and evokes the mythmaking elements of the narrative. On the other hand, she is the necessary spiritual messenger and historical reminder, but not so much about the wrongs of a people or the pain of their transcripts. More significantly, she is that vital connection to the past that the people need in order to navigate the present. Subsequently, the people are brought into the realm of remembering—no matter how horrendous it may be—what they had wanted to distill and forget. They would forget the original text of the flying African. Morrison refers to the psychological and emotional obliteration as historical amnesia. In one of their ways of protecting themselves, Morrison says that the Atlantic crossing "is not remembered at all. I did a lot of hunting in folklore and songs, but it's a big blank. What is this amnesia? I started out wanting to write a story about the feeling of Self" (Clemons 75). Of her own feelings of self and "having a belief in self that's larger than anyone's disbelief" Morrison says, "I remember the very real life-threatening obstacles people in my family faced, and whenever I would feel overwhelmed, that's all I had to think about" (Randolph 106).

The epigraph to *Beloved,* taken from the New Testament, is the following:

I will call them my people, which were not my people; and her beloved, which was not beloved. (Romans 9:25)

Margaret Atwood suggests that it may appear that Morrison rejects the people and the extent to which the Beloveds and Sethes of the New World were truly loved (50). On the contrary. Atwood maintains that "Morrison is too smart, and too much of a writer, not to have intended" meaning that moves beyond the epigraph verse. Consequently, we are reminded that the Biblical context is one that signifies conciliation, endurance, and hope, for the passage continues with:

And it shall come to pass that in the place where it was said unto them, Ye are not my people; there shall they be called the children of the living God.

In taking flight and taking foot, Margaret Garner becomes a symbol for the hope of the mother-women and their kinships. Although she did not escape slavery, her legacy would enable the progeny. New lineages would emerge. And new ways to take flight and take foot would prevail.

I embrace the meaning of *Beloved. Beloved.* As the people endure and strengthen themselves in order to reconcile, the progeny of all the Margaret Garners of the New World will yet become the children of the living God.

CHAPTER TWO

Surrogate Mothering:
Maroon Nanny, Jean Rhys, and Marronage

When your sorrow obscures the skies
other women like me will rise.
  —Lorna Goodison, "Nanny"

Columbus sail de ocean blue in fourteen hundred ninety two, an
when he did he discover de Caribbean. I just whan fe know how he
could ah discover someplace dat already had people pon it. I does
check tings out yuh know, so I pik up dis here Oxford American
Dictionary, an I see dat to discover mean to be de fust to obtain site
or knowledge of. When Columbus did lan', de Indian dem had don'
set up a society pon de islands. So I don' see how anybody in de right
min' can say dat Columbus discover de Caribbean. So leh we geh one
ting straight from de beginin', dis here Columbus wuz an interloper
an not a discover as we are led to believe.
  —Jeannette Charles, "Leh We Talk See"

Among the enclaves of the Blue Mountains of Jamaica, the Maroon
people continue to tell stories about an eighteenth-century woman called
Maroon Nanny. Mr. Sterling, a Jamaican Maroon who lives in Moore
Town, told me one of the stories of Nanny that encodes the diasporic
motif of the flying Africans: "She dead of old age. She ambushed. She
ain't dead 'cause *she could fly.* But den some dem say, when she dead,
three coffins dem make and her body place in one, rocks in de others.
She not dere where dem say. She left here and still her—flyin."[1] Again,
we have an enabling motif of death, rebirth, and transformation.

Mr. Sterling continued the legend that had been handed down to him. He said that Nanny wanted her corpse to have an unknown burial so that the British, though they held military power, would not be strengthened "in the mind" by finding her dead. Somewhere in the fertile terrain of Portland in Jamaica, one coffin was sent to Moore Town, one to Charles Town, and one to Scotts Hall. Even in death, Nanny's invisibility had to persist for the empowerment of her people. And she was never captured. Remembering her as inaccessible (a fugitive) and unseen would help them to survive because rememory would be their collective artifact. Similar to Toni Morrison's process of rememorying in *Beloved*, the Maroons themselves take an active part in the rememory process; it is their intimate recollection of the past, a past that is not distanced by historic remembrances but kept intimate and in the present by rememory. The legend of the three coffins—the unseen—underscores survival by taking foot and, when necessary, taking death. The idea of flying is an empowering and sustainable icon for the spirit of those who are left behind and the progeny waiting to be born.

Who was Maroon Nanny? Jamaican writer Michelle Cliff writes in her novel *Abeng*, "Nanny... was from the empire of the Ashanti, and carried the secrets of her magic into slavery.... Some of them were called Nanny, because they cared for the children of other women, but they did not know who Nanny had been" (14, 21). Indeed, to many people the name "nanny" suggests a governess or a contemporary au pair. That is not the meaning of the word in the history of Jamaica's resistance to slavery and colonization.

In the Caribbean island of Jamaica, the name Nanny is connected to the military battles that runaway slaves had with the British in the eighteenth century. The woman Nanny inspired and helped lead the Windward Maroons of Jamaica in their resistance against slavery during part of that island's First Maroon War (ca. 1665–1739). The European version of Jamaica's history begins with Columbus's second landing in the Americas in 1494. An excerpt from an essay by Jamaican writer Jeanette Charles is one of the epigraphs to this chapter. Whether you would agree with Jeanette Charles that "dis here Columbus wuz an interloper" or whether you see him as a true discoverer, he undoubtedly set into motion European expansion and exploitation that would have a profound effect on New World legacies. The island, then inhabited by the Arawak Indians, was claimed for Spain. In 1655, Jamaica, the "land of look-behind," was captured by the English from the Spanish. A small group of African slaves belonging to the Spaniards took advantage of the upheaval between the English and Spanish and fled to the mountainous interior of the island called the cockpits (precipitous rocks often covered with thick and thorny bushes), where they began their military struggle against the British for their freedom. They would become known as Maroons. Later joined by other fugitive slaves from the English-speaking plantations, they fought successfully against England and eventually established their autonomy. About that beginning of marronage in Jamaica, Mavis Campbell writes, "the slaves saw the British conquest as *their* opportunity to make *their* forward thrust for *their* freedom" (396).

Jamaica was called the "land of look-behind" because of the Maroons. This fairyland name is deceptive because its origin was in slavery and danger. British soldiers feared riding into the unknown, precarious, rocky terrain looking for fugitive slaves and Maroons. When they did, two men road one horse with one soldier facing front as a person would normally ride a horse and the other facing backwards watching the rear for possible ambush. Hence, he was the one who had to "look-behind" or be on the lookout for danger. Children who were in the Maroon camps were also at risk. For example, any baby who cried could be smothered if his crying risked the group's safety and hiding. One eighteenth-century account explains it this way:

> [The Maroon] men were placed on the ledges of rocks that rose almost perpendicularly to a great height, on a ground which, compared to those precipices, might be called a plain, the extremity being narrowed into a passage, upon which the fire of the whole body might bear. This passage contracted itself into a defile of nearly half a mile long, and so narrow that only one man could pass along it at a time. Had it been entered by a line of men, it would not have been difficult for the Maroons from the heights to have blocked them up in the front and in the rear, by rolling down large rocks at both ends, and afterwards to have crushed them to death by the same means.... The entrance was impregnable, the continuation of the line of smaller cockpits rendered the rear inaccessible, and Nature had secured the flanks of her own fortification. In this dell were secured the Maroon women and children.... On the open ground before the defile the men had erected their huts, which were called Maroon town, or Cudjoe's town, whence, in case of an alarm, the people could fly in a minute to the ledges of the rocks at the mouth of the cockpit. (Dallas 49–50)

These cockpits were treacherous and characterized by ambushes, betrayal, and the ruthlessness of the Maroons toward the British and often toward other runaway slaves. After the 1739 treaty, the Maroons agreed to return all other runaway slaves to the British—sometimes they didn't; many times they did.

Marronage was not unique to Jamaica. Following the establishment of slave colonies throughout the western hemisphere by the English, Danish, Dutch, French, Portuguese, and Spanish colonists, fugitives formed communities that resisted enslavement. European colonists were forced to recognize such settlements' territorial autonomy in places such as Brazil, Colombia, Cuba, Guadeloupe, Honduras, Mexico, Surinam, and Venezuela. In Honduras the Garífuna (called Black Caribs by Europeans), like the Maroons in Jamaica, refused to be enslaved and they never were. "Nunca, nunca, nunca" ("never, never, never") they proudly tell their children down to this present generation. The "negro republic" of Palmares in Brazil was one of the most famous *quilombos* or *mocambo* (Maroon villages). Palmares withstood the onslaught of the Portuguese for almost the entire seventeenth century, from 1606 to 1694! There were even Maroons, called "gangs of runaway negroes," in the great dismal swamp of the North Carolina and Virginia border during the seventeenth century, although not much is known about them. But the Maroon communities in the Caribbean and in Latin America lasted much longer and created their own realities as legends were also created about them.

There were many Maroon enclaves in Jamaica during England's forced establishment of plantations and slavery. One such place was named after Nanny, although the British called it the Great Negro Town. After the fall of Nanny Town, New Nanny Town was resettled near the site of the present Moor Town in Portland—a very beautiful, lush, and remote area in the Blue Mountains. According to Windward Maroon oral stories, the "rebel woman" called Maroon Nanny practiced obeah (African Caribbean animism)and knew the medicinal properties of local plants and herbs.[2] Her progeny would call her a "woman of science," a magico-religious woman, and a technician of the unseen. Some historians speculate that Nanny was an Ashanti who most likely was born in West Africa. Her Akan name, Nanna, could have become modified in the New World but still signify sacred characteristics of the female force as the ancestral healer and spiritual progenitor of the culture.

Maroon Nanny's identity in history and collective memory symbolizes the part and the whole: the resistance to bondage, the establishment of marronage as a geopolitical landscape, and the affirmation of island women's lucrative contributions to history and traditions. After reading about Nanny and listening to oral stories that her descendants living in the Blue Mountains of Jamaica still tell about her, I also wonder, as Lucille Mathurin Mair does:

> where on earth did such women, the "subordinate" sex, get this nerve? Perhaps it came from their very subordination—the moral force of the powerless confronting the powerful—and also from their ability to draw strength from that inheritance of ancestral spirits from the other side of the ocean. (59)

These ancestral spirits are connected to obeah. Europeans referred to obeah as witchcraft, black magic, or pagan superstitions. But as an extension of West African animism and cosmological beliefs in the New World, obeah not only influenced the personal lives of the people but their political agendas as well. That the woman named Nanny practiced obeah is emphasized in various eighteenth-century reports in the *Journals of the Assembly of Jamaica*, the official accounts from the British government of the island. Nanny was a woman who took foot from slavery and her legends remind me of the flying African because they have developed into myths that underscore the people's spiritual legacies. Legends about Nanny show that obeah also provided psychological strength for the Maroons. Maroon folklore includes stories about Nanny's military power. They said that she could shoot bullets at the British from her behind and darts from her eyes, and that she had mysterious cauldrons waiting in the cockpits for the slave hunters to fall into. These stories were told in order to frighten the outsiders and empower the insiders. In fact, because these empowerment stories arise from the Maroon belief in obeah, early historians denied that such a figure as Nanny actually existed. They took those descriptive feats literally, but, of course, the legends were not meant in the way they (the outsider historians) understood them. There is the insider reality and the outsider appearance. If their history is read as a text, then the subtext is the insider reality. Nanny, surrounded with all her legends, is an official national hero in Jamaica.

But in real history, Nanny continued to be an elusive figure for the British. In 1733 the British believed a traitor murdered her: "Cuffee, a very good party negro, claims reward for having killed Nanny, the rebels' old obeah woman."[3] Had the Maroons set out to strategically fool the British? Nanny's death turned out to be hearsay. A few years later Nanny was such a pivotal force in the treaty negotiations with the British that they deeded five hundred acres of land, "unto Nanny and the people residing with her and [their] heirs" in the parish of Portland. The magnitude of the deed transaction is evident: that the British would put the land in a woman's name and not in the name of one of the male chiefs indicates the military importance and strategy of Nanny's position. In the Spanish Town archives, a copy of the Land Patent dated 20 April 1741 reads: "wherefore the commissioners underwritten being met together do certify that the above Thomas Newland did lay an order for Negro Nanny and the people residing with her on five hundred acres of land in the Parish of Portland."[4]

The conquest of land and culture was soon transfigured into the conquest of the body—of female sexuality. Writing on the disruption and eruption of the body politic for black women, Marlene Nourbese Philip says:

> When the African came to the New World she brought with her nothing but her body and all the memory and history which body could contain. The text of her history and memory was inscribed upon and within the body which would become the repository of all the tools necessary for spiritual and cultural survival. At her most unmanageable, the slave removed her body from control of the white master, either by suicide or by maroonage. ("Managing the Unmanageable" 298)

Decidedly, the Maroon slaves were "unmanageable" for the master. Maroon women, however, not only challenged the legal institution of slavery by taking foot but they also wielded a semblance of autonomy. An ironic situation developed: as a group who refused to be enslaved and who would choose death over captivity, Maroon women eventually established a kind of mystical and cultural independence despite the adversity.

Marronage implies mental and physical suffering and perseverance, not only because of the people's resistance to captivity, but also because of the necessity of living in harsh, rural, and almost inaccessible places.

They had to turn their adverse circumstances into assets. Marronage often meant being alone and relegated to a life of solidarity and concealment. "To resist and survive means a psychology of risk-taking and a determination to brave adversity and face danger. After a certain time, many fugitives gave up and returned to servile conditions that were inhuman but secure. But the one who does not give up becomes hardened. Here lies the passage from insubordination to rebellion. He is a 'primitive rebel'" (Manigat 422). Manigat also discusses the historical text and context of marronage as "the existence of a social organization (the plantation system) with a structure and laws, within which the *servile condition* is set down, and with which the Maroon *breaks by fleeing*. This means that the threshold of acceptability has been crossed. It is the logical sequence: misfortune-threshold of tolerance-unhappiness-rupture" (Manigat 422).

In a historical context marronage connotes logistical and social ruptures that brought autonomy and hard-won freedom. Created on the threshold of the New World encounter, marronage became a new kind of indigenous living—an asset from the perspective of the marooned. Marronage then was haven and hell, resistance and sanctuary. Caribbean women writers diverse in ethnicity and generations such as Maryse Condé, Michèle Lacrosil, Myriam Warner-Vieyra, Michelle Cliff, and Jean Rhys recreate marronage as an engendered trope in their writing. These writers are engaged with issues centered on language, identity, gender, race, ethnicity, and culture within the context of transnational migrations. For example, Michelle Cliff who is also a "white" Creole and who can "pass" seeks out the Afro-Caribbean legacies that she was taught to despise. Cliff consciously recreates history as a dwelling place for knowledge—a place to visit in order to move forward. History becomes an active character in much of her work. Jean Rhys emerges from the older generation of writers. Having left the West Indies, she struggled with similar issues of transnational migrations from the vantage point of Europe. Where Rhys's self-representation in history is often problematic, Caribbean women writers such as Cliff may be viewed as the literary progeny of Jean Rhys because they come to terms with their awls of representation and reality.

Jean Rhys, a twentieth-century writer, and Maroon Nanny, an eighteenth-century African slave woman, are historical legacies of this Caribbean place. Originally from the island of Dominica and having lived in England for most of her life, Jean Rhys, who was of Scottish and French descent, was asked if she even considered herself a West Indian:

> She shrugged. "It was such a long time ago when I left."
> "So you don't think of yourself as a West Indian writer?"
> "No! I'm not, I'm not! I'm not even English."
> "What about a French writer?" I asked.
> Again she shrugged and said nothing.
> "You have no desire to go back to Dominica?"
> "Sometimes," she said. (Plante 275–76)

Jean Rhys's relationship with England was just as problematic as her connection to Dominica and the West Indies. In another instance she would write, "When I say I write for love I mean that there are two places for me. Paris (or what it was to me) and Dominica . . . where I was born. . . . Both these places or the thought of them make me want to write. . . . [T]he West Indies started knocking at my heart. . . . That (the knocking) has never stopped" (Wyndham and Melly 171). The West Indies remained an important place of being for Rhys. Although she spent her entire adult life in England, she would respond to the "knocking at my heart" with the creation of her most West Indian novel, *Wide Sargasso Sea*. It is through this novel that she returns to the homeland, wrestles with the issues of race, gender, and the legacies of West Indian plantation history.

Wide Sargasso Sea (1966) is Jean Rhys's creative dialogue with Charlotte Brontë's *Jane Eyre* (1847).[5] The novel depicts Antoinette Cosway Mason (Rhys's beautiful, young Creole), who is understood to be Charlotte Brontë's Mrs. Edward Rochester at the time of Emancipation in the English-speaking West Indies. Although it is the dawn of freedom, the backdrop of slavery persists and the vestiges of slavery permeate the action and consciousness of the principal players. Despite the attempts of the black surrogate mother, Christophine Dubois, to have Antoinette remain on the island, "Mr. Rochester" takes Antoinette to England where he attempts to hide her as the familiar madwoman in the attic.[6] Rhys cleverly never mentions the husband by name. By not naming him, Rhys consciously makes this male character a paradoxical nonentity: In one instance, because of the laws of primogeniture, he is the second-son without an inheritance; as a white Englishman he is powerful among the disenfranchised island Creoles and Africans. By not naming him, Rhys actually dethrones him, turning him into a haunted and brooding colonial on a colonized island. For him the island is over-powering and frightening. An Englishman and younger son who has been tricked and coerced into marrying a wealthy West Indian Creole, he is the perpetual explorer in colonial history. He regains a modicum of power by controlling the woman and her inheritance. Rhys has cre-ated him as Everyman the colonizer in the name of the fatherland.

Rhys wanted to give a credible West Indian voice to Bertha Rochester, the supposedly insane Creole wife of Edward Rochester. The early Holly-wood film version of *Jane Eyre*, with Vivien Leigh and Orson Welles, cap-tures the kind of madness that Brontë first depicted:

> In the deep shade, at the farther end of the room, a figure ran backwards and forwards. What it was, whether beast or human being, one could not, at first sight tell; it groveled, seemingly, on all fours; it snatched and growled like some strange wild animal: but it was covered with clothing, and a quantity of dark, grizzled hair, wild as a mane, hid its face.
> (Brontë 321)

Rhys believed that the portrayal of the so-called madwoman in the attic was superficial and that it unrealistically portrays a "paper tiger lu-natic." Rhys writes that, "I've never believed in Charlotte's [Brontë] lu-natic.... [H]e [the husband] decides that his wife is as mad as—well mad—and eventually hauls her off to England and locks her up. I've tried to make this more convincing than in *Jane Eyre*" (Wyndham and Melly 214). Significantly, Rhys states that it's the husband who declares his wife insane. She recognizes the extent to which authority forces women to be diagnosed as mad. Therein lies the tension between diagnosis and gender-oriented control. In Brontë's novel, Bertha Rochester's death al-lows Jane Eyre to finally marry Edward Rochester. Growing up fasci-nated with Rochester and Jane, I had little sympathy for the "crazy woman," Bertha. At that time I could not read how Jane is European and classed (even as a governess) while Bertha is a West Indian Creole declassed by Rochester and colonialism. How can we understand the colonial generations that created Bertha Rochester (Brontë's portrayal of her is as a "dark" heiress whose exploited wealth came from West In-dian sugar through slavery)? Bertha Rochester has been victimized by her husband who believes he has the social right to disregard her (even if the law will not allow him to legally marry Jane) because she, Bertha, is portrayed as the conventional madwoman who is kept (literally) in the attic.

In effect, what do we mean by labels such as madness? Madness, a nonclinical term for emotional dysfunction and a catch-all label for mental illness, is a marker overused to designate women who act strangely and who do not submit to the social correctness of the day; they are women circulating on the perpetual margins of their societies. Ranging from associations with temporary depression to complete bipolar dysfunction, "madness" has become a layman's all-encompassing, gender-driven metaphor for anger, depression, levels of insanity, and emotional disenfranchisement. In feminist literature, madness has been labeled as a valuable defense mechanism that subverts enforced silence and patriarchal authority. Sandra Gilbert and Susan Gubar's famous work, *The Madwoman in the Attic: The Woman Writer and the Nineteenth-Century Literary Imagination* accentuates the authorial rage of women writers who have been historically silenced. How can madness be an asset for its female victims? Do "mad" women decorously draw the curtain around them against reality and society? Is "madness" as "irrational behavior" a conduit for alienating, transforming rage? In her provocative study, *The Madwoman Can't Speak; Or Why Insanity Is Not Subversive*, Marta Caminero-Santangelo challenges the status of the madwoman and considers how "The madwoman has come to stand all but universally in feminist criticism for elements of subversion and resistance in women's writing.... [A] search for the subversive madwoman in literature not only involved some violent representations of its own ... but also is fundamentally misguided, since the symbolic resolution of the madwoman as an alternative to patriarchy ultimately traps the woman in silence." (1, 4). Brontë denies Bertha Rochester any speech of coherence or reason—Bertha can only growl and act like a ravaged animal, which highlights Jane's civility. Rhys makes irony of this: in the space of silence, Rhys's Bertha (Antoinette) will have the strength and focus to torch Rochester's ancestral estate. "Rochester's desire to shut Bertha up," says Caminero-Santangelo, "is understood by Rhys for what it implies but does not represent: his desire to rob her of the power to represent herself through speech" (16). Rhys has understood the illusion and reality of gender-oriented madness to the extent that madness is declared only by the perpetrator (Rochester) and not the victim. I find this to be a key point in the novel; Rhys intended to show that Antoinette is not the mad-woman in the attic, although she is placed there by the husband and by subsequent readers of *Jane Eyre*. In this instance, *Wide Sargasso Sea* and *Jane Eyre* are often critiqued as the quintessential novels that appropri-ate the paradigmatic trope of the madwoman raging in the house of self. In the final act, Rhys's Creole woman is angry rather than mad and out of the attic. Rhys shows that Antoinette will make the conscious choice to end her life. Rhys portrays suicide as a longing for the home-land where Antoinette (the autobiographical consciousness of Rhys) once was. Antoinette's anticipated death is propelled by that spiritual and psychological longing rather than a simplistic declaration of insan-ity. Challenging the chaos model of gender-oriented madness, Caminero-Santangelo maintains that such a model creates the illusion of escape from patriarchy. Indeed, ahead of her time, Rhys challenged the lunatic gestures of the paper tiger who transforms herself through hysteria.

The physical writing of *Wide Sargasso Sea* was a struggle for Rhys. In her foreword to Rhys's unfinished autobiography, *Smile Please*, Diana Athill writes that because of physical illness Rhys could not revise the novel to her liking and that "even though we had on our hands the manuscript of a beautiful novel which only its author could see to be unfinished, . . . she had made me promise that I would not publish it . . . until she had given her permission" (8). Rhys had recurring dreams of an unwanted pregnancy. Finally, when she dreamed that the baby was born she said, "so the book must be finished, and that must be what I think about it really" (*Smile Please* 13). She completed the novel and rec-ognized how much the metaphorical ending was a literary and cultural homecoming. In the process of writing, Rhys appears to have made a psychological and spiritual journey to her own ancestral home—in the West Indies. The complexity of the West Indian cultural landscape as a "remembered love," albeit a paradoxical one, remained with Rhys and did not reconcile with her sense of place until the book was finished. When the book was finally published in 1966, it received, and would continue to receive, an overwhelmingly positive critical response, and Rhys would triumph—from on high. As Dennis Porter writes,

> What, given its origin in literature, looks like the least personal of Jean
> Rhys's novels is, in fact, a deeply meditated work that has an intensely
> personal character. That this is the case is confirmed by the light *Wide*

Sargasso Sea sheds on all Jean Rhys's earlier works. The turbulent tale of the nineteenth-century Creole girl is crucial to an understanding of the author's frequently enigmatic modern heroines. (550)

The cultural landscapes of her homeland had taken flight.

Rhys shows us the complex and often elusive meaning of nineteenth-century gender and ethnicity in her portrayal of mothering through Christophine Dubois. Was it her own illusive sense of representation as a writer that creates Christophine as silent and silenced? That is to say, Christophine is simultaneously powerful and powerless. Most readers relegate Christophine to the background of the novel's story, which has Antoinette at the center. Yet Christophine's presence is illusive just as the Maroons were illusive in their relationship to the British and to the plantation Creoles. Like Nanny, Christophine is a technician of the unseen. And she is obeah. Christophine takes control of herself in spite of the power that the Englishman has over her. She is the mother-woman who has "spunks." For example, when asked by the Englishman what she would do if he gave her money to take Antoinette away, Christophine tells him that "I like to see the *world* before I die" (159, my emphasis). Although she may have limited legal authority, Christophine maintains her survival skills and her world vision extends beyond the island. A former slave and illiterate, she moves in the historical shadow of Maroon Nanny. Even though Rhys had reservations about the way she made Christophine unique, Christophine is articulate and resourceful. Despite Rhys's resistance, the character took on a life of her own.

Christophine is the island woman who "represents female power, wisdom and autonomy, strengths she vainly attempts to encourage in Antoinette" (O'Connor 208). Despite her position, Christophine asserts herself in the Caribbean spirit of Nanny and shrewdly attempts to take advantage of being legally emancipated by traveling to "see the world." Out of fear and intimidation, the Englishman has to struggle to maintain his composure during the confrontation. When he realizes that Christophine may be able to control what happens to Antoinette, he resorts to the only weapon he has: the power he inherits from being a white colonial male. He threatens to have her arrested for practicing obeah. He holds power and underscores what Edward Said refers to as being a "white man." During the period of colonialism such a man embodied a "very concrete manner of being-in-the-world, a way of taking hold of reality, language and thought" (Said, *Orientalism* 227). Written evidence is mockery for Christophine because concealment and not revelation is paramount in her world. Christophine finally tells him, "Read and write I don't know. Other things I know" (161). The "other things" refer to the unseen "spirits" of obeah and marronage.

"Reading" Christophine from within the attributes of marronage provides a way of reading her role as one of empowerment. It is an empowerment that has to be challenged and eliminated by the colonial manifestation of patriarchy. Christophine possesses the mother-woman's ancestral "grit and toil" that enables survival. Women of African ancestry and sensibility have personalized the "grit" of the ancestral earth-mother in spite of and because of Middle Passage legacies. Jamaican writer Opal Palmer Adisa writes in her essay, "She Scrape She Knee: The Theme of My Work," that the characteristics of the ancestral mother-woman strengths are empowering:

> As a woman I am often scraping my knee, sometimes without even falling. Perhaps it is because I dare to demand that the way be cleared for me or that I insist on leading the line at times. My choice. Always. Now as I reflect, I see that there is much in common between the little girl who frequently scraped her knee and has scars to prove it and this woman . . . who must walk . . . in defiance of the scrapes that are inflicted, often by the insensitive, the blind, the upholders of norms, traditions, and antiquated values that I had no part in setting and by which I will not abide. . . . [E]ach time I scrape my knee I learn about my potentials as well as my limitations, and I experience the Mother-God within me. (145–46)

The mother-woman who "scrape she knee" is both in context and in the text of writing. Scraping the knees is a metaphor that describes strengths and tests; that there are no victories without tests and hurts. Despite any ambivalence Rhys may have had, her authorial voice challenges the reader to move beyond her text in order to understand that unseen context of pain and recovery. Her portrayal of Christophine remains as that of the kind of woman who "scrape she knee."

How does gender and blackness and, by historical default, the consciousness of marronage as a difference that enables empowerment haunt Rhys? How does the fluidity of whiteness inform her personal and literary sensibilities? Rhys writes, "I prayed so ardently to be black, and would run to the looking glass in the morning to see if the miracle had happened. And though it never had, I tried again. Dear God, let me be black" (*Smile Please* 33). Anna Morgan, the protagonist of Rhys's 1934 novel, *Voyage in the Dark,* muses, "I wanted to be black, I always wanted to be black. . . . Being black is warm and gay, being white is cold and sad" (31). In another instance, Rhys would write,

> I would never be part of anything. I would never really belong anywhere, and I knew it, and all my life would be the same, trying to belong, and failing. Always something would go wrong. I am a stranger and I always will be, and after all I didn't really care. Perhaps it's my fault. I really can't think far enough for that. But I don't like these people, I thought. I don't hate—they hate—but I don't love what they love. I don't want their lights or the presents in gold and silver paper. . . . I don't know what I want. And if I did I couldn't say it, for I don't speak *their* language and I never will. (*Smile Please* 124, my emphasis)

Rhys had inherited this "color thing," and it burdened her and certainly created more representation questions when she first lived in Europe during the early decades of the twentieth century.

Readers have often viewed Rhys's literary women as passive. Jean Rhys felt that the powerless are relegated to self-negation. Perhaps it was Rhys's own imposing geopolitical location (England) that psychologically enabled her to make a final attempt in dealing with her complex West Indian identity during the last years of her life. In writing *Wide Sargasso Sea* had she fully arrived at accepting the diverse totality of her West Indian heritage? Was her writing therapy for cultural loss? Earlier I quoted the conversation that Rhys had with David Plant about her identity. Rhys implied that she could not deal with the diversity of her colonial, ethnic, and national heritage. Raised on the island of Dominica until she left for England at the age of seventeen, Rhys's postcolonial identity was neither here nor there. She knew that she may have been "white" but she could not be "English."

Racial traits located in phenotypes are used to categorize and dominate national and ethnic ideologies. As I mentioned in chapter 1, being white is a floating racial category in this postcolonial moment of history. Veronica Marie Gregg writes that "there seems to be a wide range of interpretive options for an analysis of Jean Rhys's writing: West Indian, Third World, British, Euro-American, European, feminist, postcolonial" (Gregg 3). Readers who view Rhys as a "problematic" woman writer who does not fit into a monolithic model nonetheless force her writing into categories that ignore the dynamics of her Creole and West Indian heritage. Jean D'Costa succinctly states:

> Critics at three corners of the triangular trade lay claim to Jean Rhys. In England scholars read her as "British woman writer," painter of grim urban settings and social subtypes, catching time, place, mood, and the values that upheld a fading imperial world.... To American critics her work speaks mostly of woman-as-victim, although they recognize her insight into British society. In the Caribbean Rhys is the exponent of the "terrified consciousness"... of the ruling class. For all three groups, Rhys presents problems of classification which disguise problems of interpretation and acceptance. (390)

Rhys's attitude about her own identity may have been "shifting, ambiguous, [and] even contradictory" (Gregg 2), but, after all, reflected in her own looking glass, Rhys undoubtedly inherited the ambivalent legacies of growing up "white" in an African Creole society.[7] Rhys used an imagination that reflected the struggles and uncertainties of an emerging postcolonial consciousness. Rhys's personal background is European and the creoleness of color. Her ambivalence should be understood in the context of a colonial subject struggling with the past—even before literary and intellectual audiences could acknowledge such a personal struggle and public ambivalence. Like many of her writer counterparts, Rhys undoubtedly had personal preoccupations with color, class, and gender in the context of being a Creole woman.

Creole. What is the meaning of this dynamic word, this word that carries so much historical meaning and cultural baggage? Columbus began the momentum for European, African, and Asian peoples to struggle with and assert coexistence in a new environment. Out of centuries of reckoning with diversity, island cultures represent many forms of creolization. To be Creole goes beyond phenotypic categories even though the history of the West Indies has formed, in part, out of the colonization and importation of race politics. Nancy Cunard believed, "[i]f all the races of the new world were finally to unite, the Creole would be the real 'American'" (397). Who really is Creole? Throughout the Americas the term Creole has had numerous historical meanings. The term has included people of multiracial descent in the Caribbean and Latin America, new generations of slaves born in the Americas (as opposed to having been born in Africa), and those Europeans who as descendents of slave owners were born in the New World. They represented European and non-European encounters—creolization, *criollismo,* créolité.

In the societies of Latin America and the West Indies, Creole representation produced prejudice and discrimination based on economic class that is closely linked to gradations of skin color (as opposed to "race") that exemplify European phenotypes. Sociologist Juanita Ramos in talking about her black Puerto Rican identity writes, "In Puerto Rico the phrase, '¿Y tu abuela donde está?' ('And where is your grandmother?'), is frequently used to imply that a white Puerto Rican is hiding his/her African heritage by not acknowledging that the fact that some relatives are black skin [*sic*]. The African heritage is implicitly transmitted through the woman and is particularly made evident by the texture of her hair" (Ramos 77). In my discussion of Margaret Garner, I mentioned the politics of gender and color prejudice—the paradox of white slave owners who could simultaneously favor, be indifferent to, and abuse slaves who were related to them through miscegenation. In the French Caribbean, there was such an urge among some women of African ancestry to assimilate into French culture that one class of fair complexioned people came to be known as "chappés" because they had *échappé* (escaped) their blackness through genetic whitening. These ideas continue to haunt and proliferate through identity and representation among those who are still caught within the confines of mental colonization.

In contrast to the West Indies, race distinctions in the United States have been predominately a matter of "black" and "white." People considered "black" by U.S. standards are not black by Caribbean and Latin American standards. I remember a graduate school friendship that I had with a woman from Peru. Carolina was predominately of European ancestry and in Peru she was "white." When she was a student in England a woman from India asked her if she would like to join some "women of color" who were organizing a political base at the university. Carolina said that she was very surprised that she was asked to join such an organization because she did not see herself as a "woman of color." She had never even thought about it. She said to me in her Spanish accent, "In my coontry, I am white." In Peru she had inherited privilege. But she decided to attend the meeting and find out what it was all about. There she came to know women who came from Pakistan, the Caribbean, India, Africa, the Middle East, the United States, and Indonesia!

After continuing to live in England she learned that, well, the English certainly didn't see her as white as they are. And from the women of color Carolina began to learn about racism from another perspective. She then went to the United States. And in the States all non-European whites are cast into being the Other, put into their places, and often called out-of-name, "*Ay, que tu eres mas negra.*" So, Carolina was seen as a "woman of color" here, not to her dismay, but to her curiosity. Being a friendly person, it was not difficult for her to befriend other women of color. The politics of color was a learning experience for her. She told us that when she finished graduate school in the States she would return to Peru where she would become "white" again. Now, after those experiences in England and the States, she would know what it means to identify and speak with the Peruvian women of African and Indian descent (the women of color in Peru) who are discriminated against because of color, class, and sex. New World history produced a kind of carnival that is either taken very seriously or simply laughed at when color is an issue.

I would like to imagine that, had Jean Rhys been a part of our current postcolonial consciousness, she would have articulated cultural ambivalence, identity, and passion from an all-encompassing historic view. Maybe she would have learned and gained new ways of thinking like Carolina and Juanita Ramos. She certainly would have had a supportive literary and cultural climate in which to explore her most personal story. Rhys was an interpreter of change and continuity, about much of which she was personally insecure. Rhys was both ahead of her time and a product of her time. We can still wonder if she had come to terms with what she regarded as the intimacy of self in her writing. Regardless of any reservations she may still have had about her Creole identity, it seems that she found refuge and latent healing in shaping the two central women characters in the novel of her most West Indian historical and personal Creole consciousness.

Miscegenation was one of the practices that brought European and African women into not only precarious emotional relationships but also hidden biological ones. Who was related to whom? One nineteenth-century Creole from Martinique declared, "Many of the women and children did not know whether they were Creoles or whites, nor could the whites themselves tell who was white and who was Creole, so generally was the population mixed, while the city was largely French in manners and life" (Cunard 397). In spite of the "trickle up" theory of color, white Creoles throughout the islands continued to be influenced by the African persistence. In one of Jean Rhys's short stories, "The Day They Burned the Books," the central theme focuses on the meaning of being "white" for two young Dominican playmates. The narrator says that "whenever the subject was brought up—people's relations and whether they had a drop of coloured blood or whether they hadn't—my father would grow impatient and interrupt. 'Who's white?' He would say. 'Damned few'" (156). Throughout the Caribbean, white Creoles didn't want "mixed blood" in the family. These attitudes have caused inner conflicts and public ambivalence among West Indians who look toward the "motherland" (the European country) for identity representation. The expression, "¿Y tu abuela donde está?" indicates the extent to which color prejudice permeates lineage with a focus on gender and place. In her autobiographical writings, Rhys suggests that her own Dominican family may have had an interracial heritage. For example, she writes with pride about her great-grandfather (who owned a slave estate). As a child she heard stories about his beautiful Spanish wife. That she does not believe the story about the woman's European origin is evident when she remarks, "Spanish? I wonder" (*Smile Please* 36). Rather than concede a possible African heritage, West Indians would cite the influence of "Spanish" characteristics to explain the presence of "color" in their family. This propensity for "Spanish" ancestry can also be seen in Gustave de Beaumont's 1835 novel, *Marie, or Slavery in the United States*, where, in the foreword, he writes, "I made out in the balcony for whites a face which was very dark. I asked for an explanation of this new phenomenon; the American answered: 'She is white . . . local tradition affirms that the blood which flows in her veins is *Spanish*'" (5, my emphasis).

Any "type" in the Caribbean signifies the triangular trade route—Europe, Africa, and the Americas—of Columbus's voyages and of the Middle Passage that produced the West Indies and its Creole middle passages. Indeed, unlike the race situation in the United States, being "white" in the West Indies and other places in Latin America is a flotilla of expression, practice, perception, and legacy. Is Rhys the epitome of cultural chaos because she has a so-called difficult fit? Trying to make her fit into boxed categories limits the scope of her historical consciousness. Making her fit accentuates only what is visible and what we all know—that skin color, the ubiquitous epidermal factor, still remains only skin deep. Gregg gives us another way of looking at this complexity:

> Far from ignoring social and historical formation or separating herself, Jean Rhys's writing demonstrates that the "identity" of the Creole is made of the sociohistorical, discursive fabric of the colonial West Indies. The articulation of the Creole Subjectivity is at one and the same time a discursive self-destruction articulated within the historical specificity of racialized slavery in the Caribbean. Rhys does not have a choice. One of the achievements of her fiction is that . . . it calls attention to and opens up for examination the historical and discursive processes by which the white Self in the Caribbean is constructed over and against that of the black Other. (38)

Rhys is one of the race chameleons whose alliances shift. The themes of Rhys's writing affirm that kind of personal and historical ambivalence.

Throughout the first section of her autobiography, Rhys refers to the ambivalent relationships she had during her childhood with "coloured" and black relatives and neighbors in Dominica. Selwyn Cudjoe writes that "in *Voyage in the Dark* and *Wide Sargasso Sea* she locates her hero-ines in the slave history of the Caribbean and from that vantage point tries to work out their relationships with the black people of the soci-ety. . . . She empathized with their (blacks) slave past but felt repulsed by their assertive present in the postemancipation era" (*Caribbean Women Writers* 17). In life (and in her fiction) Rhys had a distinct fascination—what would amount to prejudice from our contemporary perspec-tive—about "dark" West Indians. One of her well-known remarks in an interview with David Plante underscores her attitude:

> At the start I hated my nurse. A horrid woman. It was she who told me awful stories of zombies and *sucriants,* the vampires; she frightened me totally. I was a bit wary of the black people. I've tried to write about how I gradually became even a bit envious. They were so strong. They could walk great distances, it seemed to me, without getting tired, and carry those heavy loads on their heads. They went to the dances every night. They wore turbans. They had lovely dresses with a belt to tuck the trains through that were lined with paper and rustled when they moved. (50)

Rhys shows her unfamiliarity. She is distanced from the black people of her community even as she is amid them believing in and creating stereo-types of the black Dominican. That was her personal paradox. Given Rhys's conflicting identity regarding her Creole, that is to say African, and European heritage, this ambivalence about identity and representation can be understood. "Although Rhys cannot claim fully to understand the 'otherness' of most West Indian women, because most are African-Caribbean rather than white Creole, she does seem able to return to the West Indian Bertha Mason the dignity taken away by Charlotte Brontë. Bertha Mason was a victim of the sexism and imperialism of British culture.... [I]n Rhys's fiction, we do see a successful syncretism between the white Creole woman Antoinette and the black Creole woman Tia" (de Abruna 96).

While exploring what she thought were her own inadequacies, Rhys believed that the individual has to earn death. She felt that only after writing all that was possible could she deserve death. The only completed chapter (about her West Indian childhood) in the autobiography seems to allow the curtain to gently fall because with *Wide Sargasso Sea* she had followed her bliss. Like Janie in Zora Neale Hurston's *Their Eyes Were Watching God*, Rhys pulls in her horizon and tells the world to come and see; Rhys's final novel also celebrates the mother's land and undeniably lays claim to the enabling modalities of mother-women searching within the matrilineal diaspora.

> If your mother doesn't nurse you, your grandmother will.
> —Caribbean Proverb

If you stay long enough on any of the Caribbean islands you will hear variants of proverbial beliefs such as "if your mother doesn't nurse you, your grandmother will" or "it's my mother who fathered me." Many of us who come from New World African cultures know that if the natural mother is not able to provide, another woman will. We learned the lesson from our mother-women that a woman does not have to bear children in order to speak and act the gift of mothering. Many of us can remember when there was always someone in the neighborhood to take care of you, to help you if there was trouble, and if you made trouble, these mother-women would certainly let your own mother-woman know. When something happened, good news and bad news traveled so fast; even though we didn't have voice mail, e-mail, faxes, or sometimes telephone, the news traveled. We understood that this was the way it was supposed to be.

We understood that our mothers did the best they could do for us. They were the women who could create ways out of no way. In her anthology *The Woman That I Am,* Soyini Madison writes, "I remember my mother standing, in a 'colored woman' style, her arms akimbo and her head tilted to the side, speaking quietly but forcefully in a tone that could scare a bull. She would willfully declare: 'Being the woman that I am I will make a way out of no way.' These were ... the words and the will of all women of color who assert who they are, who create sound out of silence, and who build worlds out of remnants" (1). Toward the end of her life, my own mother looked back over the years of her life and would say, "I always did the best that I could do for you children." That was an absolute among few absolutes in life. Many times I have read and heard of women whose lives may have been interpreted as not fulfilling much of anything. Yet these women knew that, regardless how others would deem them unsuccessful, they could trace their lives and say, "I did the best I could."

Rhys was ambivalent about the mother that she wanted to be and that she became. She had chronic interpersonal problems with her biological mother, her nannies (who were West Indian black women), and later in life with her own daughter. She would remember how, "Once I heard her [my mother] say that black babies were prettier than white ones. Was this the reason I prayed so to be black?" (*Smile Please* 33). As a girl, does she want to be black in order to be more loved by her mother or in order to be pretty? Remember that, elsewhere in the autobiography, Rhys claims that she "prays ardently" to be black not for the sake of blackness, but because it is a concrete identity connected to family and happiness. The ambivalence carried over into her portrayal of the black surrogate mother, Christophine. Considering her autobiographical writings, it seems that the writing of *Wide Sargasso Sea* was an attempt to purge this psychological conflict, the psychological resolution of her West Indian sense of both the mother's legacy and the African presence in her personal history. Rhys wrote *Voyage in the Dark,* which may be viewed as the labor pain of another birth that took a long time coming in the form of *Wide Sargasso Sea.* Here Rhys abandons the biological mother-daughter reconciliation, and another kind of mother bonding takes place.

How does biography inform the writer's creative imagination? What meaning is there between the juxtaposition and contradiction of biography and autobiography? How can autobiography be a vehicle for fiction and vice versa? Jamaica Kincaid's novel *The Autobiography of My Mother* takes place on the island of Dominica—Jean Rhys's homeland. Although

I have never been to Dominica, I felt an overwhelming sense of familiarity as I read Kincaid's description of the hinterlands of Dominica and
the roads to and from Roseau and Massacre—all places that I'd "visited"
many times through Jean Rhys. I was intrigued by Kincaid's title. Does
Kincaid come to terms with the "fractured mother-daughter bond" that
permeates her writing? Referring to *The Autobiography of My Mother*,
Kincaid tells an interviewer, "My mother is an overwhelming presence
in my life and in my brothers' lives. . . . She's jealous of our being alive.
She doesn't quite want us dead, but rather in a state of perpetual dying"
(Weathers 100). The narrator's story is autobiography because she tries
to come to terms with her own life as she attempts to reconstruct the
memory and life of her mother who died in childbirth. The mother remains unknown to the narrator, but she says, "This account of my life
has been an account of my mother's life as much as it has been an account of mine, and even so, again it is an account of the life of the children I did not have" (227). The narrator constructs a created memory of
the mother in order to come to terms with her own childless (by choice)
life. Thus the ideas of biography and autobiography are merged into
one voice. An incomplete sepia image of a woman begins each chapter.
As the narrator begins to understand her inner self, the image of this
woman unfolds and in the end the picture is completed. Is this a picture
of the mother or of the daughter? Is the picture what the daughter wanted
it to be? Likewise, in what way does Rhys's literary Creole inform the
autobiographical consciousness of Rhys?

> Mirror, mirror, off the wall
> mirror mirror break my fall
> Let me return
> Let me fly
> Let me journey
> before I die.
> Mirror, mirror, I'm not wildly leaping
> I only want Coulibri. . . .
> Let me return
> Let me fly
> Let me journey
> before I die.
>
> —Anonymous

Throughout the West Indies, precarious relationships among island
women arose out of the ambivalent emotional relationships caused by

slavery. In her discussions of those relationships Barbara Bush tells us how white West Indian women held a peculiar power. Although not legally enslaved like the bonded women, they were victims of gender oppression. The peculiar power they had over enslaved women (and men) produced relationships such as those that Rhys vividly portrays between Christophine and Antoinette and between Antoinette and the young black girl, Tia. Creole women of European descent, who "in practice . . . were not afforded much consideration or respect" (Bush 246), had what I refer to as logistical friendships with their female slaves or black comères. White women often abused at whim black women who helped them and whom they needed. Both white and black women shared peculiar logistics that extended into cautious and strained civility, if not direct animosity, after Emancipation. Rhys depicts a gender-oriented bonding and rejection through the tentative liaison between Tia and Antoinette and the surrogate relationship between Antoinette and Christophine. In Michelle Cliff's *Abeng* there is a similar social statute of limitation between the central character, Clare Savage, and Zoe. Zoe is dark complexioned and knows her place next to white-complexioned Clare. Their childhood friendship can't endure because of color and class prejudice. Cliff writes that Clare "is a light-skinned female who has been removed from her homeland in a variety of ways and whose life is a movement back, ragged, interrupted, uncertain, to that homeland. She is fragmented, damaged, incomplete" ("Clare Savage as a Crossroads Character" 265). Significantly, toward the end of *Abeng*, Clare has a dream that mirrors the stone-throwing scene in *Wide Sargasso Sea:*

> That night Clare dreamed that she and Zoe were fist-fighting by the river in St. Elizabeth. That she picked up a stone and hit Zoe underneath the eye and a trickle of blood ran down her friend's face and onto the rock where she sat. The blood formed into a pool where the rock folded over on itself. And she went over to Zoe and told her she was sorry—making a compress of moss drenched in water to soothe the cut. (165)

The dream in *Abeng* and the stone-throwing episode in *Wide Sargasso Sea* are mirror reflections that evoke the historic images of gender and Creole ethnicity. While Clare may question and challenge race and class differences, Tia refuses to accept Antoinette's sudden recognition of their cultural kinship. The often quoted lines from the novel, "we stared at each other, blood on my face, tears on hers" (45), indicates not only a wounding, but a connection through bloodlines. Regardless of color and potential status, Antoinette is just as much an "island girl" as Tia. Furthermore, at this early juncture of establishing relationships, Rhys is teasing out hidden blood ties that would, indeed, cause social hatred. Despite any kinship ties, potential bonding between the girl-children cannot continue once the conflict between the former slaves and the white Creoles has flared into an uprising. The adult world's conflicts of class and color prejudice establish an emotional obstacle between them. Seeing this violent gesture as motivated by hate and envy oversimplifies the complex reality of ethnic sensibilities and juvenile confusion. As adolescents on the threshold of going in separate social directions, neither Antoinette nor Tia can articulate the reasons for their confusion—they simply imitate adults. The blood on Antoinette's face and the tears on Tia's face dispel the friendship between them. And their Creole kinship ties remain in denial. The moment embraces and repels kinship and lineage. They are doubly marginalized as girl-children within the restrictions of the colonizer and the colonized. This pivotal scene is complete with the complexity of the colonizing gaze, kinship images (i.e., the "looking glass"), and Tia and Antoinette who lock eyes under the realization of truth. Given the hidden and ambiguous lineage relationships at Coulibri, the gaze positions Antoinette as an unrelated kin. *Tía* is the Spanish word for aunt. Spanish, English, and French markings are coded on the ambivalent cultural landscape. Is Rhys embedding another trace of kinship—hidden in plain view? The paradox is that Tia, a metaphorical progeny of Nanny, has already usurped Antoinette's trust, has betrayed their girl-sharing despite any kind of kinship. That Antoinette nevertheless runs to Tia underscores the significance of the cyclic return to kinship. Remember that Tia's image also has been in the pool—the symbolic mirror that reflects who is related to whom and "who is white"—only a few really are.

Like the metaphorical sister Seseku in Michelle Cliff's *Abeng,* who is searching out a doubled heritage, Antoinette Cosway eventually finds the means by which to express her hidden strength and earn death. There is no doubt that Antoinette is an island child. Christophine, the obeah mother-woman and inscriptive progeny of Nanny, tells Antoinette's English husband that "she [Antoinette] is Creole girl and she have the sun in her" (158). Furthermore, Christophine insists on self-definition and eventually takes foot when Rhys writes her out of the story. But Christophine Dubois signifies the embedded consciousness in *Wide*

Sargasso Sea, that of the woman who could enable herself and not succumb to European male domination; she is the inaccessible Maroon mother-woman written out of the story, but whose presence remains a necessary force for Antoinette's spiritual return. Certainly while Antoinette vacillates between otherness—somewhere else—and holding on to loss, Christophine, the mother-woman to whom she turns for comfort and survival, is secure about her inner ability to cope with reality. Whereas Antoinette portrays what is done to her by a patriarchal, slavery-haunted system of values, Christophine signifies what enables her into action in spite of what has been done. Christophine's empowerment is generally ignored in discussions about *Wide Sargasso Sea* or simply not seen. Yet this character's empowering presence in the narrative is her silence. Her limited speech and clandestine action are assets in the land of look-behind.

While Antoinette's English husband (the symbolic Rochester) does not like Christophine, he recognizes and fears her unseen powers. Christophine is another technician of the unseen. Furthermore, she makes it clear that she does not have to speak *his* language in order to understand the "letters of the law." Did Rhys intend Christophine to echo her own stream of thinking—not caring about "monied white men" and their laws? She probably did, given her own life circumstances. Marginalized, Christophine tells Antoinette, "All women, all colors, nothing but fools. Three children I have. One living in the world, each one a different father, but no husband, I thank my God. I keep my money. I don't give it to no worthless man" (110). Regardless of color and class, Christophine believes that women have a shared denominator: the men who control or attempt to control them. I see that her motivations reveal something of the author's alter ego. Rhys wrote to her friend and editor Diana Athill commenting that "the most seriously wrong thing with Part II is that I've made the obeah woman, the nurse, too articulate. I thought of cutting it a bit, I will if you like, but after all no one will notice. Besides there's no reason why one particular negro woman shouldn't be articulate enough, especially as she's spent most of her life in a white household" (Wyndham and Melly 297). Is Rhys referring to Christophine's way of speaking or to her independent spirit? Regardless, from that remark, Rhys appears to believe that nineteenth-century black women had to be influenced by Euro–West Indian values in order to shine. "The forms of (Creole) selfhood that Rhys's writing elaborates are racially inflected. The profoundly racialized, even racist, structure of her imagination insistently reveals itself in her use of West Indian 'black people' as props to the Creole identity and as cultural objects" (Gregg 37).

Indeed, the Creole can't be represented or even referenced without the "prop" of blackness as subject or object. Despite Rhys's consistent literary and personal reservations, Christophine takes on a life of her own historical truth. Such is Rhys's indelible cultural imprint of blackness, regardless of any affinity for something else. Indeed, "there is in all of Rhys's writing a knotted dialectic tension between the ontological negation/appropriation of 'black people' and a formidably critical intelligence that understands and analyzes the constructed nature of the colonialist discourse that passes itself off as natural and transparent. This tension underwrites her fiction, in particular, in subtle, ironic, and fruitful ways" (Gregg 38). Christophine astutely knows that, despite the fact that the Emancipation Act has legally abolished slavery, the former slaves are still objectified through psychological imprisonment:

> No more slavery! She had to laugh! "These new ones have Letter of the Law. Same thing. They got magistrate. They got fine. They got jail house and chain gang. They got tread machine to mash up people's feet. New ones worse than old ones—more cunning, that's all." (22–23)

In the previous chapter I mentioned Esteban Montejo's autobiographical narrative *The Autobiography of a Runaway Slave*. Lamenting similar feelings about freedom but from real history, Montejo says of his own reality after Emancipation,

> When slavery ended, I ceased being a maroon. From the people's shouting I knew that slavery was over and I came out. They shouted: "Free at last." But I didn't truly believe it. For me it was all a lie. (62)

The former slaves experienced a different kind of colonialism—the "post-plantation order." Christophine may not know the letter of the law but she is a seer of the law. In the consciousness of gender-oriented marronage, she has to see further than authority will allow her to read. I connect Christophine to ancestral legacies that abound in the West Indies. Like the wild, green, tropical fruit after which she is named (chayote, cho-cho, or christophene), she embodies a utilitarian configuration of ritual, myth, and physical survival. In his exploration of pre-Columbian, Amerindian, and African connections in *Wide Sargasso Sea,* and of the food-bearing "tree of life," Wilson Harris writes that "whereas Jean

Rhys plotted an obvious correspondence with the 'garden in the Bible,' it is unlikely that she was consciously aware of the pre-Columbian image that seems to me to secrete itself in the margins of her fiction and, as a consequence, there exists in the narrative indirections of *Wide Sargasso Sea* that particular blend of opacity and transparency that alerts us to the force of the intuitive imagination in building strategies of which it *knows* and yet does not *know*" (Harris 115). Harris places these specters in the context of the cultural vernacular. Rather than being in the "margins of her fiction" these ideas permeate Rhys's fiction like invisible, but empowering traces of marronage. Later in the novel Antoinette calls out to the mother-woman, "Oh, Christophine. O Pheena, Pheena, help me" (154).

Like the author who created her, Antoinette is also a "difficult fit" for many readers. The reality of the terms "creole" and "mulatto" are really blended images. Certainly by the 1840s, the setting of *Wide Sargasso Sea*, being white was more in the eyes of the beholder. Rhys implies, through the husband's musings and by way of Daniel Cosway, that Antoinette is a woman of color—Creole. Recall that Daniel Cosway writes the letter to Antoinette's husband claiming that he is her "brother by another lady, half-way house as we say. Her father and mine was a shameless man and of all his illegitimates I am the most unfortunate and poverty stricken" (96). The question that readers and critics ask is "should we believe him?" Considering Rhys's care in crafting the narrative, the problematics of Daniel Boyd Cosway's story are plausible. And considering the nineteenth-century laws of primogeniture that Rhys incorporates into the novel, it is possible for him to believe that he could very well have some kind of claim to his father's name—not as a right, but as a privilege. Yet as a "half-way" child, the most he could claim is the name because the wealth is not his to take. Daniel wants others to believe that Antoinette is a person of color like he is—mixed and not "pure." Indeed, the husband begins to see Antoinette as "dark" and laments: "She never blinks at all it seems to me. Long, sad dark alien eyes. Creole of pure English descent she may be, but they are not English or European either" (67). The "pure" English planters reject her family because they are Creole. Indeed, this is one of the reasons why Antoinette internally resists her European heritage and attempts to place herself within the framework of the island's mixed Creole heritage.

The motif of marronage permeates the text and context of *Wide Sargasso Sea*. In one episode, Antoinette's mother, Annette, finds that their horse has been poisoned and laments, "Now we are marooned . . . now what will become of us?" (18). The Cosways (are they also "castaways"?) are not only logistically isolated, but socially alienated. They are West Indian, English-speaking Creoles marginalized by the history taking place around them. They are even alien to the marginality of marronage because they are unable to embrace it. Christophine, in contrast, does not ask, "what will become of us?" She is not marooned in the sense of being stranded; rather, through language and association she is the Maroon. In what appears to be a nonsensical world, marronage is the empowering center. Marronage is based to a great extent on irrationality, disruption, upheaval, and isolation by choice. Inevitably such human chaos, framed as social and cultural madness, could be reappropriated and become the basis for individual and group cohesion. Slavery forced a communal way of being in the world: see and not see, hear and not hear, be and not be. Lack or absence of a coherent female voice in the text is substance and presence when grounded in a cultural vernacular reading of the text from the inside out. In the historical milieu of marronage, lack was an asset for survival, accommodation, and resistance. The Maroons lacked sufficient land for food crops, accessibility, stability, and so on. All of this "lack" seems ironic because they did accommodate themselves, they did resist, and they did survive. The geopolitical space of the metaphoric cockpits is the place of madness, or chaos and order—simultaneously haven and hell. Chaos is an asset for the safe haven of the Maroon estate, whether it is in the wilderness, the swamps, the mountain hinterland, or in the metaphoric wilderness of the postcolonial woman straining to resist and to accommodate. In *Abeng*, Michelle Cliff describes marronage as "Places to hide. Difficult to reach. Not barren but deep and magnificent indentations populated by bush and growth and wild orchids—collectors of water—natural goblets" (21). These natural estates are simultaneously barren and fertile helping the Maroons to function in the midst of chaos. Hence, out of what appears to be madness is a functioning system of order and transformation. Madness is an illusion. Antoinette has an extended kinship with those who are marooned by choice; she creates her own transformation out of New World chaos. Antoinette is betwixt and between self-representation and autonomy, the difficult spaces from which to come out of hiding or in which to further retreat. Of Antoinette Cosway, Mary Lou Emery writes,

> Rejected by her mother, betrayed by her black friend, and submitted to the neo-colonialist . . . Antoinette cannot place herself among the island's people or her family. She resorts, in her pain, to a trick of her own imagination, recreating and replacing herself. . . . She has learned something about survival and internal resistance from the culture of slavery that preceded this period in the island's history. . . . Antoinette's ability to be elsewhere, learned early in her childhood, gives her voice a formal power in the novel even as she becomes most socially powerless. (30)

We cannnot read Antoinette without reading the context of slavery in the West Indies. As Antoinette becomes socially powerless, she gains empowerment like the Maroons who preceded her. Because of this kinship to metaphoric lineage and a shared New World history, gender is not the only unifying force for sisterhood and identity. Speaking about women's cross-cultural experiences and their "unrelated kinship," Gwendolyn Etter-Lewis writes, "while gender can be a source of bonding between women, the additional variable of race/ethnicity should not be overlooked as another critical factor" (Etter-Lewis 6). Slavery and colonization force us to see how we can identify these other distinct ways that represent women through the multiplicity of unrelated kinship.

> The apparent struggles of the agonal moments are like some violent outburst of protest arising deep in the primitive unconscious, raging against the too-hasty departure of the spirit.
> —Sherwin B. Nuland, *How We Die*

In her novel, *The Chosen Place, the Timeless People*, Paule Marshall tells the story of the unsuccessful slave rebellion led by Cuffee Ned on the fictitious Caribbean island of Bournehills. Every year at carnival the Bournehills peasants put on a mas' (or performance) honoring their hero Cuffee Ned, who led his people in resistance to slavery. According to their history, however, he enjoyed a short-lived (*petit*) marronage before he was captured and executed by the colonists: "But Cuffee had died content. . . . For he had seen his life and deeds as pointing the way to what must be. And man that he was, a true believer, he believed that death was not an end but a return, so that in dying he would be restored to the homeland. . . . 'Him feel joy,' he was known to have said of himself at the end, 'Him ready fuh to die now'" (310). Again we see the motif of the spirit returning to the homeland.

There is a humble but resounding gallantry that Marshall ascribes to Cuffee Ned through words like "joy" and "ready fuh to die now" when describing his preparation for violent death by decapitation. That is fiction. How did the real Cuffee Neds, the real babies and women and men of slavery face that violent and painful outburst of death that often resulted when they resisted or were victims? What does the trope of Cuffee Ned tell us about the discourse of pain and violent death? Some slaves chose the immediacy of painful dying over prolonged enslavement. In my earlier discussion on aspects of suicide and the flying African I indicated how the early New World slaves saw death as a welcome alternative to the political and physical atrocities of slavery. Many of the slavers writing or telling narratives in the seventeenth and eighteenth centuries didn't mince their words when describing torture and death connected to the slave trade. Historian Colin Palmer asserts:

> Some [slaves] would come to terms with their situation, but others would offer a stoic resistance to defining themselves as chattel. When it is recalled that the majority of the slaves were teenagers, their experiences appear all the more tragically poignant. No historical record can ever completely recapture their pain and do justice to their story. (158)

There was a remarkable source of endurance that the New World Africans had for, in a word, life. The horrific physical pain arising out of resistance that many of these people went through caused me to think about intersections of their spirituality of death and the physiological import of death. It is one thing to understand an ontological belief (seeing death as a return to the well being of a "homeland") that would motivate the acceptance of one's own suicide or execution; it is another to understand from a clinical perspective how the body deals with the fatal onslaught of pain and brutality. Most of us are familiar with various religious preparations for death, but what is the clinical and physiological explanation of the body's "preparation" for the onslaught of pain that will terminate through death? The mind and body are protected and connected by certain defense mechanisms. Understanding the physiological preparation against torture may help to understand the ontological fortitude that enables the body to withstand physical pain and violence.

The recent interest by medical science and its relationship to spiritual reality is exemplified in *How We Die* by the renowned surgeon and historian of medicine Sherwin B. Nuland. In his discussion on "Murder and Serenity," Nuland clinically explains how the human body struggles to hold on to life even after vital organs and blood vessels have been irreversibly traumatized through "hemorrhage, exsanguination, cardiac arrest, the agonal moments, clinical death, and finally irretrievable mortality" (Nuland 124). Medical practitioners use the term 'agonal phase' to describe the visible actions that take place when the body can no longer sustain its life force. Yet in the moments of actual "death agony" or the terminal seconds of urgency and desperation brought on by violent trauma and pain, an interesting phenomenon occurs that scientists have only recently began to identify. To induce tranquillity to help the agonal passage of dying while in pain and physiological violence, the human body is capable of generating what is called endogenous morphine-like compounds. The hypothalamus, the periaqueductal gray matter in the brain, and the pituitary gland can all secret endorphins in response to acute stress and trauma. "Together with ACTH, a hormone that activates the adrenal glands, endorphin molecules are known to bind themselves, as do the other narcotics, onto foci, called receptors, on the surfaces of certain nerve cells. The effect is to alter normal sensory awareness. Endorphins seem to play a significant role not only in raising pain threshold but also in alerting emotional responses" (Nuland 131). Medical practitioners don't know how much trauma the body has to undergo before the endorphins "swing into action," but they do. In other words, when the body's vital systems are in arrest, in the agony of death, and on the threshold of mortality, endorphins act as self-generated opiates to produce a level of serenity that raises the pain threshold during those final moments of life. In this instance, it seems that the body has generated the ability to increase its threshold for pain and fear. "Endorphin elevation appears to be an innate physiological mechanism to protect mammals and perhaps other animals against the emotional and physical dangers of terror and pain" (Nuland 133). Dr. Nuland goes on to say that, "to some endorphins would seem to involve matters of the body, and to other matters of the spirit" (Nuland 133).

Nuland describes a vicious attack on a nine-year-old girl that took place a few years ago in an urban American city. After being repeatedly stabbed with a hunting knife by a paranoid schizophrenic whom she didn't even know, the child died of acute hemorrhage from hypovolemic shock—her carotid artery had been completely torn. The child's mother,

who "stood about twenty feet away, rooted there by disbelief and horror" witnessed the attack, which lasted only a few minutes. "She [the
mother] would later remember that the air seemed too thick to let her
move through it—her body felt warm and benumbed, and she was enveloped in a dreamy mist of insulation" (Nuland 125). When the mother
could finally move out of her consternation, she ran to her daughter as
two passersby grabbed at the attacker and pulled him off the dying child.
The mother relates the final moments she had with her daughter:

> How much pain did she feel? I needed to know that. I saw her bleed all
> the blood out of her body.... Her chest and face were covered with cuts
> and gashes. She must have been moving her head from side to side,
> struggling to get free of this man.... Do you know what she looked like?
> It looked like a release.... [I]t gave me a sense of peace to see that look
> of release. She must have released herself from this pain, because her
> face didn't show it. She looked surprised, but not terrified. (127)

Nuland contends that in the child's terminal seconds of physical and
physiological crisis her body released endorphins to raise her threshold
of pain and trigger what appeared to be "release" or tranquillity. "It is
not farfetched to believe that the human body itself knows how to make
those morphine-like substances and knows how to time their release to
correspond with the instant of need" (Nuland 132). Of the child who
was attacked and murdered, Nuland says, "We will never know the level
of Katie Mason's endorphins . . . but I am convinced that nature stepped
in . . . and provided exactly the right spoonful of medicine to give a measure of tranquillity to a dying child" (132).

The phenomenon of self-generating biochemical endorphins is viewed
by some as mystical and as an occurrence that cannot be scientifically
demonstrated every time it appears to happen. Even if answers to the
physiological occurrence are, as Nuland contends, "spread out over a
philosophical terrain as wide as the distance between spiritualism and
science" (132), there remains the fact that the human body indeed has a
self-generating physiological response that enables it to turn the physical
agony that could occur in dying into that measure of physical endurance
or "release." It's as if the body is controlling the threshold of violent
pain so that the dying person is able to endure the insurmountable pain
in a painless "twilight zone" of serenity without the assistance of exter-
nally prescribed medication. The endorphins are biochemical reactions
to the trauma of the agonal moment. After the body and mind have been

violently assaulted through pain, we say, from a layperson's perspective, that the person is "dying in peace" or "being made ready for death" or "crossing over." The clinical phenomenon—the endorphin response—creates a space in which the serenity of death signals the return to stasis and harmony. Thus spirituality (and religious beliefs) and clinical phenomena are not so far apart—neither is mutually exclusive of the other. The agonal moment dissipates through chemical intervention. Therefore the "release" of the spirit and the harmony that signals the beginning of the end through death is complemented by the stasis caused by the endogenous biochemical release.

Although endorphins have only recently been identified, these biochemicals have been a part of our human capacity, a part of the "primitive unconscious." Endorphins have always been in place to respond to the agonal moment, to act as a biochemical mediator between pain and death. From the clinical perspective of the "body shutting down," suffering is shielded within the agonal moments of dying. For the enslaved, pain was endurable. Many aspects of slavery and dying may be beyond our understanding. The reality of endorphins, stasis, and chaos suggests one way to understand terminal mental and physical suffering. Endorphins allow the human body to withdraw from physical and mental acknowledgments of pain. Endorphins bring about a communion with life itself and the beginning of the next world.

> My spirit is straining for another beginning in a place where there will be new eyes and where things that will remain unsaid here will turn to a glad welcome and my ghost will find the beginning that will be known here as my end.
>
> —Ayi Kweh Armah, *Fragments*

Antoinette's flight from Thornfield is an endorphinous moment that anticipates death. Her psychic moment allays any fear of death. Antoinette's imminent death represents transcendence. Death is the mere termination of the physical life and a profound beginning of another kind of existence. Rhys may not have had any scientific models about endorphins in front of her, but as a writer she could articulate the agility of the body's physiological protection against fear and pain in terms of metaphor and psychic transcendence. Antoinette's "agonal moments" take place in her dreams in the attic (as prison) at Thornfield. She is the daughter who wants to return to the mother—the surrogate protection of Christophine. Her agony is mental suffering that sees death as a release from the pain of alienation and exclusion. Physical death and the return to the homeland ensure the ontological outlook that Nanny and her people left behind for the New World descendants. The return allows empowering journeys on new realms of being. Antoinette's focus seems to be "straining for another beginning in a place where there will be new eyes and where things that will remain unsaid here will turn to a glad welcome and [her] ghost will find the beginning that will be known here as [her] end" (Armah 123).

Taking flight, Antoinette will return to her homeland through the enabling spiritual connection to Tia and Christophine. In the context of historical and symbolic marronage, at the intersection of ontological and biochemical responses, Antoinette's moment of decision defeats agony. We remember the legend of Nanny's three coffins. Death may be viewed as an enabling continuum. Antoinette sees her own Atlantic homeland in the Caribbean where she wants to be. She is no longer without capacity. Despite the diagnosis (made by the husband) of "madness," she thinks clearly in terms of community, homeland, and security: "I am because we are, since we are, therefore I am." In the final dream of thought and action, she prepares to torch Thornfield, which is a gesture of cleansing. Mother-centered memories invade her consciousness: "As I ran or perhaps floated or flew I called help me Christophine: help me and looking behind me I saw that I had been helped" (189). Dreams are the oracle's voice guiding the return:

> Then I turned round and saw the sky. It was red and all my life was in it. I saw the grandfather clock and Aunt Cora's patchwork, all colours, I saw the orchids and stephanotis and the jasmine and the tree of life in flames. (189)

In her dream vision, Antoinette retrieves her past through flying—the life-taking force of the flying African: self-chosen death. The spirits of Christophine and Tia participate in Antoinette's agonal moments that comprise dreams, reality, and spiritual longing. *Your mother is there to protect you. She is buried there. And that is why we say mother is supreme.* Antoinette spiritually and psychologically communicates with these island women and their beliefs. She will have the gift of flight.

Dreams are part of that visionary experience connecting spiritual and physical worlds. Like Nanny and the flying Africans, Antoinette will take flight. We remember what Mr. Sterling said of Maroon Nanny: "She dead of old age. She ambushed. She ain't dead 'cause *she could fly.* But den some dem say, when she dead, three coffins dem make and her body place in one, rocks in de others. She not dere where dem say. She left here and still her—flyin.'" Death is not the end of her journey, only another part of it. The spiritual return to Coulibri, to Christophine, and to Tia provides healing for Antoinette in the spiritual and psychological rejoining. Like Sethe in *Beloved,* Antoinette moves backward in order to move forward. Like the historical women who had to take foot, Antoinette finally pulls "strength from that inheritance of ancestral spirits from the other side of the ocean" (Mair 59). Through naming and remembering, she reconnects with the women of her island homeland.

Through her ironic reclaiming of ethos, longing, and placement, Jean Rhys lamented that the Caribbean "is where I belong and . . . where I wish to stay." Those of us who have emigrated, who have been displaced, who have settled elsewhere, who make new diasporas, who are new generations, who have left home for whatever reason seem to need to go back in order to move forward. We are the migrating subjects in this postcolonial moment of uncertainty, of determination, of perseverance: We are Garífuna, Asian, Persian, Indian, West Indian, African, and more. In solidarity with our sister-mothers we want our legacies to be empowered throughout the matrilineal diasporas that we call home.

CHAPTER THREE

Refusing to Live on Scent: Textures of Memory by Way of *Pluie et vent sur Télumée Miracle*

> To write! To put her hips, her sex, her heart, into motion in order to give birth to a world inscribed in her obscurity.
> —Maryse Condé, "Three Women in Manhattan"

Here on the West Indian island of St. Thomas, a certain Negro woman writes a letter to our Queen of Denmark:

> *Nú is ons hope, de konings Majestait ons sal die order geven, dat ons dúrf voortgaan te leeren den Heere Jesus. Ons staan vast tot noch tœ, als het God den Heere geliest, schon ons seer gedrukt* [sic] *word van all, en komen ons slagen en kappen, as ons by den Heyland leert, en Bœk verbranden, en doop Honde Doop nœmen, en Brœders Beesten, en Neger moet niet zaalig worden, een gedoopt Neger is Brandhout in de Hell. En hebben ons Brœders, sonderlyk Bas Martinus, die God aan ons al had gebruikt, en die van twentig Brœders overgebleven is, (die gestorvenzyn,) met syn Brœders, over drie Maant op deFort gesett, en wil sy van de land bannen. . . . Ons wil ons Meesters in all ding gehoorsam zyn, enkel ons siel na de Hemel by den Heer Jesus stúúren. Want ons heeft ons Heere gestoolen, Maron geloopen, na Porto Rico gegaan.*

[It is our hope now that His Majesty the King will give the order [for] us that we may go on learning [about] the Lord Jesus. We are steadfast until now, if the Lord God wants it, even though we are oppressed heavily by all; [they] come to beat and kidnap us when we learn about the Savior; and [they] burn our books, call our baptism dog's baptism and Brethren beasts; a Negro should not be saved; a baptized Negro is firewood in hell. And they have put our brothers, especially Bas Martinus, whom God had already used for us, and who is the one left out of twenty brothers

(who died) with his Brethren in the Fortress for three months, and they
want to expel them from the country. . . . We will obey our masters in
everything, we only want to send our soul to heaven to the Lord Jesus.
Because we were stolen by our masters [from Africa], the Maroons
escaped and went to Puerto Rico.][1]

She speaks and writes Creole Danish—the language in general use in
this mission station. It is a singular and very imperfect dialect, not unlike the Negro English spoken by the Negroes of Surinam.

The day is February 15th and 1739 in the year of our Lord. Mary Magdalena is a pious Negro woman of medium build, of dark hue but with
an intelligent portrayal of the forehead. In her daily activities, she con-
ducts herself with exemplary diligence and the excellence of her character is many times acknowledged. She clutches her Bible as she writes.
Because her love for the Lord Jesus is so fervent it is with a great searching and yearning of the heart that she writes to the Queen.

Count von Zinzendorf, Moravian Ordinary and leader of our movement in these West Indies, will be the bearer of Magdalena's letter on
behalf of the Negroes. God has appointed some to be masters, and others to be slaves. Slavery is not a matter for the Brethren to question and
slave-owning is not a sin. Count von Zinzendorf counsels that "Their
dark understanding becomes enlightened; their wicked ways they for-
sake and become ashamed of, and by the love of God they become willing and learn their duty to God and men and are reconciled with the
dispensation of God in their situation of being slaves in this world."

Scarcely a day passes in which Mary Magdalena does not weep in
love for her Lord, for her sins, and for everlasting grace after death. She
achieved the highest station that any of the slaves can attain from the
Brethren: baptism. Baas Martin baptized her on May 4, 1738. He renamed
her Mary Magdalena. She is no longer called by the heathen name of
Marotta. She attains the pleasure of Holy Communion in the name of
the Lord Jesus. It is with the benign influence of the Gospel that she
prays and sings with the Brethren and her fellow sisters in praises of the
Lord. Led by Brother Dober, all the Brethren missionaries rejoice every
day that at least two hundred and fifty Negro women slaves accepted
the Lord Jesus.

Magdalena rejoices because, although she is a slave, she esteems the
power of the pen and writes. She ventures to believe that writing is the
mark of her own humanity alongside us, her masters. There are adver-

saries on the island who do not want that the Negroes receive these instructions for reading and writing. But the work and word of God is bound, and the Negro men and women want to meet for edification and for that instruction of learning. It is an esteemed privilege to learn ciphering, and it appears that a great desire to learn has been excited among both the young and old Negroes on the island. Indeed, Mary Magdalena has distinguished herself as an articulate and useful native assistant. Thus it is she who writes for the women sisters.

Our hut faces the beach and the Atlantic Ocean. Our Negro fishermen are coming back with their day's provisions. There will be much merriment on the beach with the fishmongers and girl servants who run to meet the boats—they will palaver, cajole, and buy for the evening meal. Night comes quickly in these tropics, and she wants to finish the letter before darkness closes in. From time to time as she writes, she looks up and out beyond the beach, and memories from her childhood across the ocean appear to form the gist of her efforts to write . . .

> *Groote Koniginne.*
> *Die tyd mi a wes na Poppo op Africa, doen mi a dint die Heer Mau, nu*
> *kome na blanco land, mi no wilt gu din de Heere. Mi no ha di grond vor tú*
> *dien die Heere; mi ben bedrœv na min herte, voor dat Negrinne no kan*
> *dien die Heere Jesus in Thomas, die Blanke no wil dien die Heere. Lat so as*
> *sili wil, maar soo de povre swarte Brœders en susters wil dien de Heer Jesus,*
> *so mœt zilli dœn, as si bin maron volk.*

> [Great Queen.
> When I was in Poppo *[sic]* in Africa, I served the Lord Mau. Now that I
> come to the white people's land, I do not want to serve that Lord anymore.
> I do not have reason to serve that Lord. My heart is saddened because
> Negro women cannot serve the Lord Jesus on St. Thomas. The whites do
> not want to serve the Lord. Let it be as they want; when the poor black
> Brethren and sisters want to serve the Lord, they are treated as Maroons.]

Magdalena turns away from the heathen god of her African people Mau, and accepts our God. She accepts her place on the plantation as a Negro slave woman, but her greatest desire is to continue with unshaken faith in the instruction of ciphering. It is a gift that she has acquired. Yes, she is a gifted Negro of our sex, and she also possesses the blessing of utterance; her discourses are impressive and listened to not only by the Negroes but also by many of the whites. And she is conversant in the manners, superstitions, and customs of her people. She desires to write her story and those of the other Negro women, for now she has obtained the knowledge of the Holy Scriptures as well as other books of acclaim. Magdalena asks that Her Majesty be an intermediary. Her Majesty could act on her behalf to the King.

Our sister Mary Magdalena happily departed His service on earth in 1763 by means of the prevailing bilious fever. She would be with the Savior and would kiss his wounds for all the bounties that He had given during the miserable times of her life. After the blessings of the congregation of sisters, she said to us, "Now I am finished with the world and free of everything." Several hundred persons gathered at the burial ground to show their grief that sanctified her removal and their tokens of love for that departed servant of the Lord.

> It has been a long time since our people walked to Africa, they say.
> The sea, it has no back doors.
> —Edwidge Danticat, *Breath, Eyes, Memory*

The opening section of this chapter presents an imagined African Moravian narrative that creates a memory of Mary Magdalene, an African slave woman who lived on the island of St. Thomas in the eighteenth century. I created a memory site, "Mary Magdalena," that gives another cross-cultural perspective on slavery in the New World by way of a specific gender construction, that of an African Caribbean Moravian slave woman. In what kind of historical context did the real Magdalene (as her name is spelled in the Periodical Accounts of the Brethren) articulate an identity for herself? How was Magdalene viewed as an individual considering she had the empowerment of literacy provided by the same people who, though religious, still had jurisdiction over her? To what extent did the Brethren maintain slavery and justify it with the Word and world of Christianity? To answer such inquiries requires a look at gender and race issues. The "heathen" is in the process of becoming an empowered Other.

Magdalene of St. Thomas was a contemporary of Maroon Nanny from Jamaica. In keeping with the mother-woman paradigm, I present Magdalene as an African Moravian woman creating a new journey for herself as a Christian bonded to the legalities and abuses of slavery. While Nanny sought marronage, Magdalene rejected it in favor of what literacy and Christianity offered. Magdalene appears to have learned that she could approach another woman, the Queen in Europe, who could mediate on her behalf to the King.[2]

In addition to the major British, French, Spanish, and Dutch participation, Denmark was also involved in the African slave trade. In 1671, the Danish West India Company was established. The majority of the merchants who went out with the company were Dutch, and they had more direct communication with the slave population than the Danish colonists. Although Danish was the official language on the main islands of St. Thomas, St. Croix, and St. John, the Creole language that developed among the slaves was largely influenced by Dutch-speaking entrepreneurs.[3] For that reason, it was more related to the "Negro English of Surinam" (Surinam was the principle Dutch colony in South America). The Creole that Mary Magdalene could speak and write could be referred to as "Dutch" Creole, though as long as the Danish were controlling the islands, they would call the emerging New World language Creole Danish.

The Moravian Church has its origin in the Unity of the Brethren, or Unitas Fratrum, a Protestant denomination founded in 1457 in Eastern Bohemia. The United Brethren came to the West Indies as missionaries in 1731 under the religious leadership of Count Nicholas Ludwig von Zinzendorf (1700–1760). In 1739 the Count himself traveled to the island of St. Thomas. (Mary Magdalene could very well have met him, although in the Brethren periodicals there are no references to their meeting.) That same year the Brethren published the narrative of Mary Magdalene in the original Creole Danish.[4]

How does Magdalene organize her perception of the world through writing? She wrote that she was born in Popo, which is located in what is presently the Republic of Benin in West Africa. A division of the ancient kingdom of Dahomey, Popo was well known during the time of transatlantic slavery. She could have been from any of the ports along the infamous Slave Coast: Ouidah, Grand Popo, or Aneho (Little Popo). Many youths were taken from their homes and forced into slavery. It is quite possible that she arrived in the Caribbean as a youth, traumatized from the Atlantic crossing. The Brethren missionaries record that she came to the Caribbean in 1712. In her narrative, Magdalene refers to a deity named "Mau." Her spelling is an eighteenth-century variant of "Mawu," who is the supreme god, the Christian equivalent of the "God

Almighty," among the Fon of Abomey in Benin.[5] Magdalene indicates that, out of her new learning, she came to prefer living on the plantation as a slave rather than in the hinterland as a "Maron geloopen" (Maroon). Remaining with the Brethren for the rest of her life, she died a slave in 1763.

When I first read Mary Magdalene's narrative, I found it rather remarkable that she petitioned for literacy and did not want to be like the "free" Maroon fugitives of the island. Putting her narrative back into history, I speculate that legal freedom was not a personal quest for her and her fellow converts at that historical moment. She had few choices as an enslaved woman. The slaves on St. Thomas must have heard about the brutal slave rebellion that had taken place on the Danish island of St. John in 1733, where the rebel slaves had managed to hold off the slave owners for six months. When the rebels realized their defeat was coming, they committed suicide, knowing that the slave owners were going to kill them anyhow. That final defiance was a major strategy of resistance for the rebels. But, it appears that armed resistance was not an issue for Magdalene and her compatriots on St. Thomas.

From my perspective on history and memory, the conditions of slavery should have been challenged. Furthermore, from our contemporary perspective, von Zinzendorf was exceedingly racist. He, however, has to be recontextualized into the history and memory of his time. Zinzendorf was a baroque nobleman and believed in his mission of educating the soul and intellect of the "slaves of the world." Magdalene of St. Thomas was among numerous African Moravian slave women who had access to the "magical alchemy of writing."[6] Through her quest for literacy, she became a significant precursor in the matrilineal diaspora of writing.

The Brethren kept meticulous journals and church records. It was customary for believers to write his or her memoir or have someone write it as an "as told to" memoir. In fact, Count von Zinzendorf encouraged the "writing of the life" for posterity and for church missionary records. At the time of the believer's death, the memoir or life narrative was read to the congregation and additional biographical information was added by someone who knew the deceased or by the minister. Mary Magdalene of St. Thomas does not follow this paradigm because her narrative is not an extensive account of her life. Her narrative elicits the objective of immediate life rather than the conclusiveness of death.

The Brethren were quite keen on teaching their slaves how to read and write.[7] Literacy training was a part of the conversion process; it allowed individuals to have direct access to the Bible for reading and religious contemplation. In her introduction to *The History of Mary Prince, A West Indian Slave, Related by Herself,* Moira Ferguson writes about Mary Prince, a slave woman from Antigua, who became a Moravian convert: "Her conversion to Moravianism allied her with other slaves, with free blacks, and with the minority of whites who believed in spiritual equality. . . . For Mary Prince, religion built a bridge to freedom and social acceptance" (18–19). Published in 1831, Prince's narrative is considered to be the first by a slave woman from the British West Indies. And although this nineteenth-century narrative is secular, the Moravian influence is evident. Narratives written under the auspices of the Moravian teachings were indications of the "civilizing" religious mission of the missionaries. These memoirs and autobiographical narratives are precursors to the nineteenth-century African American slave narrative.

The non-Moravian plantation owners on the island realized how the tools of reading and writing were powerful; therefore they created laws that made it illegal for slaves to receive an education. Their beliefs matched the European worldview of that era:

Literacy = intellectual capacity and reasoning = citizenship in the human race

Africans were seen as "things" that could not rationalize or *think*. It was necessary to maintain them as property and objects. In her essay "Codes of Law and Bodies of Color," Joan Dayan explains that "the thinker of Descartes' *Meditations* in 1640 sets the stage for the 1685 edict [*Le Code Noir*] of Louis XIV. Or, to put it another way, the making of enlightenment man led to the demolition of the unenlightened brute. . . . Once you establish who is a rational man, you can ascertain what is not. . . . What is this thing that does not think or feel, and cannot will, refuse, deny, or imagine?" (45–46). From this perspective, the colonizers could not tolerate slaves who demonstrated thinking, knowledge, and rationality signified by self-definition through writing.

During the formation of new cultures in the Americas, slave women may have viewed the writing process as something remarkable—as a door opening into a another kind of New World. Despite the power imbalance that remained, they could have had more negotiating power that superimposed an alternative agency. Hilary McD. Beckles discusses how literacy can be viewed as an attainment "designed to improve the efficiency of the system so as to extract greater material, social and ideological rewards with the logical effect of rendering the quality of life more free than slave" (*Natural Rebels* 157). Most scholars agree that, among slave populations in the Americas and especially in the United States, acquiring literacy was paramount. Others challenge that general perspective about literacy. For example, Winifred Morgan maintains that men and women experienced slavery according to their gendered roles, and therefore literacy did not have the same value for women as it did for men. Essentially, "the drive to become literate appears to be gender-based; unlike the narratives written by men, women's narratives do not emphasize this factor. While male narrators accentuate the role of literacy, females stress the importance of relationships" (76). Because they emphasized the importance of domestic relationships and social roles in their narratives, ex-slave women could not benefit from the public sphere of literacy that often changed the lives of ex-slave men:

> Male slave fugitives might earn a living lecturing on the abolitionist lecture circuit and writing slave narratives, but for women fugitives, publishing narratives frequently meant a certain amount of infamy.... For women narrators, literacy was useful, but it only marginally advanced their "independence."... [I]n telling their stories, women were motivated by the need to build communities. (Morgan 91)

Morgan's analysis brings a new focus to representative slave narratives from the perspectives of racism and sexism.

On another level, however, reality was complicated by the intersections of gender, class, and the significance of education/literacy. To say that black women were not as interested in literacy as black men of that time period underestimates the intelligence and pragmatism of those women.[8] Literacy provided the potential for material advancement. In one sense, literacy was a symbol of hope (for the "race" woman). In another sense, it provided intellectual legitimacy. If literacy could not always offer power, freedom, and economic advancement for women, its attainment enabled empowerment—that development of the inner capacity of the mother-women. Literacy for once-enslaved women was not only a matter of "respectability," it was a tool of hope. Although "women narrators could not show that they had been the 'perfect wives' that the cult of domesticity demanded, [and] emphasized instead the ways in which their relationships with their families allied them with their white reading audience" (Morgan 90), literacy offered black women the opportunity to better the conditions for those relationships. Black women recognized the extent to which domesticity honored women who could read, write, watercolor, embroider, and do other domestic arts associated with literacy. "Letters" allowed these women to move from object to agency, albeit still within the parameters of relationships and familial roles. The "first mothers" valued reading and writing to the extent that they became foundations for the pursuit of "schooling" at paramount costs and sacrifices. Literacy was directly related to the efforts of black women to promulgate education for their children, and within their communities—not losing sight of the importance of their relationships within their families and communities. Thus reading and writing were keys to citizenship on a very fundamental level.

To what extent did the African Moravian women in the Caribbean use literacy for economic and social survival? Did their conversion to Christianity mean that they also contributed to maintaining slavery? Magdalene's narrative has a sense of urgency for God and literacy. Undoubtedly Magdalene realized how her religious standing would improve her economic condition. She could have understood that it helped to improve slavery conditions. She could find a modicum of freedom within the legal slavery system. Whereas eighteenth-century marronage seemed to offer more opportunity for permanent freedom from slavery, literacy could offer possible social and economic bounties, while ensuring new alliances within slavery. With the date of 1739, Magdalene's narrative is among the first formal writing by an African slave woman in the New World. From the perspective of sheer literacy, Mary Magdalene is in a remarkable union with Phillis Wheatley, Ann Plato, and Lucy Terry— *American* women of African descent who first inscribed themselves into humanity and then into history.

When I visited that part of equatorial Africa where the river Popo still runs along its course, I remembered the slave woman Magdalene of St. Thomas and her narrative. This is today. How much of the cultural landscape has changed? She came from Popo on the Old World side of the Atlantic. She came from one of the villages that had been pillaged by slave catchers. Europeans. Her own people. Many of the people who live here are illiterate; but from the textures of history they know that many of their people were forced across the ocean and would never return. Their descendants make the return journey. We know some of them as Aguda—others are recent arrivants. Do they know this Middle Passage memory through the songs and laments of their griots, oral chroniclers of history? Indeed, their belief in "huenoho" or the memory-telling of history continues because everything has its historical significance, and the griots assume roles as "historic place-holders."[9] The progeny of King Béhanzin (the last of the great Dahomean kings who fought against the French but was defeated and exiled to Martinique) make their annual return from the Caribbean. Antigua. St. Thomas. Martinique. Marie Galante. Guadeloupe. Brazil. Descendants from one side of the Atlantic. Descendants on the other. The door opens and they return. Do they know all this from the laments and memories of their historic place-holders? Do they really know?

The Atlantic side of Grand Popo beach is beautiful with shimmering sand dunes untouched by litter and only occasionally by people. In many places, the stretch is remote and forgotten. Here, they don't pay as much attention to what the beach offers as they do in the Caribbean. Here, the ocean is not a thing to play with; therefore the people don't swim along the beach. The forceful waves are elegant and dangerous. Because of the abrupt slopes of the beach and the submerged sand dunes along the coast, the rushing of runback water from these crashing waves becomes treacherous and violent. If you are caught in the rushing, the undertow is menacing and eventually pulls you out into the ocean. Even a champion swimmer will most likely drown. That is why most of the locals stay away. But the vast span of the beach remains beautiful.

This late afternoon is still rather hot, and I perspire despite the whims of the breezes whisking from the Atlantic. The fishermen know how to deal with the ocean for the sake of making a meager living. I watch them bringing in the day's catch. Night comes early and fast here in the tropics. It's four degrees above the equator which makes the sunset fleeting and done with after only a few minutes—no lingering colors to awe and inspire the watcher. And so the fishermen hurry as they sing, laugh, cajole, and palaver each other, pulling their ragged, weather-beaten boats onto the beach. Their feet dig into the sand. Their black torsos are wet and taut and supple with the strain of the pulling. This is the place, now poor and neocolonized with subsistence capitalism, now left with France's colonial legacies, that Magdalene remembered when she wrote to the Queen of Denmark in 1739. I was intrigued by her capacity, as I am now. Her faith. She was in the house of self with 250 other sister-women. I am humbled by her struggles and the choices she made. A mother-woman. The sun is already on the other side of the horizon. The tide is coming in faster and more powerful, covering up and destroying the sand dunes. I feel the vastness of the Atlantic and the collective memories of the African people who are linked to the Americas and to those events that happened here centuries ago. I quickly walk toward the beach road away from the danger zones of the tide; a feeling inside of me bows down in remembrance of all the Magdalenes and their descendants who struggled for wholeness on both sides of the Atlantic.

> All that humankind has created down through the ages shows that human beings are capable of doing wondrous things. Your great challenge is to believe this about yourself.
>
> —Susan L. Taylor

Indeed, the eighteenth-century Moravian women of African descent in the Caribbean inscribed themselves into the beginnings of Creole identity.

In chapter 2 I explored the shifting meaning of the word "Creole." This word, continuously loaded with manifestations of colonial history and non-European cultures, is in the matrix of postcolonial debates that focus on the Caribbean. The authors of the well-known manifesto, *Éloge de la créolité* [*In Praise of Creoleness*], Jean Bernabé, Patrick Chamoiseau, and Raphaël Confiant, assert a new modality of being "Creole" in the Caribbean. Their version of *créolité* vigorously shuns, for example, Léopold Senghor's Negritude consciousness and the symbolism of "mother Africa." As a cultural manifesto, *Éloge de la créolité* is their intellectual reference point for "being in the world"—as Creoles. Bernabé, Chamoiseau, and Confiant claim that because of its "geopolitical" consciousness "la Créolité est doce le fait d'appartenir à une entité humaine originale (31) [Creoleness is the fact of belonging to an original human entity (92)].[10] Accordingly, *créolité* signifies the New World plantation system that was created by language (French) and privilege. But the intellectuals-three miss the boat. They do not consider the presence of women or gender issues in their articulations of a new Caribbean identity. As James Arnold affirms, they belong to a movement that "permits only male talents to emerge within . . . to carry its seal of approval. . . . [I]t pushes literature written by women in the background. In a word, *créolité* is the latest avatar of the masculinist culture of the French West Indies, which is being steadily challenged by the more recently emerged . . . womanist culture" ("The Gendering of Créolité" 21). Further highlighting this characteristic of *créolité*, anthropologists Richard Price and Sally Price state that "If . . . the *créolists* tend, in their depiction of the past, to erase women as active agents of cultural production, and if they tend to depict themselves as heirs to the (male) conteur of slave days, it should not be surprising that they tend to deal with living female writers and critics by simply silencing them" (17).[11] In another manifesto, *The Repeating Island*, Antonio Benítez-Rojo redefines the foundations of the Caribbean as a "plantation machine" that promulgates a metaphoric "repeating island." Benítez-Rojo theorizes that, from the scientific perspective of Chaos and order, "the Caribbean space is . . . saturated with messages—'language games'. . . sent out in five European languages (Spanish, English, French, Dutch and Portuguese) and different local dialects. . . . [with] the features of an island that 'repeats' itself, unfolding and bifurcating" (2–3). Although these contemporary intellectuals who expound on issues of *créolité* and repeating plantation systems may exclude the issues of women and gender from their discussions, Caribbean women actively participated in the shaping of Caribbean identities and consciousness.

Unsung, illiterate women who could not "write" themselves onto the plateau of humanity nevertheless inscribed themselves into these early Creole cultures. They fulfilled economic and social capacities such as clan mothers, market women, seamstresses, traders, healers, nurses, fugitives, oral historians, and Maroon abolitionists. Indeed, as Maryse Condé affirms,

Le rôle de la femme au sein des luttes de libération antérieures et postérieures à l'abolition de l'esclavage a été largement occulté. Vivant souvent dans l'Habitation à titre domestique . . . elle a dans bien des cas été responsable des empoisonnements collectifs des maîtres et de leur famille, participé aux indendies des plantations, terreur du XVIIIᵉ siècle et a marroné en nombre important. (*La Parole des femmes* 4)

[The central role of women in the liberation struggles both before and after the abolition of slavery has been largely concealed. Often living in the Plantation House as a domestic . . . it was often she who was responsible for the mass poisonings of masters and their families, for the setting of terrifying fires on the plantations, the terror of the eighteenth century, and for frequent marronage.]

We know some of their names from such places as Barbados, Cuba, Guadeloupe, Haiti, Jamaica, Surinam: Nanny Grigg, Solitude, Cubah, Dédée Bazille, Mère Colombas, Nanny, Jaja Dandé, and Mama Cató. Does this mean that deeds are only deemed important in documented history when the subject is a public figure? What about the private and significant roles that women have performed? Women have been involved not only with public rebellions but with personal battles as well. In another instance, because these sisters and mothers were not known, they did not have a voice, they were *"sans histoire"* and *"sans papiers"* (Mckinney 30).[12] And so they remained excluded, anonymous, or even executed without traces. Considering what the mother-women had to endure, their survival tactics were accomplishments that they passed on to future generations. The unsung women of our past, however, wanted justice; they wanted peace; they wanted to move beyond survival. "When a woman insists 'I am a survivor' over and over again," writes Clarissa Pinkola Estés, "once the time for usefulness is past, the work ahead is clear. We must loosen the person's clutch on the survival archetype. Otherwise nothing else can grow" (195). Not wanting to remain as mere survivors, such women want to thrive. Thriving means expanding energy levels and establishing a different kind of perspective toward life. This motivating principle extends to the mother-women in the Caribbean. Therefore I continue to think about and search for some of the invisible mother-women in cross-cultural perspectives. If we know even snippets of their stories and history, we can be inspired and perhaps even be awed by our own individual capacity.

Toni Morrison compares memory to the site of the dammed up river that remembers its ancient course—the collective consciousness of nature—and tries to return in order to reestablish its identity with time and the landscape. We need to know the past in order to move forward without the burdens of history. Among the Caribbean writers who also visit and recreate sites of memory is the Guadeloupean writer, Simone Schwarz-Bart. Schwarz-Bart grew up in Guadeloupe in the French West Indies and went to school in France soon after World War II. Her first novel with André Schwarz-Bart, *Un plat de porc aux bananes vertes* (1967), is about an aging woman, Mariotte, living out her last days in an institution for the aged in Paris. Left only with her memory, Mariotte claims the past by returning to a site that is both personal and historical. In the novel, the Guadeloupean dish of pork and plantains becomes an extended metaphor for nostalgia and remembering the island home. Schwarz-Bart also captures the fictional history of the legendary Guadeloupean Maroon woman, Solitude. At this juncture she creates another tension between memory and history. A fugitive slave woman, Solitude was with Louis Delgrès at the slave revolt of 1802 at Fort Matouba. There, about three hundred Maroons tried to fight off the French. When they realized defeat was coming, they attempted mass suicide by blowing up the fort. There were, however, survivors. Solitude was among them, and she was pregnant. The French allowed her to deliver her baby because it was the property of the slave owner. After the delivery, she was executed on November 2, 1802. Like many of her Maroon sisters and mothers, Solitude, if even mentioned or known about, was a footnote in history. André Schwarz-Bart's novel *La mulâtresse Solitude* recreates Solitude as a Maroon in her struggle for freedom. In *Pluie et vent sur Télumée Miracle*, and in her six-volume encyclopedia *Hommage à la femme noire* (in collaboration with André Schwarz-Bart), Simone Schwarz-Bart again pays homage to the historical figure of Solitude. Today in Guadeloupe, Louis Delgrès, Solitude, and the other rebels of the Matouba revolt are memorialized with monuments and renamed streets and plazas. These modern sites witness collective memory. Memory then is also a contested site for emotional struggles because it challenges ways that New World interpretations of history have excluded a certain part of humanity because of race, class, and gender differences.

Textual Healing

New World Caribbean women have progressed from writing with the raw functions of "letters" to writing with the textures of the "lettered." Through creative writing, Schwarz-Bart returns to a certain memory site in *Pluie et vent*. With the narrative, she conjures the presence of a certain woman who produced an archival collage for her:

> Je l'ai connue pendant mon enfance.... Nous nous sommes intimement liées quand je suis devenue femme.... Elle racontait sa vie comme quelque chose de nostalgique, de perdu, qui disparaîtrait á tout jamais. Elle sentait que c'était une vie qui avait vraiment sa signification....
> Pour moi, elle était d'un courage extraordinaire... Je pense, voyez-vous, comme les Africains, que lorsqu'un vieux meurt, toute une bibliothèque disparaît. (Toumson 15)

[I knew her during my childhood. . . . We had close ties when I became older. . . . She would tell her life story as something nostalgic, something lost, which had altogether disappeared. She felt that her life had its importance. . . . For me, she had extraordinary courage. . . . You see, I believe as the Africans do that when the old people die, a library disappears.]

Schwarz-Bart's objective then is to keep the "archives" active, to keep them read and well-attended through the handing down of the folk's narrative lore. Likewise, with the paradigm of memory, French historian Pierre Nora believes that "modern memory is . . . archival. It relies entirely on the materiality of the trace, the immediacy of the recording, the visibility of the image" (Nora 13). And while Fanotte's stories represent *lieux de mémoire* (sites of memory), *Pluie et vent,* as a work of the creative imagination, arises from what Nora calls the *milieux de mémoire* "a real environment of memory" (ibid.). Schwarz-Bart recreates a real environment from the Guadeloupe that once was. In isolated places like the hinterlands of the island (the back of beyond), real environments do exist because, in those places, memory has not been assaulted by the "acceleration of history" (Nora 8). The memory site is not only a reference within another history that can be, as Nora writes, "material, symbolic, and functional," but it is also a *space* for exploring emotional, intellectual, and psychological attributes of personal history. Furthermore, "*lieux de mémoire* are created by a play of memory and history, an interaction of two factors that results in their reciprocal over determination. . . . The *lieux* are mixed, hybrid, mutant, bound intimately with life and death, with time and eternity; enveloped in a Möbius strip of the collective and the individual, the sacred and the profane, the immutable and the mobile. For if we accept that the most fundamental purpose of the *lieux de mémoire* is to stop time, to block the work of forgetting, to establish a state of things, to immortalize death, to materialize the immaterial . . . it is also clear that *lieux de mémoire* only exist because of their capacity for metamorphosis, an endless recycling of their meaning and an unpredictable proliferation of their ramifications" (Nora 25).

These sites of memory as "libraries" often disappear when the old people die. Extraordinary sites and ordinary places evoke and encourage our wanting to know. Schwarz-Bart's access to these "little histories" of Guadeloupe is taken from many different women's stories. With her knowledge of the real environment, she transforms that collage into a textured memory by way of a first-person, fictional narrative. Significantly, the sites evoke both memoir (narrative) and memory (the process of remembering). This narrative memory site belongs to Fanotte, to Schwarz-Bart, and to the historical collage of mother-women in Guadeloupe. Revisiting the paradigms of memory, Schwarz-Bart also creates a narrative of "textual healing."

Textual healing. I evoke this phrase from Farah Jasmine Griffin who explores the learnings[13] of healing and fortitude in the texts of black women writers. In her essay "Textual Healing: Claiming Black Women's Bodies, the Erotic and Resistance in Contemporary Novels of Slavery," Griffin discusses how contemporary women of African descent are in the historical process of healing from the legacies of slavery and patriarchal oppression. Taking place on spiritual, psychological, and emotional levels, healing is a healthy and progressive response to historical wounds. An enabling metaphor of sound, sensuality, and image, textual healing conjures up the memory of Marvin Gaye's timeless song that celebrates "sexual healing." Healing is rhythmic and flows with the movement of our minds, bodies, and spiritual sites. When we heal, we take care of the divine attributes that are within us—that inner life that talks to us. Healing is a process that is honored and accompanied by time. Griffin says that "in addition to its literary merit and theoretical implications, part of the power of some writing by black women is its transformative potential for the lives of all of us who continue to be haunted by the legacy of white supremacy and male patriarchy" (Griffin 521). By creating a dialogue with Caribbean history, Schwarz-Bart gives agency to the power of healing and the resilient spirit of women who are responsible, not only as biological mothers but as mother-women. Kitzie McKinney asserts that the "gift of being" allows women to "teach others how to live; at the same time, they derive support and strength from the 'invisible threads' that link them to each other and to their neighbors" (30). In the configuration of textual healing their texts and artifacts are also "sites of healing, pleasure, and resistance" (Griffin 520). Schwarz-Bart's mother-women may never be rich with material power, but they find ways to emotional and spiritual enrichment despite their economic powerlessness.

There are many popular "inspirational" self-help books for women's psychological, spiritual, and mental wellness. These works include Maya

Angelou's *Wouldn't Take Nothing for My Journey Now,* bell hooks's *Sisters of the Yam: Black Women and Self-Recovery,* Iyanla Vanzant's *Tapping the Power Within: A Path to Self-Empowerment for Black Women,* and Susan Taylor's *In the Spirit.* African American women's autobiographical and creative narratives gain ascendancy and are connected to Caribbean mother-women through the kinship of communal textual healing. The narratives may be read as inspirational texts for contemporary women of African descent recovering from the everyday repercussions of slavery, patriarchy, and colonization. The legacies of literacy have paved a way for writing the stories of these memories. For writers like Schwarz-Bart, textual healing comes out of knowing the memory sites and knowing that other women could still embrace life despite the hardships. Inspiration comes from the words and the images of the text. By using autobiographical storytelling as a narrative vehicle, Schwarz-Bart profoundly enjoins the demarcations of imagination, reality, and cross-cultural experiences.

Bella Brodzki writes that "in all its variety, literature in the late twentieth century reflects an almost global obsession with the transmission, preservation, repression, and potential effacement of memory as an instrument of historical consciousness" (220). The interest and debate about ideas on memory, history, and representation continue from different perspectives. In *Framing Silence: Revolutionary Novels by Haitian Women,* a refreshing study on the topic, Myriam J. A. Chancy has this to say about memory, history, and orality and the link to women writing in the African diaspora:

> [O]rality equals survival. Language, song, and stories have been the means by which enslaved peoples have maintained a sense of culture as they have been denied access to their very roots. Out of necessity, new codes were created out of converging and conflicting cultural matrices: creole languages are but one aspect of this mechanism of survival. Acts of memory are another. Memory, both personal and collective, provides the basis for cultural cohesion in societies where chaos, as defined by those outside those societies, appears to be the only constant. (74)

For many of us, memory through storytelling is what inscribes our history. Similar to Paule Marshall's mother-women, whom she calls "kitchen bards," they reclaim segments of the past and look to the future in order to fulfill themselves. Marshall writes about the West Indian women she grew up with, and she calls them "bards" because of their creative use of language. By referencing the Bajan community of her childhood, Marshall also returns to the *lieux de mémoire* where "the quest for memory is the search for one's history" (Nora 13). She advocates that we explore and rediscover history by reorganizing memory and its complex relationship to history. Haitian American writer Edwidge Danticat also has a dialogue with memory: "I look to the past—to Haiti—hoping that the extraordinary female storytellers I grew up with—the ones that have passed on—will choose to tell their story through my voice. For those of us who have a voice must speak to the present and past" (Casey 524).

With the imagination and construction of textual healing, Caribbean women writers bring a new vitality to perspectives on collective memory and history through personal encoding and decoding. In such novels as Michelle Cliff's *Abeng*, Edwidge Danticat's *Breath, Eyes, Memory*, Maryse Condé's *Les derniers roi mages* (*The Last of the African Kings*), and Ghislaine Charlier's *Mémoire d'une affranchie*, the writers decode memory and bring history to the forefront of intellectual discussion, reading, and thinking. Memory is archival as a collection of tangible and intangible artifacts that include our emotions in the context of history, culture, and intellect. Memory is secular and spiritual. Memory is empowerment. Memory belongs to the individual and to the group. Memory invokes the things that were and the things that are not. Memory opposes history and embraces it with ordinary things and extraordinary artifacts. In the larger context of the lives of women of color, Myriam J. A. Chancy affirms: "Mémoire is the thread that links generations of people whose various histories have been ignored, displaced, silenced: its invocation continues to place the absence of women's collectivity at the center of feminist discourse. Remembrance is thus at the crux of the reconstructive moment, and the 'text' becomes the intermediary between private and collective consciousness" (103). There are people of African descent in the Caribbean who do not want to pass on stories of slavery. They don't want the rememory of telling on history. Deliberate amnesia. One Caribbean-born observer is quoted as saying, "The central problem of blacks in the Caribbean is their total inability to accept the slave experience" (McKinney 30). They are still ashamed of the slave stories that are too strong, too near in time, and too painful to keep alive. They want to keep the memories buried because things are getting better. The children are better off not knowing about the brutality, the beatings, the rapes, the hunger, and the work their ancestors were forced to do from sunup to sundown, from can't see in the morning to can't see at night in the cotton fields in the south and in the sugar cane fields in the West Indies. They can now send the children to London, Paris, Amsterdam, New York. "Yep," they say, "you better off not knowin' nothin' about it." And sometimes they say, "Ain't no slavery 'appen 'ere, mon."

We all are selective about our memories, in particular when the selectivity becomes protection and defense mechanism for wellness. An elderly woman recently said to me, "When you get as old as I am, the only thing that you have left is the memories." This affluent woman lives alone in a beautiful but empty house—empty not of material things, but of kindred spirits. Toward the end of her life, her memories are comfortably wrapped around material things. The central character in *Pluie et vent*, Télumée Miracle, wraps her memories around emotional fulfillment and the enrichment of her life.[14] With the first section of the novel, entitled "Présentation des miens" ["My People"], Schwarz-Bart establishes Télumée as an elderly woman who is waiting to join her ancestors in the spirit world. Télumée has become the village mother. Basking in the sun of memories she reminisces how

> Le pays dépend bien souvent du coeur de l'homme: il est minuscule si le coeur est petit, et immense si le coeur est grand. Je n'ai jamais souffert de l'exiguïté de mon pays, sans pour autant prétendre que j'aie un grand coeur. Si on m'en donnait le pouvoir, c'est ici même, en Guadeloupe, que je choisirais de renaître, souffrir et mourir. Pourtant, il n'y a guère, mes ancêtres furent esclaves en cette île à volcans, à cyclones et moustiques, à mauvaise mentalité. Mais je ne suis pas venue sur terre pour soupeser toute la tristesse du monde. A cela, je préfère rêver, encore et encore, debout au milieu de mon jardin, comme le font toutes les vieilles de mon âge, jusqu'à ce que la mort me prenne dans mon rêve, avec toute ma joie. (11)

> [A man's country may be cramped or vast according to the size of his heart. I've never found my country too small, though that isn't to say my heart is great. And if I could choose it's here in Guadeloupe that I'd be born again, suffer and die. Yet not long back my ancestors were slaves on this volcanic, hurricane-swept, mosquito-ridden, nasty-minded island. But I didn't come into the world to weigh the world's woe. I prefer to dream, on and on, standing in my garden, just like any other old woman of my age, till death comes and takes me as I dream, me and all my joy. (2)]

As a life-story narrative, the language is simple and poetic, ordinary and extraordinary. Real or imagined, life story is one of the ways to give breath to the memory sites. Télumée looks back on the past and her personal relationships connected with it. At this point in her life, she not only lives on memories, but she untangles their meaning. The garden motif symbolizes how death is only another beginning, not a final departure. The rains and winds have fertilized life's tribulations and triumphs through that sense of place and being. The doubts and uncertainties that Télumée had as a child have been transformed into the ability to understand the kind of moral courage that characterizes women in many cultures. Therefore textures of memory refer to the multiplicity of ways in which memory returns and the different layers of remembering the past in storytelling. Through textures of memory, Télumée traces her journey to the beginning site by remembering the Lougandor woman, Minerva. Minerva's *lieux de mémoire* are the village places in turn-of-the-century Guadeloupe. Slavery is legally abolished, but the peasants continue to experience racism, economic oppression, and class prejudice because of the inherited injustices.

I am particularly attracted to the storytelling narrative in *Pluie et vent*. Storytelling is one way of accessing the memory sites. In *Woman, Native, Other*, Trinh T. Minh-ha tells us that "storytelling, the oldest form of building historical consciousness in community, constitutes a rich oral legacy, whose values have regained all importance . . . especially in the context of writing by women of color" and that women as storytellers make the compelling link to the past and present lessons in life "by re-establishing the contact with [their] foremothers, so that living tradition can never congeal into fixed forms, so that life keeps on nurturing life, so that what is understood as the Past continues to provide the link for the Present and the Future" (148–49). Also writing about the storytelling powers of women, Clarissa Pinkola Estés says, "Among the best of the teller-healers I know . . . *their stories grow out of their lives* as roots grow a tree. The stories have *grown* them, grown them into who they are. We can tell the difference. We know when someone has 'grown' a story facetiously and when the story has genuinely grown them. It is the latter that underlies the integral traditions" (471).

The metaphoric rain and wind that the Lougandor women have to contend with signify emotional, spiritual, and moral courage. They stay on the nurturing ground or they leave, as Victoire does. In another sense of the metaphor, the rains and winds nourish the women who stay; the women find "ways out of no way" to overcome obstacles. Because of her perseverance and fortitude, the villagers rename Toussine, Reine Sans Nom—an image of magnificence that is all-empowering to the extent that her attributes cannot be assumed by one name:

> Nous avons cherché un nom de reine qui te convienne mais en vain, car à la vérité, il n'y a pas de nom pour toi. Aussi désormais, quant à nous, nous t'appellerons: Reine Sans Nom. (29)

> [We have tried and tried to think of a name for you, but in vain, for there isn't one that will do. And so from now on we shall call you "Queen Without a Name!" (15)]

Following in her grandmother's footsteps, Télumée attains and merits the right to serve as the community's handmaiden of miracles, and she is renamed Télumée Miracle. Her profound kindness and guidance inspire awe in the villagers. Maryse Condé writes that

> Toujours est-il que la grande supériorité des Lougandor réside dans leur capacité de supporter la tristesse, la folie et l'absurdité du monde sans baisser la tête.[15]

> [In any case, the superiority of the Lougandors rests in their capacity to support the sorrow, the craziness, and the absurdity of the world without lowering their heads.]

If it were not for the adversities, how would they know how to "ride the horse"? Télumée moves from the dreaded cane fields to the isolated *mornes* (hills) reminiscent of marronage. As she moves from place to place in the back of beyond, she also journeys from fear into tranquillity, from powerlessness into empowerment, and from doubt into certainty.

Along with Simone Schwarz-Bart, Caribbean women writers such as Maryse Condé, Edwidge Danticat, and Françoise Ega create women characters who act as participants in and witnesses to the diverse histories of black women's cultural kinships. Indeed, as Christiane Ndiaye writes in *Danses de la parole* , "C'est le cas, en fait, d'un grand nombre de personnages féminins du roman antillais: tout en étant 'vivants,' 'réalistes' ils glissent subtilement dans la légende, dans le mythe; ils dépassent l'humain et acquièrent une dimension suréelle, merveilleuse" [In fact, it is the case of a number of women characters in Caribbean novels; all being 'alive,' 'realistic,' they go quietly into the legend, into the myth; they surpass being human and acquire a marvelous, surreal dimension].[16] They depict women who, by trying to move beyond survival, live on the edge. They redefine paradigms as they recreate our histories. What kinds of awls do they leave for our generations to tell stories about? Women certainly left their own stories and memories for us to dwell on. How do we interpret them? Women relate to the fundamental and essential aspects of culture as oral historians and New World griots. Our stories personify indelible perseverance. Through memory and storytelling linkages, we know about them and ourselves. Just as many African Americans are connected to southern American cultures, many are also connected to the Caribbean landscapes. Such are the lineages of shared kinships. Slavery and marronage are counterpoints in the larger histories of New World Africans. The ancestors are in a special convocation with the progeny, many of whom attempt to thrive despite the adversity that surrounds them. They refuse to live on the scent of life.

What do I mean by refusing to live on the scent of life?

Reine Sans Nom tells Télumée a fable about a horseman, Wvabor Hautes Jambes (Wvabor Longlegs). Wvabor saw only evil in life and with his mare rode the countryside keeping a safe distance from evil as well as any love humanity could offer. Eventually the horse takes over Wvabor's life—the horse takes control and begins to "ride" the horseman. From the mare, he is able to look down on humanity and live on the scent of the human condition. He sees the decay and the odors of humanity from a distance: "Plus il observait les hommes, plus il les trouvait pervers et la méchanceté qu'il voyait en eux l'empêchait d'admirer quoi que ce fût" (80) [The more he saw of men the more perverse he found them, and the wickedness he saw in them prevented him from admiring anything whatever (49)]. The human condition can also offer hope and love. Therefore when he meets love, it's too late. The horse has gained control of its rider. But this fable can be confusing. With much integrity, Reine Sans Nom decides that Télumée needs another angle in order to understand. Toussine's words carry thousands of years of learnings: "'ma petite braise', chuchotait-elle, 'si tu enfourches un cheval, garde ses brides bien en main, afin qu'il ne te conduise pas. . . . derrière une peine il y a une autre peine, la misère est une vague sans fin, mais le cheval ne doit pas te conduire, c'est toi qui dois conduire le cheval'" (82) ["'My little ember,' she'd whisper, 'if you ever get on a horse, keep good hold of the reins so that it's not the horse that rides you. . . . Behind one pain there is another. Sorrow is a wave without end. But the horse mustn't ride you, you must ride it'" (50–51)]. Toussine uses the fable's image to enable Télumée. This powerful image is the force that propels Télumée through life. I appreciate Kitzie McKinney's marvelous interpretation of the fable as an "explanation to Télumée of 'good' and 'bad' ways to live.... Preferring an abstract world of essence to the complexity of bodily existence, substituting one dimension of human nature for its entirety, Wvabor reduces human pleasure, ambivalence, multiplicity, and nuance to identical terms of the Same ('wickedness'), thereby destroying all sense of difference, including his own"(28). The fable is another canon to live by. Its modality is psychological, emotional, spiritual, and even spatial. With the telling of the fable, Schwarz-Bart gives us this narrative as an inspirational text. She has created a space of textual healing. We also face rains and winds that challenge our spirits and our faiths. In our own lives, we need awls that will show us beneficial pathways toward fulfillment.

Wvabor's lesson is a "reversed apocalypse" in that it does not trigger an ending but rather a beginning. When she forgets the fabled horseman, Télumée looses her footing on the nurturing ground. For example, Télumée goes into a deep depression because of Elie's abandonment, or she mourns her grandmother's death—these are expected kinds of reactions to disappointment and loss. Yet the image of the horseman is there to remind her that life can be "éblouie par l'éclat du faste de l'incertitude humaine (254)" ["dazzled by the splendour of human uncertainty" (172)]. She shares her synergy with others, and when she does, she is elevated because of that capacity. By applying the significance of the Wvabor legend to her life, Télumée gains ascendancy. The villagers recognize her attributes as a miracle woman of spirit and endurance. As they did with Toussine, they honor Télumée because, as they tell her,

depuis que tu es arrivée au morne La Folie, nous avons vainement cherché un nom qui te convienne... aujourd'hui, te voilà bien vieille pour recevoir un nom, mais tant que le soleil n'est pas couché, tout peut arriver... quant à nous, désormais, nous t'appellerons: Télumée Miracle. (246)

[Ever since you came to La Folie we have tried in vain to find a suitable name for you. Now you are very old to be given a name, but until the sun has set, anything may happen. So as for us, henceforth we shall call you Télumée Miracle. (166)]

She does not become lost in the forest nor does she turn her back on life by living off the scent of life. Christiane Ndiaye similarly writes that "Télumée a un rôle bien précis à jouer dans ce roman; ramener le Soleil, ramener la Magie de l'univers dans la vie humaine. . . . Voilà le Miracle de Télumée, voici sa petite Magie: aider les gens à vivre, ou sinon, du moins à mourir" (32) [Télumée has a very precise role to play in the novel; bringing the sun, bringing the Magic of the universe into human life. . . . That is the Miracle of Télumée, here is her little Magic: helping the people to live, if not to die]. The metaphor of scent of life is visceral. Horsemen are in possession of a necessary arrogance. They are in control of the reins. Thinking about the tale even more, I see that there is an ironic magnificence about the lesson of the horseman as a knight.

The image of magnificence is meant to evoke the memory of something visceral and regal, the image of the thing that will empower. When I was an undergraduate, I had a drama teacher, *une grande dame*, Ms. Minnie Gentry, who came from Kalamazoo. She had been a part of another kind of black migration during the early decades of the twentieth century—that of talent from the Midwest going to the cultural mecca of New York City to search for fame and fortune in the theater. By the time I met her, she had not accumulated any fortune, but in the theater world she was known and much respected. Between gigs, she taught acting to a motley group of young adults from both the inner city and suburbia. One day Ms. Gentry gave us an exercise to do, an exercise of a high order because at the time we did not realize that this exercise was meant to be significant beyond the limits of the theater and acting. This exercise would carry over into our lives, if we were smart enough to understand it as a touchstone of faith in ourselves.

Here we are trying to understand the hidden words of Stanislavsky's An Actor Prepares: *Eric. Cheryl. Cashmir. Sandra. Luke. John. Luther. Kevin. Daryl. Sherry. And the others. Acting is life itself for Ms. Gentry—she always tells us that. She has told us that it is what she wants to do as much as she wants life itself; as much as she wants to breathe. Now, she tells us to think about something very beautiful, empowering, exultant. As she sets the mood of silence for us, she talks. She tells us to keep a secret image in our mind and our consciousness. These two forces merge and become the soul of the instrument. (The instrument is the actor's entire body.) We should never tell anyone that there is an image with us and in us—it is like a special middle name and at the same time that which cannot be named. "It will be a magnificence without a name to anyone but you," she says. And*

*she says that the image of magnificence will be our personal talisman. She
knew that she could not give each of us an image, we had to find it for self.
We had to create our own possibility out of the strength of imagination.
Our secret fetish.*

*Ms. Gentry is from the Stanislavsky school of acting and she continues in
that precise accent of the stage that still hints of Kalamazoo."Always keep
your image of magnificence with you. Whenever somebody tries to cut you
down, you use that image; the image is power; you don't let them ride you,
because the image of magnificence won't let them. You don't ever let them
know the source of your empowerment. Always keep it inside of your body,
the instrument; in front of you—the instrument; use it! And they will
never be able to ride you!" Her voice raises with impatience as some of the
not-so-serious students snicker. "Shut up! I want absolute silence! You will
create the image of magnificence. Now get started."*

*It's summer time and very hot. All kinds of noises and odors from the
Harlem streets intrude up into our loft space; Olatunji's dance troupe
practices to his drums of passion in the next studio. She has taught us
how to block out sounds and noise and how to concentrate against even the
decibels of sound. Now she teaches us to listen inwardly. She wants us to
hear the silence that we must create around us. We step into the silence of
our own creative spirit. The windows are open but it's hot; no air condi-
tioning here. The heat is more distracting than the noise outside. Stuffy.
Dusty hardwood floors in this large space. A few pieces of old furniture for
stage props. A few secondhand chairs to sit on. Our elevated stage made
from ware-house packing crates. She wants us to be artists and to learn how
to create illusions with the inner and outer strength of our bodies. We listen
to our inner life and begin to conjure up the image without a name. It will
invent something new and wonderful to surround the self like a force field
of spirit that can't be touched by outsiders. Ms. Gentry sits down with her
ubiquitous cigarette and can of coke, leans forward looking at us, locking
eyes with our closed eyes, purses her lips, and waits for us to complete what
she has commanded. Consumed in her own silence, she will wait for as long
as it takes.*

Another memory site. That *grande dame* is no longer among us, but
I've always remembered what she told us as a lesson for living and giving. Likewise, Toussine's fable of Wvabor Hautes Jambes is a teaching
story and exercise. Wvabor Hautes Jambes is an image of magnificence
that will, indeed, allow Télumée to "rise over the earth like a cathedral."
It's an image for her to keep because, as she begins to understand its
meaning, it transforms her inner life. She learns how to apply it to her
life. That is the paradox of the fable. Wvabor's tale is a lesson for keeping our feet on the nurturing ground.

Ne prie pas pour une vie facile. Prie pour être fort.
[Pray not for an easy life. Pray for strength.]

—Proverb

Not all of us grow from the pains that have been inflicted upon us. There are those who fall prey to hardships and injustices in spite of what our ancestors wanted to preserve in their lineages. Some of us succumb. Depression, drugs, alcohol, abuse, suicide: modern-day pains are all around us. How to avoid the injustice of pain? Don't we want life to be without adversity? "The sufferer who possesses but is not possessive," writes Alice Walker, "is not exempt from pain and enslavement, but she, unlike her slave counterpart, does not passively endure or accept pain; she actively experiences and encounters it. Because she is capable of action, movement toward transformation, transcendence, she can invoke 'God.' That is, the inner spirit, the inner voice; the human compulsion, when deeply distressed to seek healing counsel within herself, the capacity within herself both to create this counsel and to receive it" ("A Letter of the Times" 32). Out of her own heritage of hardships, Reine Sans Nom creates counsel for herself and in turn is able to teach Télumée, who rises to the challenge of her legacy. "[D]errière une peine il y a une autre peine, la misère est une vague sans fin, mais le cheval ne doit pas te conduire, c'est toi qui dois conduire le cheval" (82) [Behind one pain there is another. Sorrow is a wave without end. But the horse mustn't ride you, you must ride it" (51)]. For many women, hearing another woman's healing story brings about new capacities for life and its enrichment. In Zora Neale Hurston's *Their Eyes Were Watching God*, Pheoby is empowered after listening to Janie's story. She says to Janie, "Lawd, Ah done growed ten feet higher from jus' listenin' tuh you, Janie" (158). And to further echo one of Hurston's characters in *Their Eyes, we're not blind*, we have *heard* the story and understand it as textual healing.

This literary lineage of textual healing and memory wellness includes Dany Bébel-Gisler's *Léonora: L'histoire enfouie de la Guadeloupe*. While Schwarz-Bart constructs her novel with a first-person narrator, Bébel-Gisler's *Léonora* is a nonfiction, first-person narrative. Its title indicates that Bébel-Gisler is conscious of how a woman's collective and personal histories have been excluded from master discourses. Bébel-Gisler herself writes the memory through the storytelling artifacts (the narrative strategy) of an elderly Guadeloupean woman named Léonora, who is illiterate. Bébel-Gisler is the collaborative editor and narrator. About the written version of her life story, Léonora tells Bébel-Gisler (in the English translation), "In this book made up of my words, it is my very self that is present. Just as I have told my story, you have written it" (261). While *Léonora* can be read as an autobiographical *testimonio* because much of the story focuses on the central figure's adult political life, *Pluie et vent* is a narrative meant to simulate autobiography and indirect *testimonio*. Télumée's memories and Léonora's life story reflect the textures of Guadeloupe's history and memory sites.

Again, I ask the question, what does this all mean? Télumée is her grandmother's shadow, her footfalls; she is the pulse that intensifies the love between them. She is the apprentice who endures. She is the female cavalier trying to hold on to the reins of life even after her beloved grandmother dies. Therein lies the spirituality of Schwarz-Bart's work. Crossing the bridge is certainly the difficult passage. The crossing, however, is not only about Télumée, "vaillante petite négresse à deux coeurs" [a valiant little negress with two hearts], but about a lineage; an exceptional dynasty of women: the blind woman, Minerva, born during slavery, Reine Sans Nom, and then Victoire, the mother of Télumée. When we speak of dynasties, we think of wealth and political power. *Their* lives are impoverished. Their wealth, however, resides in their attitudes toward life: In spite of the poverty they find the resilience with which to deal with what has been thrown to them. As metaphoric progeny of that dynasty, our spirit is rooted in a New World ethos that our foremothers created: "Ne prie pas pour une vie facile. Prie pour être fort." The women pray for fortitude in order to make a way out of no way, to just get through one more day, to be able to carry the load, to be able to cross the bridge, and to be able to jump at the sun. I explored some of the stereotypes that have characterized the strength of black women in the Americas. Despite these negative images, it seems that the mother-women want to celebrate perseverance even if they continue to be denounced because of it. The ethos embodies dynamic properties of the mother-women as they negotiate individuality and communal identity. Schwarz-Bart aims to present cultural memory as a slice of reality. Remembering the image of Wvabor helps Télumée to be less willing to accept her powerlessness. And so the image of magnificence is an enabling one. Télumée creates her own counsel within the community because some legacies should be passed on.

> Ignorance is indisputably the principal reason for the decline and fall of peoples and the perpetuation of prejudice. No nation can achieve success unless education is accorded all its citizens. . . . The decision-making agencies involved would do well to consider giving first priority to the education of women and girls, since it is through educated mothers that the benefits of knowledge can be most effectively and rapidly diffused throughout society.
> —The Universal House of Justice, *The Promise of World Peace*

Rain and wind. Like Fanotte, we have memories of the mother-women of our personal and collective heritage. We write about them and tell their stories. We must conjure up the images of magnificence. We celebrate the rains and winds of life. We create the collages. Healing is part of finding fulfillment because it allows us to live from within rather than from outside of ourselves.

Do remember the spirit of the Magdalenes, mother-women from another era. Remember their plights. Remember the learnings they embraced, their distress, their loves, their efforts to negotiate adversity, their efforts to read and write their stories. In this postcolonial moment, there are kinfolk in the large and small villages of our homelands who do not want their daughters to be schooled. They will only put their daughters to work in the fields or tell them they must cook and clean and add children to the lineage. They will not allow their daughters to claim their full achievements. Their daughters cannot read or write. The hinterland communities do not understand that to remember the past is one thing, to live in it is another. They do not understand that the girl-children have many capacities. The girls cannot remain ignorant and uninformed—they must be able to grow into mother-women who will be the first educators, mother-women who will undeniably diffuse the energy of learning and teaching throughout their societies. Writing is no longer a gift of privilege or an enunciation of human qualities. In many ways these truths *are* self-evident. Reading and writing establish and maintain enabling identities. Literacy commits to the power of nommo, the empowering word. Whereas literacy is a foundation for knowing, knowledge is informed by literacy and justices associated with learning. Remember the girl-children and the women who created pathways and roadways for them. And remember their fictional progeny: Télumée Miracle, Reine Sans Nom, Minerva, the Others. Remember our magnificence in the matrilineal diaspora. We have the capacity to create enabling words and stories that will provide textual healing. Let us read. We will write. And we will create. Refusing to live on scent, we know that our capacities are life affirming.

CHAPTER FOUR

Crossing Bridges and Memory-Telling:
Une si longue lettre

To all women and to men of good will.
—Mariama Bâ, *Une si longue lettre*

With the arrival of the new millennium, the progeny of the flying Africans continue to bridge black Atlantic cultures and connect back to the homelands of the ancestors. Our transatlantic crossings are tied to memory, identity, transformation, and transmission. We are the definers. From one side of the Atlantic to the other, we've exchanged our music, culinary arts, performing arts, literature, and haute couture from jeans to kente and bogolan. Our Atlantic cultures are mutually exchanged through Internet technology, intermarriages, and multilingual fluency. The crossings evoke fiction and real-life experiences. There are mythic memories of Africa that the ancestors left behind in the Americas. On the African side of the Atlantic are contemporary societies in economic and cultural transitions that are still influenced by the immediacy of ancient traditions and beliefs. To what extent does memory contest gender-oriented cultural borders that connect new diasporas? To what extent do modern New World people of African descent engage historical *lieux de mémoire* when we cross bridges and reconnect? How can we use gender awareness to disengage certain practices in order to initiate new traditions?

One symbolic place of memory connected to Africa and African diaspora cultures is the island of Gorée located off the coast of Senegal.

Gorée, indeed, is not just a quaint island off the westernmost point of the African continent. Europeans knew that Gorée existed as early as 1433, when Portuguese ships first began to stop here in order to reprovision with supplies from the mainland. Its strategic location, without doubt, influenced the destiny of Gorée. The island eventually became an exit port for an indeterminable number of Africans who were captured and taken to the Americas. With the historical momentum of Africans who collaborated with the Europeans, the slave trade flourished at various points along what was called the Slave Coast. Ouidah. Old Calabar. Elmina. Cape Verde. Gorée. The island became infamous not so much because of the number of Africans who departed from here as slaves but because its history was tumultuous and brutal with extensive European ownership. Portuguese, Italian, English, Dutch, Spanish, and French traders all participated in the profitable trade in human beings. Gorée constantly reminds its visitors of slavery, and for some people it has become a symbol of the history of the slave trade.

Is it Gorée's contemporary serenity that confirms its brutal past? The island is cozy, slow-paced, and beautiful in varying colors of sand, stone, and tropical foliage. A ferry shuttles back and forth between Dakar, the capital city of Senegal, and Gorée with tourists, official visitors, and local people. They visit the historical attractions, museums, seafood cafes, and open-air art markets; or they meander through the cobbled streets and tucked-away courtyards visiting friends and relatives. Private cars and other motor vehicles are not allowed on the island. Walking initiates curiosity and a sense of place, and it's easy to strike up a conversation in French or Wolof with the islanders. About fifteen hundred people live here now: Americans, Europeans, Senegalese. And métise descendants of the *signares*—multilingual African-European women who were involved in the slave trade as sellers and buyers of slaves.[1] The *signares* were known for their beauty, elegance, and for being sophisticated entrepreneurs. Their activities and connections to the Atlantic world introduced other lineages of African "mothers" and developed commercial affinities along the coast. They were Magdalene's sisters on this side of the Atlantic.

Undoubtedly the island is a unique site of memory. On Rue St.-Germain, one of the main streets, there is the well-known Maison des Esclaves (House of Slaves) that overlooks the ocean. For a time during the eighteenth century, the house was owned and operated by one of the *signares*. The house has been comfortably renovated to accommodate tourism. At night, La Maison becomes an open-air theater with dramatic lighting for dance performances, plays, readings, and concerts that reverberate with traditional African drumming and contemporary world beat music. During the day, La Maison is a monument to historical grief. The famous door of no return opens into one of its passageways.

Some people believe that the door is an imagined reference point. But the door exists. During the era of the triangular trade routes that connected Africa, the Americas, and Europe in the misery and profits of slavery, there was the vastness of the Atlantic ocean on one side of the door. On the other side were the wretched holding pens that held the African cargo before they were hustled through the door and forced into the waiting slave ships. Some people say that it was impossible for the slave ships to dock so close to the house because of the precarious rocks that encircle this small area of the island's coast. Myths continue to intersect with historical circumstances. The Africans would return in spirit because most of them would never physically see their homeland again. Hence, the passageway became known as the final place of exit. Progeny from the Americas would embrace their history and make the symbolic journey of return. The door becomes charged with historical and spiritual significance as well as with irony because, as it was an infamous exit point along the coast, it is now a defining point of return. The people come from homelands in all parts of the Americas. New York. Chicago. Montreal. Rio. Jamaica. San Pedro Sula. Travésia. Nevis. Guadeloupe. They are well fed and dressed, and relatively well educated. They are unrelated kin whose beliefs and values have inevitably been influenced by social and political progress. These descendants continue to arrive at Gorée as New World pilgrims. To return is to honor the flying Africans. But as we evoke memory and narrative, how do we disengage from the burden of memory?

Today it's hot with occasional breezes skipping across the island. I watch clusters of tourists circulate about the Maison. They listen in various languages to their guides, who retell the history of Gorée. There are Africans from other countries of the continent, Europeans, Japanese, West Indians, and Americans of both European and African descent. The Americans of African descent are eager to meet the famous curator, Monsieur Joseph Ndiaye, who strives to keep the historical and symbolic memory of Gorée alive. Monsieur has hung framed commentaries about slavery throughout the Maison. Their presence (that of the African Americans and the framed pictures) creates textures of memories. Some stories must unfold over generations before they can be understood profoundly because "there are years that ask questions and years that answer."[2]

Sometime during the 1930s, anthropologist Melville J. Herskovits listened to a priest from King Béhanzin's court in Abomey (in present-day Republic of Benin) chant about how the milieu of slavery was a distinct tribal memoir for him: "Oh ancestors, do all in your power that princes and nobles who today rule never be sent away from here as slaves to Ame'ica. . . . We pray you to do all in your power to punish the people who bought our kinsmen whom we shall never see again. . . . Send their vessels to Whidah [Ouidah] harbor. When they come, drown their crews, and make the wealth of their ships come back to Dahomey. . . . The Americans must bring the cloths and the rum made by our kinsmen who are there, for these will permit us to smell their presence."[3] The Dahomean priest is like the voices of some African Americans who become angry and remorseful when they visit the door of no return. They are wounded by the smell of a presence that once was—slavery. People frequently get emotionally invested in things that don't make sense to others. Emotional investments, however, make Gorée an intensely spiritual place. And there are those who acknowledge the past in order to move forward: This is a history to pass *on*, to echo Toni Morrison in *Beloved*. In order to reconcile and bury the hatchets, it's also a history to *pass* on. Hasn't there been enough wounding? Monuments are memories for celebration.

From the famous, or infamous, doorway I look down below to where the Atlantic waves are crashing up against the rocks. For the moment nobody is around, and I'm the lone silhouette in the passageway. There's a ship moored not too far away. It's a yacht—anchored, white, and shimmering in the sunlight. These are the kinds of sea vessels that come now. This modern vessel of affluence is framed by the same doorway that framed slave ships centuries ago.

Madame Salla Niang, an energetic Goréan businesswoman, kindly offers me hospitality one afternoon during my stay on the island. I sit with the Niang family and eat a wonderful Senegalese lunch. We talk about our families and our lives. She lets me know that her middle-aged brother, who lets her do all the talking, needs a wife. I ignore her comment. Although remaining involved in our conversation, he says nothing. Madame, who is delighted to have an unexpected visitor says, "Beaucoup de Noirs Américains viennent chez moi ... [she gestures with her hands to indicate the cool and rather comfortable surroundings.] J'aime vraiment rencontrer mes frères et soeurs Américains qui viennent visiter notre île. Mais, ils ne doivent pas être blessé et fâché à cause de l'histoire. . . . l'esclavage, colonialisme et tout le reste. Enterrons le passé! Ce qui importe c'est le présent. [Many African Americans come to my home. . . . I really enjoy meeting my American brothers and sisters who come to visit our island. But they should not be hurt and angry because of the past ... slavery, colonialism, and all that. Let's bury the past! The important thing is life right now.] The tranquillity of island hospitality lingers on into the late afternoon. Thanking Madame Salla Niang and her family, I leave them and continue my walking exploration of the island.

The history of slavery may be a symbolic chapter on Gorée, but only a historical epigraph elsewhere in Senegal and the rest of West Africa. Can Gorée be a site for burying the past and healing? Can it help to foster a reconciliation with Atlantic history? And what about the descendants who remained on this side of the Atlantic? How do their diverse memory sites interact with postcolonial attitudes? Gorée can represent new ways to think about the Atlantic world. It is no longer a point of no return. It is a site of reentry and welcome. I arrive at the girls' school that bears the name of the late Senegalese writer, Mariama Bâ: Maison d'Education Mariama Bâ. The paved courtyard is swept clean, and potted tropical plants add to the sense of order and stateliness. Do the young women who attend this school know that many of us across the Atlantic offer literary tributes to Mariama Bâ's legacy? What kinds of traditions do the girls adhere to? Is it easier for this new generation to accept the past as the past?

Madame Bâ is no longer physically with us. Her legacy, however, remains. She has written about some of the contemporary gender-oriented issues that profoundly challenge traditional values and ways of thinking. In her novel *Une si longue lettre* (*So Long a Letter*),[4] Mariama Bâ crosses many cultural bridges and shows how aspects of African mothering demand new values and new ways of thinking about the sites of memory and history. She presents the dilemma: how do we engage memory as we attempt to disengage from it?

Souvenons-nous . . . tous les poètes, et lecteurs et lectrices de
poètes . . . car si depuis des décades il ne s'agit plus d'expliquer le
monde, mais de le transformer pour le bien de tous, déjà maintenant
il ne s'agit plus seulement d'écrire de la vie quotidienne et de lire des
poèmes, mais de transformer en poèmes tous les gestes.[5]

—René Depestre

Mariama Bâ received the prestigious Noma award in 1980 for *Une si
longue lettre*. The novel has become a contemporary classic of African
women's literature. Her second novel, *Un chant écarlate*, was published
posthumously in 1981. While the latter is about the dynamics of an interracial marriage in Senegal, the former depicts a Senegalese widow's
emotional and spiritual rebirth after the death of her estranged spouse.
As a new generation of idealistic "nation builders," Ramatoulaye and
Modou Fall held their marriage vows within monogamy. Years later
Modou Fall takes a second wife and abandons Ramatoulaye and their
children. *Lettre* is not exclusively about polygamy; it is more about a
middle-aged woman's inner exploration of her life through the therapy
that memory-telling provides by way of writing a letter. The central
character's transformation is crafted by Bâ's sense of memory and her
illuminations as a Senegalese and as an African woman who wants to
valorize the coexistence of the particular and the universal. The epistolary voice and the voice of memory-telling in *Lettre* are representative
multiple voices of the irreversible currents of global feminisms. Written
in the first person, the narrative develops an indigenous feminist thinking that crosses cultural boundaries. In what milieu can African women
begin to reshape their lives, which have been dominated by traditional
gender roles and patriarchal definitions of womanhood? In a 1979 interview, Mariama Bâ said, "J'ai voulu donner au roman une forme originale. En général, l'auteur se met en dehors des personnages et raconte.
J'ai choisi la forme d'une lettre pour donner à l'oeuvre un visage humain. Quand on écrit une lettre, on dit je. Ce 'je' s'identifie à Ramatoulaye et non à l'auteur" ["I wanted to give an original form to the
novel. The author generally puts himself outside of the characters and
tells the story. I chose the form of a letter in order to give the work a human face. When you write a letter, you say I. This 'I' identifies itself
with Ramatoulaye and not with the author"] (Dia 12). While the narrative is not an autobiography, there is an autobiographical consciousness
that is connected to cherished values. "Je" enables the consciousness for

actualizing the process of writing. "Je" sets the stage for memory-telling. On one stage is the author herself crafting the book; on another is the persona who is memory-telling through writing. In this instance, memory-telling takes shape through the cross-cultural continuity of epistolary writing. Women's epistolary writing continues to be a literary vehicle or an author's strategy for gender-oriented "authenticity" and for engaging the reader in the initial suspension of disbelief.

While *Lettre* is not an autobiography or a work of nonfiction, it is the consciousness of autobiographical sites of memory and cultural arti-facts. The letter belongs to Ramatoulaye (and Aïssatou), and it expresses Bâ's autobiographical perspectives about the intersections of ethnicity (in the form of caste prejudice), mothering, tradition, and nation. Rep-resenting a space for privacy and introspection, *Lettre* is about the nar-rator's journey of discovery and ascendancy through *mémoire* (the letter) and memory-telling (the process of telling story). Mariama Bâ creates the central character through writing, who in turn creates her own ther-apy through writing memory. What I refer to as memory-telling com-plements Pierre Nora's concept of *lieux de mémoire*. What is memory-telling and how does it accentuate the process of writing the story? Memory-telling is another dynamic of storytelling generated by remem-bering the past. Memory-telling has the guise of informality; its narra-tive boundaries expand; the "memory" is open and fluid. Memory-telling is an exchange of personal relationships to public history. Memory-telling thrives on the dynamics of orality and audience. Like the ancient griots, a memory-teller carries thousands of years in her memories. Memory-telling enables ascendancy.

The consciousness of global feminisms has undoubtedly affected tra-ditional paradigms about mothering in Africa. Where lie the new chal-lenges of mothering in these cultures where the mother-women have been proud and revered as they have also been relegated to inferior po-sitions? Although the status of women is improving universally because of the irreversible currents of feminisms, I agree with Jacqueline S. Sol-way, who says that "the fact remains that some degree of male dominance strikes many of us as a cross-cultural reality in the contemporary world" (49). Attitudes of reverence bestowed on African women are ambiguous because, on the one hand, mothers are supreme (to echo Chinua Achebe from *Things Fall Apart*), and on the other hand, women as mothers and wives continue to be subordinated and dominated by patriarchal traditions. With the themes of mothering, polygamy, nation-building, and the empowerment of middle-aged women, Mariama Bâ dedicates *Une si longue lettre* to "all women and to men of good will." The qualifier is significant: while Bâ may embrace all women cross-culturally, she wants solidarity only with the men who will respect the equality and empowerment of women's lives. The global issues of equality and personal fulfillment continue to be relevant to the transformations that are taking place cross-culturally in the lives and consciousness of women.

Lettre is personal and political. Its epistolary form gives the impression of an intimate outpouring of the heart that is essentially a private written communication between two women, Ramatoulaye Fall and Aïssatou Bâ. On another level, one within the postcolonial moment, Ramatoulaye's ambitions and aspirations move across national boundaries. Toward the end of her letter, Ramatoulaye writes that she is aware of the women's movement in the world and its struggle for stability and permanence. Indeed, she identifies with the global emergence of women as recognized contributors to progress and the transformation of their societies. African women writers depict how the consciousness of equality affects women from all levels of education and articulation. In Aminata Sow Fall's *La grève des bàttu, ou Les déchets humains* (*The Beggars' Strike, or the Dregs of Society*),[6] Lolli, who despite being illiterate,

> avait vu que les femmes n'acceptent plus d'être considérées comme de simples objets et engageaient une lutte énergique pour leur émancipation; partout, à la radio, dans les meetings, dans les cérémonies familiales, elles clamaient qu' au point de vue juridique, elles avaient les mêmes droits que les hommes; que bien sûr elles ne disputaient pas à l'homme sa situation de chef de famille, mais qu'il était nécessaire que l'homme fût conscient que la femme est un être à part entière, ayant des droits et des devoirs. (42)

> [had seen that women no longer accepted being treated as simple objects. They were engaged in an energetic struggle for emancipation; everywhere, on the radio, at meetings, at family gatherings, they were claiming that, from a legal point of view, they had the same rights as men. Naturally, they were not disputing the man's position as head of the family, but the man had got to realize this his wife is an independent human being, with her own rights and obligations. (30)]

Within the span of writing, Ramatoulaye arrives at a new destination and eventually sees herself as part of a global alliance with feminisms. Although they are fictional characters, Ramatoulaye and Lolli echo the sentiments of real women who hear the prevailing debates of feminisms that challenge time-honored traditions. They know that stagnant values thwart the ambitions of women who want to define themselves on the nurturing grounds of family, community, and nation. Women, to a certain extent, have to disengage so that new foundations can start new traditions. Ramatoulaye abruptly decides not to post the letter, yet as a novel, *Une si longue lettre* is like a forwarded letter that continues to be sent to the rest of the world in many languages with its message of gender equality and good will.

> "Que mon conte soit beau et se déroule comme un long fil...."
> "May my story be beautiful and unwind like a long thread...."
> [This is the standard ... introduction the Kabyle folksingers in the Algerian mountains recite before beginning their tales.]
> —Charlotte H. Bruner, *Unwinding Threads*

Mariama Bâ sets her literary stage with paper and a pen as tools of the craft.[7] She elegantly creates Ramatoulaye as a woman in the transitional life course of middle age with the onset of menopause who has a story to tell.[8] At this juncture in her life, how does Ramatoulaye come to terms with the crisis of her spouse's death and the pain of remembering during middle age?

Medical and cultural anthropologists generally concur that most societies view menopause as a gradual life-course transition. The transition is not ritualized or demarcated, as is the recognition of events such as puberty, initiation, birthing, or death. Among Western cultures (i.e., North America and Europe), menopausal women generally believe that they suffer during this period of significant physiological and social transition because of the overwhelming lack and loss of the feminine mystique. In this context, menopause is often characterized as psychosomatic, and "the menopausal transition period is generally felt ... to be fraught with physical and psychological stresses of various kinds" (Vatuk 163). Beyond the universal biochemical changes that women experience during middle age, attitudes about and gender responses to menopause are culturally constructed.[9] Therefore, compounded with cultural perceptions, menopause is a biocultural occurrence. Social and clinical descriptions of menopause often reflect the manner in which menopause is seen as an organic disability in Western cultures with such descriptions as "regression, decline, atrophy, shrinkage and disturbance loss, inability and resignation" (Martin 43).[10] Western women have been led by the Western medical construct of gender identity to submit to the "menopausal syndrome"—social and physiological occurrences that regard menopause as a "traumatic and problematic" stage of the female life course (Kaufert and Lock 204).

Western feminists are challenging stagnant attitudes and beliefs regarding female menopause because middle age can fundamentally be "the time in which a woman enjoys her greatest power, status and autonomy.... [W]hether it is seen in relation to a woman's own life or in relation to the lives of men of her culture and generation, middle age is a woman's prime" (Sacks 2). Cross-cultural patterns demonstrate that non-Western societies in general have viewed menopause as a positively transforming time for women. It has its own vitality. Throughout the majority of nonindustrialized societies, when women reach middle age and menopause, their status in the community improves and is changed positively, if not elevated, for a variety of reasons. For example, women can be beyond the childbearing years (this period includes not only birthing but adopting and fostering dependent children), but that reality does not signal the syndrome of loss. Cultural variables enable middle-aged women to find new avenues for creativity, and their families and communities support their potential to be harbingers of new ventures. The onset of middle age signals enhanced possibilities for personal fulfillment. Viewing African societies cross-culturally, we recognize that aging is an honor and a positive attribute. Menopausal women are respected because of the aging process. Regardless of the patriarchal customs that may continue to dominate, middle-aged/menopausal women have the spiritual and psychological space to generate new aspects of empowerment and honor. Menopause is, therefore, a passage that can enable new ideas, autonomy, and achievement. Despite cross-cultural variables, African middle-aged women are seen as even more attractive by the community (by women and men) not only because of their physical attributes and sexuality but also because of the inner spirit that has been nurtured by life-course achievements and responsibilities. In this sense, menopause is a metaphor for fulfillment, empowerment, and creativity. Menopause, seen as the beginning of another

stage of the life course, is an empowering transitional moment that carries women into culturally valued old age.

What are the cultural and contextual dynamics that highlight Ramatoulaye as a middle-aged, menopausal woman? Writing provides a space
through which Ramatoulaye can actualize her potential. Via the letter,
she crafts a space for the immediacy of mother-centered memory-telling.
Through soul-searching and the voices of memory-telling, Ramatoulaye
indeed gains ascendancy and becomes responsible for her own spiritual
wellness. She gains a unique awareness of what she can offer to her
family, community, and nation. Ramatoulaye's letter, however, is not
only a narrative of nation. It's a narrative of a life course that has been
propelled by ideology, idealism, perseverance, and rejuvenation. Furthermore, memory-telling through writing a letter allows Ramatoulaye
to be introspective and to be the interpreter; she assembles, dismantles,
and recreates meaning out of memory-telling.

In the larger context of literary history, epistolary fiction became successful in eighteenth-century England and France when European readers wanted to believe that published romances and stories of intrigue
were "real" and that public "letters" were authentic. These "authenti-
cated" letters were often "found" and admitted the public into the private arenas of scandal and intrigue among the upper classes. The "found"
letter (or diary) was a popular vehicle that women writers used to convey the narrative line.[11] Spontaneity, privacy, and familiarity rather than
formal presentation and arrangement characterize letters. (Journal en-
tries, although intimate, are methodical and more strategically arranged.)
Contemporary gender-oriented epistolary writing is produced cross-
culturally and causes similar reader responses. The very nature of epistolary writing generates feelings of "truth," authenticity, and intimacy.
What I refer to as perceived truth develops out of both real letters and
epistolary fiction. This semblance of truth demonstrates "a pragmatic
approach which accepts the text as a document laden with information
which is real. . . . Yet there are letters . . . which serve another and equally
vital function: that of creating illusion and fiction" (Bossis, *Methodological Journeys* 68). As readers we suspend our disbelief, and epistolary
fiction becomes another trope for illusions of reality and truth. Yet epistolary fiction continues to create a continuous movement between illusion and reality because the illusion underscores some part of reality
that the writer wants to convey.

Taking advantage of the epistolary form, Mariama Bâ contextualizes immediacy, intimacy, and the wide movement of time that is encapsulated in a memoir. The letter (addressed to Aïssatou) is also a *mémoire* because it provides textual healing for Ramatoulaye. Furthermore, Ruth Perry maintains that

> One effect of telling stories about the consciousness of the characters is that it gives a continuous sense of time even where there is no formal unity of time or place in this genre. The reader soon disregards the formal dislocations and paces himself instead to the inward rhythms of the epistolary characters who are always reacting to the present. The immediacy of such writing also encourages the inclusion of all the psychological particulars ... when writing about an event while living through it, all the immaterial psychological nuance seems potentially relevant and deserving of attention. (120)

Ramatoulaye writes about pivotal events that happened in the past as she continues to redefine how those events have affected the choices she has made. As a *write* of passage, the letter becomes Ramatoulaye's artifact of affirmation for personal truths. As an artifact reflecting a rite of passage (she has recently become a widow), the letter allows Ramatoulaye to see ways in which she can disengage from the past. Mireille Bossis points out that epistolary writing can be seen as "truth" and "for ideological reasons the critic may select a series of elements consistent with his or her subjective interpretation and, through a process of rationalization, may from them construct a figure which accords with what he or she expects to find" (*Methodological Journeys* 66). From such a perspective and given its epistolary structure, *Lettre* may be viewed as representative ideological "truth" that highlights mother-centered experiences of a middle-aged, middle-class woman in modern Senegal.

With the changing roles of Senegalese women as mothers and wives in mind, Madame Bâ creates two distinct prototypes of mothering in *Une si longue lettre*. One creates misery and jealousies in the name of caste and tradition. These women as mothers seek prestige and power through the marriages their sons and daughters will make. They cause calamities and try to build happiness on the unhappiness of others— which they have often caused. They often disrespect and take advantage of younger sister-daughters. They are women who define themselves through the authority of men who are socially well placed.[12] Their mothering habits define patriarchal beliefs. For these women, the personal is also very political. They are like Tante Nabou, who is bent on destroying her son's first marriage, and Dame Belle-Mère, who is the catalyst for Ramatoulaye's marital break up.

Tante Nabou grooms and prepares her young niece (also named Nabou) for the destruction of the monogamous marriage of her son Mawdou to Aïssatou, whom Tante Nabou did not accept in the first place. Tante Nabou sees marriage as social mobility and an opportunity for material gain. Because of inheritance laws, marriage enforces rigid caste discrimination. Tante Nabou,

> Elle vivait dans le passé sans prendre conscience du monde qui muait. Elle s'obstinait dans les vérités anciennes. Fortement attachée à ses origines privilégiées, elle croyait ferme au sang porteur de vertus et répétait en hochant la tête, que le manque de noblesse à la naissance se retrouve dans le comportement. (42)

> [She lived in the past, unaware of the changing world. She clung to old beliefs. Being strongly attached to her privileged origins, she believed firmly that blood carried with it virtues, and, nodding her head, she would repeat that humble birth would always show in a person's bearing. (26)]

Dame Belle-Mère arranges and sanctions Modou's marriage to his daughter's school friend. Tante Nabou exerts control through manipulating her relationships with other people. Women like Nabou and Dame Belle-Mère uphold the premise that the first quality in a woman is docility because a wife owes her husband submission and provides for his pleasure and well-being. They cause distress among others in their efforts to enforce traditions indiscriminately. Tante Nabou and Dame Belle-Mère personify the antagonistic woman. Such mothers in *Lettre* like Yaye Khady in *Un chant écarlate* are prisoners of tradition and are obstacles to transformation not only within themselves but in their societies as well.

Those women live by ancient, worn-out wisdom and resist the dynamics of change with the resilience of tradition. They can't feel or accept the winds of change. They can't disengage from certain traditions of the mothers. They cling to what they know and what their foremothers wrongly or rightly did. Such women cling to timeworn traditions out of fear and loyalty. Those women are amazing: they want their daughters and sister-women to be images of them! They don't realize that certain prejudiced beliefs and practices can no longer serve their daughters, who seek new beliefs and ideas.

Such mothers exist across cultures and across different textual narratives. For example, in Fauziya Kassindja's autobiography *Do They Hear You When You Cry?* the aunt, Aweye, is just that kind of mother and woman in Togo. After the sudden death of Fauziya's father, the aunt attempts not only to manipulate a marriage for her niece but also plans to have Fauziya undergo *kakia* (female genital cutting), neither of which the seventeen-year-old Fauziya wants.[13] According to Fauziya Kassindja, "My aunt and uncle would find me and claim me. I was their property now. They could do with me as they liked. That was tribal law. . . . 'Fauziya . . . you're not going to school. You're getting married.' I was yelling at her now, screaming out of control . . . 'I'm not getting married, I won't!'" (102). Women like Aweye believe that the ancestors' customs are just as viable for this historical moment as they were centuries ago. These women are cunning and forceful.

There are, however, the mother-women in our cultures, the kind of women to whom Mariama Bâ pays homage in *Lettre*, who acknowledge the transformation of new ideas and new ways of thinking. Like Fauziya Kassindja, they have faith in themselves. They want the society to change because everyone has something at stake. They are cross-cultural feminists. They are pathfinders. Madame Bâ depicts these women as intellectual and unapologetically spiritual and sexual. Because of caste and stifling traditions, such women struggle with the challenges of making choices that overrule ancient modalities. They challenge the complacency that lingers in the shadows of patriarchy. They appreciate the bounties that their mothers and grandmothers have given. They respect them, even if those women are clingers. These women know they cannot build happiness on top of another person's distress. Out of kinship ties, they do not abandon those who cling to ways that need to be abandoned, yet they are critical of the ancestors' errors and those practices that are out of sync with today's societies. If they must reject the laws of the ancestors' religion, then so be it. Nevertheless they remain spiritual as they seek new ways to define spirituality and religion. They want to make new pathways for wellness.

These women believe in educating the girls. If the family must make a choice to send the boy or the girl to school, the girl will go because she will be the first educator of the next generation. These women create new kinds of mother-centered friendships. These women have the power to rebirth themselves and forge opportunities out of adversity and distress. Mariama Bâ creates Ramatoulaye as one such woman, who has become a middle-aged widow by the virtue of her estranged husband's sudden death.

Ramatoulaye is mourning this death when she begins her letter to Aïssatou. "Modou est mort. Comment te raconter? On ne prend pas de rendez-vous avec le destin. . . . Modou Fall est bien mort, Aïssatou" (8, 10). [Modou is dead. How can I tell you? One does fix appointments with fate. . . . Modou Fall is indeed dead, Aïssatou (2, 3)]. His passing re-opens emotional wounds for Ramatoulaye that had not completely healed: "Cette situation d'extrême tension aiguise ma souffrance" (10) [This condition of extreme tension sharpens my suffering" (3)]. She loved him. Because she had not divorced Modou Fall after he left her for another woman, at his death Ramatoulaye is still legally married to him, and therefore she is the first widow. Through this memoir of intimacy, Ramatoulaye recaptures the story of thirty years of her life: twenty-five of marriage to her husband Modou and five years in an estranged relationship, during which time Modou lives with his second wife. As a widow Ramatoulaye now remembers how the years had passed; she had to deal with the polygamous marital status and the economic difficulty of providing for twelve children and taking care of herself. She mourns more than his death; she mourns the memories.

Writing intensifies Ramatoulaye's friendship with Aïssatou. As sister-friends they come together through Ramatoulaye's memory-telling: "Je t'invoque. Le passé renaît avec son cortège d'émotions" (4) [I conjure you up. The past is reborn, along with its procession of emotions (1)]. These emotions appear like ghosts flinging themselves in front of her; then the memories become just that: on paper. The ghosts turn into ancestral strengths. "Conjuring" is the nommo of words and power. "Black women speak/write in multiple voices, not all simultaneously or with equal weight," Mae Henderson tells us, "but with various and changing degrees of intensity, privileging one parole and then another" (36). Ramatoulaye's memory speaks as it connects immediacy and intimacy. At the engagement of pen and paper—"En guise de réponse, j'ouvre ce cahier" (7) ["By way of reply, I am beginning this diary" (1)]—the intimate connections between the tangible and the spirit, between words and things are established. Writing transcends its material quality when Ramatoulaye writes: "Amie, amie, amie! Je t'appelle trois fois" (8) ["My friend, my friend, my friend, I call on you three times" (1)]. There's the sorrow and compassion of the moment. Ramatoulaye's decision to write the letter is similar to what Madame de Sévigné writes to her daughter: "J'aime à vous écrire; je parle à vous, je cause avec vous" [I like to write to you; I speak to you, I talk with you] (Duchêne 264).

Aïssatou, from whom a response is implied but not given, is the active listener. Therefore Ramatoulaye tells a story (her own) as she simultaneously retells Aïssatou's story: "J'ai raconté d'un trait ton histoire et la mienne" (81) ["I've related at one go your story as well as mine" (55)]. Ramatoulaye consistently invokes the importance of addressing the person to whom she is "speaking": "Aïssatou, mon amie" or "Aïssatou, ma soeur" or "Aïssatou, Aïssatou. . . ." Through pleadings, through these nommo connections, Ramatoulaye crosses temporal boundaries of emotion and urgency with Aïssatou: "Tu m'a souvent prouvé la supériorité de l'amitié sur l'amour" (104) ["You have often proved to me the superiority of friendship over love" (72)]. The foundation of love that existed between Ramatoulaye and Modou was shattered. Ultimately, their sisterhood, the spirit of childhood and womanhood together, is sustaining; she understands how the depth and lasting quality of women's friendship can transcend threatening and competitive love.

Through letter writing, Ramatoulaye creates her own artifact as both *mémoire* and site of memory: "Si les rêves meurent en traversant les ans et les réalités, je garde intacts mes souvenirs, sel de ma mémoire" (7) ["If over the years, and passing through the realities of life, dreams die, I still keep intact my memories, the salt of remembrance" (1)]. Memoir as memory and writing is an organic process. Mariama Bâ evokes memoir/memory on multiple levels of gender sensibility during the life course from youth to middle age. Madame Bâ celebrates middle-aged women who overcome obstacles that once stood in the way of hopes and accomplishments and who gain ascendancy through memories of the life course despite what the past may have been. Ramatoulaye reclaims integrity and reaffirms herself in society. As a middle-aged mother-woman, she reaffirms and reclaims writing and the real environment of memory. With these strengths she creates new foundations. Everyday acts become heroic, and heroic acts are accepted as the norm. The therapeutic act of writing evokes these places of memory that affirm endurance and courage.

Toward the end of her letter, Ramatoulaye is undoubtedly aware of her social and spiritual status as a mother-woman. Ramatoulaye's testimony to her life, in part, celebrates customs that have sustaining value and identifies those that must be given up. Her perspective encapsulates the difficult position of the contemporary non-Western feminist caught between a valuable heritage that she will not forfeit and an opposing need to express herself as a progressive woman who can deny those patriarchal traditions that are detrimental to her and women in her society. In this respect, her worldview becomes all-encompassing: As a Muslim woman, she grows into a heightened awareness of herself and of her relationship to the family and to the nation in transition. She can connect herself to global and feminist ways of being. For her, transformation is spiritual, cultural, and political.

Within the frame of memory-telling through writing, Mariama Bâ's use of different narrative voices allows her central character to write the memory that is transforming. Mae Henderson's observations about identity and voice in an African American context of gender and culture are on target for contemporary black women's writing in African contexts:

> What is at once characteristic and suggestive about black women's writing is its interlocutory, or dialogic, character reflecting not only a relationship with the "other(s)," but an internal dialogue with the plural aspects of self that constitute the matrix of black female subjectivity. (17–18)

The black woman speaks as a mother, wife, potential lover, and woman-friend. She speaks against the public and private voices of tradition. In beginning the letter, Ramatoulaye is not convinced of her own inspirations. Through memory-telling, she finds the way to claim an identity by defining her own form of self-relatedness. The narrator as memory-teller returns full cycle to the beginning when, at the close of the letter, she writes: "Le mot bonheur recouvre bien quelque chose, n'est-ce pas? J'irai à sa recherche.... j'ai encore à t'écrire une si longue lettre..." (131) ["The word 'happiness' does indeed have meaning, doesn't it? I shall go out in search of it.... again I have to write you so long a letter..."(89)]. Ramatoulaye's memory-telling takes place in a profound amount of time and space: she is in the official forty-day period of mourning that is observed by Muslims, and she is "coming out" emotionally and spiritually.

Epistolary fiction has an African diasporic and gender consciousness of its own. Miriam Warner-Vieyra's epistolary novel *Juletane* is written in the form of a letter to herself by a young Caribbean woman undergoing a mental breakdown. The setting is in a francophone African country. Juletane's demise begins when she finds herself in a polygamous household as another wife. She is the "crazy" intruder into the modern rhythm of polygamy. She is not able to deal with the demands of polygamy and the challenges of life in a Muslim culture. Devastated, Juletane eventually returns to Paris where she dies. Another Caribbean woman, Hélène, accidentally discovers Juletane's journal. The novel centers on the paradigms of memory-telling as Hélène, also a psychiatric nurse, begins a memory dialogue with the dead woman's journal. The lonely voice of Juletane enables Hélène, who has been emotionally wounded in her relationships with Caribbean men, to heal.

On the African American side of epistolary fiction, Celie, in Alice Walker's *The Color Purple,* writes to God in her efforts to understand why she is the victim of painful physical and sexual abuse. The letters to God are sent through the spirit of epistolary prayers and supplications—Celie believes they will arrive and be heard. Her letters are written to God-the-father. Her woman-centered friendship with Shug Avery transforms Celie. She later discovers real letters from her sister Nettie in Africa that Mr. _____ had kept hidden for years. By the time she reads them, the letters are telling memory.

Similar to Walker's strategy, Bâ also develops intertextual epistolary messages—letters within letters. When Aïssatou decides to divorce her spouse, Mawdo, she leaves him a letter that defiantly states her position: "Je me dépouille de ton amour, de ton nom. Vêtue du seul habit valable de la dignité, je poursuis ma route" (50) ["I am stripping myself of your love, your name. Clothed in my dignity, the only worthy garment, I go my way" (32)]. Does Ramatoulaye, by remembering how Aïssatou confronted the situation of polygamy, come to terms with the reality of her own widowhood? Although Ramatoulaye decided to remain married to Modou after he married again, her decision takes as much courage as Aïssatou's. Ramatoulaye admires her friend's courage. Later, working as a well-paid diplomat in her country's foreign service, Aïssatou is able to assist Ramatoulaye financially with a car for transportation (Modou had taken all cars from the family). By reconstructing Aïssatou's own letter, Ramatoulaye bears witness to its message, gives additional substance to it (a contrast to her own marital decision), and once more provides the raw material for memory-telling.

Another epistolary voice emerges when Ramatoulaye remembers a letter that she has sent to Daouda Dieng, the man who wanted to marry her during their youth. After the respectable length of time has lapsed since Modou's death, Daouda again asks Ramatoulaye to marry him. Daouda Dieng, educated and handsome, already has a wife. Because of his marital status and because she does not love him, Ramatoulaye rejects his proposal:

> Tu crois simple le problème polygamique. Ceux qui s'y meuvent connaissent des contraintes, des mensonges, des injustices qui alourdissent leur conscience pour la joie éphémère d'un changement. Je suis sûr que l'amour est ton mobile, un amour qui exista bien avant ton mariage et que le destin n'a pas comblé. . . . A bientôt, n'est-ce pas? (100)

> [You think the problem of polygamy is a simple one. Those who are involved in it know the constraints, the lies, the injustices that weigh down their consciences in return for the ephemeral joys of change. I am sure you are motivated by love, a love that existed well before your marriage and that fate has not been able to satisfy. . . . Shall I hope to see you again? (68)]

Ramatoulaye, at this point, is naïve; she attempts to compromise on his love for her and hopes to continue a platonic friendship when he wants marriage and a sexual relationship. Despite her ideals, or rather because of them, Ramatoulaye insults Daouda Dieng. She may want a friendship without sexual intimacy, but he wants to be a friend and lover. Mariama Bâ is consistent and insistent about her stance regarding polygamy: it has outlived its usefulness in society even when the man is a "catch." Daouda will not compromise. Daouda, rejected by Ramatoulaye on his terms, consequently, writes back: "All or nothing. Adieu" (69).

Despite their emotional impasse, Daouda Dieng supports Ramatoulaye in affirming her position in the progressive generation of Senegalese women—pathfinders who acknowledge the past as they contend with the present and future. Ramatoulaye repeats what Daouda has said concerning these women and their relationship to the nation:

> La femme est la racine première, fondamentale de la nation où se greffe tout apport, d'où part aussi toute floraison. Il faut inciter la femme à s'intéresser davantage au sort de son pays. Même toi qui rouspètes, tu as préféré ton mari, ta classe, les enfants à la chose publique. Si des hommes seuls militent dans les partis, pourquoi songeraient-ils aux femmes? La réaction est humaine de se donner une large portion quand on partage le gâteau. (90–91)

> [Women are the nation's primary, fundamental root, from which all else grows and blossoms. Women must be encouraged to take a keener

interest in the destiny of the country. Even you who are protesting; you preferred your husband, your class, your children to public life. If men alone are active in the parties, why should they think of the women? It is only human to give yourself the larger portion of the cake when you are sharing it out. (61–62)]

Daouda's intellectual and political integrity (he is even called a feminist among his political colleagues) along with his distinguished stature causes Ramatoulaye to realize how much of a "rebel" she is in not accepting his marriage proposal. Ramatoulaye continues to view monogamous love as the ideal. Both Daouda and Ramatoulaye are strong-willed and, ironically for both of them, it is indeed "all or nothing."

Mariama Bâ writes beyond the emotional politics of male infidelity. She is more concerned about the redemptive and spiritual make-up of self-expression among and between women as friends and mothers. Her perspectives on women's bonding and sisterhood can be placed in the larger context of postcolonial writing by women of color. Toni Morrison's novel *Sula* also illustrates this notion of sister-women friendships. South African novelist Bessie Head similarly illustrates the bonding of two mother-women in her short story "The Collector of Treasures." Like Sula and Nel, Dikeledi and Kenalepe possess the "deep and old meaning" of intimate sharing: "It was not long before the two women had going one of those deep, affectionate, sharing-everything kinds of friendships that only women know how to have" (94). In this cross-cultural tradition of women-friendships, in the spiritual bonding between mother-women, Ramatoulaye writes and reconciles. She spiritually and emotionally navigates the circumstances of the past. Undoubtedly, the need to bond increases in moments of crisis. Our need for guidance and assurance arises out of crisis and stasis. Just as Ramatoulaye finds solace in women-centered friendships, so does she embrace daughter-friendships. Before women can be capable mothers, they must learn how to be daughters. How do the mothers enable their daughters with the skills necessary for attaining *their* goals and in order to define *themselves*?

Mothering Daughters . . .

In the majority of African societies, it is of paramount importance that women have children. Men want children because it assures their lineage. But women also place a high premium on having a family with children. Having children manifests well-being and social satisfaction.[14]

Madame Bâ focuses on the spiritual being of mother-women who, despite having undergone emotional crisis and humiliation, are able to reaffirm faith in themselves and in their families through the daughters—the next generation. Throughout Africa women are primarily responsible for the school fees for their children's education, and they progressively want their daughters to have access to formal education. And the partners of these daughters will also be of a new generation of men because they will have been taught by progressive mothers. Daba is Ramatoulaye's eldest daughter, and Daba's husband tells Ramatoulaye that "Daba est ma femme. Elle n'est pas mon esclave, ni ma servante (107) ["Daba is my wife. She is not my slave, nor my servant"] (73). These daughters, along with their husbands, are the hope of the next generation. They will carry the ideals of their parents further into practice and belief. The daughters will make errors, but they will find their way because of the mothers.

During the aftermath of Modou's death, Ramatoulaye learns that one of her unmarried daughters is pregnant. In her strengthening role as a mother-woman, Ramatoulaye does not disown the daughter, who is named after Ramatoulaye's sister-friend, Aïssatou. The griot Farmata is surprised that Ramatoulaye will not reject her daughter despite the violation that has taken place. Madame Bâ is at her most eloquent rendering of a mother's love for her daughter-child when Ramatoulaye intones:

> Me souvenant, comme d'une bouée de sauvetage, de l'attitude tendre et consolatrice de ma fille, pendant ma détresse, mes longues années de solitude, je dominais mon bouleversement. Je recourais à Dieu, comme à chaque drame de ma vie. . . . Et puis, on est mère pour comprendre l'inexplicable. . . . On est mère pour aimer, sans commencement ni fin. (120)

> [Remembering, like a life buoy, the tender and consoling attitude of my daughter during my distress, my long years of loneliness, I overcame my emotion. I sought refuge in God, as at every moment of crisis in my life. . . . And also, one is a mother in order to understand the inexplicable. . . . One is a mother in order to love without beginning or end. (82, 83)]

Ramatoulaye embraces her daughter with all her energy and support. She will not allow patriarchal laws to create havoc for her daughter.

Daba wanted her mother to divorce rather than stay in a polygamous marriage. More than Ramatoulaye or Aïssatou, Daba represents the caliber of yet another generation—for her it is also "all or nothing." When Daba learns that her father has married her school friend, Binetou, Daba is overwhelmed with anger, disappointment, and embarrassment. Infuriated, she tells her mother: "Romps, Maman! Chasse cet homme. Il ne nous a pas respectées, ni toi, ni moi. Fais comme Tata Aïsssatou, romps. Dis-moi que tu rompras. Je ne te vois pas te disputant un homme avec une fille de mon âge (60)" ["Break with him, mother! Send this man away. He has respected neither you nor me. Do what Aunty Aïssatou did; break with him. Tell me you'll break with him. I can't see you fighting over a man with a girl my age" (39)]. Daba has a counterpart in Aminata Sow Fall's *La grève des bàttu,* where Lolli's university-educated daughter, Rabbi, has no sympathy for her father: "Rabbi a essayé de convaincre sa mère qu'elle doit se battre, qu'elle ne doit pas accepter une situation ambiguë, qu'elle a le devoir de ne pas laisser une intruse lui disputer sa place, et pour cela 'il faut prendre tes responsabilités et demander à papa de choisir'"(46) ["Rabbi tried to convince her mother she ought to fight back, tried to persuade her not to accept the ambiguous situation, telling her it was her duty to prevent an intruder taking her place, that she must 'assume her responsibilities and tell Papa he's got to choose'" (33)]. It is interesting to see how African women writers juxtapose the responses of middle-aged mother-women with those of the younger sister-daughters regarding the actions of their mothers to marital infidelity. The daughters do not sanction polygamy and view it as infidelity. The daughters do not understand why their mothers, who believe in monogamy, remain married to their unworthy fathers. The daughters represent the new generation of women who have been reared to think like this. And yet for the African mother-women who have reared them, it is not a simple matter of divorcing the fathers of their daughters. The mothers reared their daughters for a new generation and a new method. The daughters care about their mothers, and they cannot abide by the old self-sacrificing ways. The daughters want and demand equality because they are educated and believe and practice that men and women are, indeed, complementary. The daughters have little patience because they are daughters following the new pathways their mothers have forged.

The world of humanity has two wings—one is women and the other men. Should one wing remain weak, flight is impossible. Not until the world of women becomes equal to the world of men in the acquisition of virtues and perfections, can success and prosperity be attained as they ought to be.

—Abdul Abbás, *Women*

With dignity and a quiet constitution of will, Ramatoulaye confronts not only the immediate crisis of her husband's death but the other significant events that follow. Now that she is a widow, to what extent can she determine her own life course after the rituals of her husband's passing have been carried out? Whereas Ramatoulaye laments the passing years: "Mon ventre saillait sous le pagne qui dissimulait des mollets développés par l'impressionnant kilométrage des marches qu'ils avaient effectuées, depuis le temps que j'existe. L'allaitement avait ôté à mes seins leur rondeur et leur fermeté" (62) ["My stomach protruded from beneath the wrapper that hid the calves developed by the impressive number of kilometres walked since the beginning of my existence. Suckling had robbed my breasts of their round firmness"(41)]. Now she begins to see herself beyond the physical attributes that once defined her as a young woman. The body of the middle-aged woman is unique in a different way. The physical attributes may no longer be in top form, but the menopausal woman has experience, creativity, and the knowledge of empowerment. Regardless of the way she once interpreted her image in the mirror (she will not maintain these transitional feelings of old age), the irony is that Ramatoulaye is a "catch" because of her economic status as a widow.

In some cultures that carry on certain marital traditions, it is assumed that widows will remarry through the levirate inheritance; that is, marriage to one of the brothers from the deceased husband's family.[15] "Marital possibilities for African widows range from remaining a widow or marrying for ritual purposes only... through the levirate, widow inheritance, and 'full' marriage with the usual rights and obligations.... Both the levirate and widow inheritance may be less commonly practiced these days, especially as women themselves are resisting these customs and even resisting marriage altogether" (Cattell 75). Despite the fact that cultures subscribe to an ancient support system for widowhood, that system can be corrupted and taken advantage of. In the context of the levirate, the new husband also claims the widow's inheritance and material possessions, a patriarchal dominance that African women are resisting. By the time women reach middle-age, with or without husbands, they realize the extent to which they can manage their own resources because, "having reached the top rung of the kinship ladder, older women have the confidence and assurance of age and experience, and can be leaders in this aspect of the politics of gender relations" (Cattell 83).

Decidedly, Madame Bâ makes a direct social and political comment on the need for middle-aged women to take a stance regarding assumed marriages. As a Muslim woman, it is a bold step for Ramatoulaye to take when she refuses her brother-in-law Tamsir's marriage proposal. He assumes that she will accept him: "Après ta 'sorti'... je t'épouse. Tu me conviens comme femme.... Tu es ma chance. Je t'épouse (84)" ["When you have 'come out'...I shall marry you. You suit me as a wife.... You are my good luck. I shall marry you" (57)]. She refuses him on her terms: he is already married, he wants her because of her economic status, and she doesn't love him: "Tu [Tamsir] oublies que j'ai un coeur, une raison, que je ne suis pas un objet que l'on se passe de main en main. Tu ignores ce que se marier signifie pour moi: c'est un acte de foi et d'amour, un don total de soi à l'être que l'on a choisi et qui vous a choisi. (J'insistais sur le mot choisi)" (85). ["You [Tamsir] forget that I have a heart, a mind, that I am not an object to be passed from hand to hand. You don't know what marriage means to me: it is an act of faith, and of love, the total surrender of oneself to the person one has chosen and who has chosen you (I emphasized the word 'chosen')" (58)]. Abandonment forced Ramatoulaye into self-reliance, and now she is very satisfied that she has finally spoken out after "thirty years of silence, thirty years of harassment" (57, 58). She says no to a possible marriage that goes against her beliefs and newfound capacity. She sanctions her reply by dismissing Tamsir and his entourage.

One Western reader has viewed polygamy as "the most glaringly inequitable and sexist feature of traditional African society" (Frank 18). It is debatable whether polygamy could be regarded as the most sexist feature in African traditions. Polygamy, however, continues to be a central issue with Westerners regarding male/female relationships in Africa. Mariama Bâ judiciously demonstrates how the levirate is a built-in practice that retains polygamy—a practice that has outlived its purpose and design. At the 1972 international conference on "La civilization

de la femme dans la tradition Africaine," the first of its kind on the continent, women from Africa and the African diaspora discussed, among
the many and diverse topics, the dynamics and repercussions of polygamy
in Africa.[16] How does polygamy affect African women in their intermediate societies?[17] In the past, the general consensus was that polygamy
had its place and purpose. Today, many African women are caught within
the dilemma of tradition and changing values. How do we negotiate the
two realities? Are they mutually exclusive of each other? Does this
dilemma resolve into a binary response across the spectrum of accepting or not accepting traditional versus modern values? Speaking about
polygamy, Bâ said,

> Men and women are complementary.... Of course Ramatoulaye's
> husband was not just any man. He was enlightened and knew his duties.
> It was an ideal marriage. In the book we feel that it was very good before
> there was a second wife.... They had worked together and had comple-
> mented each other. (Harrell-Bond 8)

Complementarity. Not until it is recognized globally that men and women
are complementary can we all prosper and success, however it is defined, be fully attained. Like the two wings of a bird, we must be equally
developed before we can fly. Madame Bâ eloquently appeals to and strives
for this complementary empowerment of men and women. African
women realize how their futures will inevitably reflect change as well as
continuity. Mothers may be supreme, but they are not superwomen because, as Madame Bâ tells us, "what women are searching for is not so
much to destroy everything from the past. But the man must abandon a
part of his power, his privileges from the past" (Harrell-Bond 8). Working in a complementary relationship that accentuates dignity, friendship, and purpose is life-affirming for everyone involved. As an idealistic
young woman who wanted to marry for love, Ramatoulaye saw herself
in a new kind of marriage. The ideal was that she and Modou would
not only have a family to create and a nation to help develop, but would
have each other to nurture. She resolves that these ideals will find hope
and nourishment in the marital relationships that her daughters will
have. She continues to hope and endure.

Ramatoulaye writes that at one time she believed in the pursuit of
happiness through marriage: "Je n'ai jamais conçu le bonheur hors du
couple..." (82). ["I have never conceived of happiness outside marriage..." (56)]. As part of a new generation of educated Senegalese,

Ramatoulaye wants to marry from her own choice of love and not through an arrangement based on traditional class obligations or parental decision. She marries Modou for love and for an ideal of love. She recalls paradoxical advice and wisdom from her own mother: "une femme doit épouser l'homme qui l'aime mais point celui qu'elle aime; c'est le secret d'une bonheur durable" (87) ["a woman must marry the man who loves her but never the one she loves: that is the secret of lasting happiness" (59)]. Yet Ramatoulaye does not adhere to her mother's advice even years later when Daouda Dieng, the man who loves her and whom she does not love, again asks her to marry him. What some critics may refer to as conservatism may also be viewed as Ramatoulaye's stubborn refusal to give up an ideal. Yet she somehow understands at the close of the letter that happiness is, after all, a relative state of being and that her rebirth is not from the failed monogamous marriage but from the affirmation of the redemptive qualities of her own decisions. In this regard, memory-telling again reflects Ramatoulaye's collective psyche—that of her foremothers and the spirit of her own fulfillment in middle age.

Mariama Bâ may seem to illustrate ambivalence as part of the pathway to understanding self—not as the end product of issues that cannot be resolved. African women are confronted with ambivalence because their cultures are changing and holding on to the continuity of traditions. On a more profound level of commitment and personal memory-telling, Ramatoulaye is actually a reflection, a mirroring of Aïssatou in that Ramatoulaye realizes how her decision not to divorce was just as worthy as Aïssatou's decision to leave her husband. Each woman has made the decision to do what was best for her personal circumstances. For some, marriage is no longer the ideal partnership. Gender-oriented disillusionment with marriage is a transcultural problem that occurs because of ambivalent marital vows that clash because of modern-day circumstances. In Buchi Emecheta's novel *The Joys of Motherhood* the female protagonist learns that her husband has taken another wife when he unceremoniously brings the new wife home. The title character in *Juletane* marries her husband in Paris. It is not until they are en route to his home in an unnamed francophone African country that she learns he has other wives. In her journal, Juletane writes that "La gorge serrée, je me sentais paralysée par ce que je venais d'apprendre. . . . Une fois de plus je retrouvais mon angoisse d'orpheline. Perdue,

seule au monde. Mon désarroi était immense" (34). ["My throat tight-
ened; I felt paralyzed by what I had come to know.... Once more I felt
my anxiety about being orphaned. Lost, alone in the world. I was totally
confused" (15)].

In Aminata Sow Fall's *La grève des bàttu*, Mour surprises his wife by
simply telling her that he has made plans to take another wife the next
day, "on me 'donne' une femme demain" (40). He sheepishly makes his
decision without informing Lolli, his first wife and mother of his children as, at least, decorum requires. Likewise, Ramatoulaye learns second hand from her brother-in-law Tamsir and the Imam that they have
come from the mosque in Grand Dakar where Modou has married another woman. Both Mour and Modou take a new wife without respect-
ing and conducting the proper arrangements with the first wife that are
required in Islamic and polygamous customs. The first wife should be
respected with consultation, and she should know from the husband
before the marriage takes place.

Whether university-educated or uneducated and from the village,
African women have been collectively disrespected and disenfranchised
by patriarchal convictions and opportunity. What are the African women
writers telling us? Despite being caught up in the upheaval of modernization, men like Modou insist on maintaining traditional practices that
are challenged in urban African settings. Compared to Aïssatou's decision to divorce, for Ramatoulaye to remain married to a polygamous partner may appear as an acceptance of the practice. On the contrary. In *La
grève des bàttu*, although Lolli had expected to be monogamous, she
does not divorce Mour when he marries again. Likewise, Ramatoulaye
believes in marriage as an ideal. Their choices become challenges. Lolli's
spouse returns to her after he becomes disillusioned with the younger
wife. Ramatoulaye eventually triumphs (despite all that has happened,
after Modou's death, her place at the head of the immediate family is
recognized), and she is able to resolve her grief and disappointment.

What are the path-making challenges for middle-aged women as feminists? Carole Boyce Davies writes that "the very fact that it is necessary
to qualify feminism or limit it with the word 'African' indicates implicitly the relationship between the two.... [T]herefore, African feminism
is a hybrid of sorts, which seeks to combine African concerns with feminist concerns. This is the nature of the 'balancing' which has to take place"
(*Ngambika* 12). To what extent does Bâ voice an African feminist con-

sciousness while honoring women in the middle age of the life course? How do African feminisms complement tradition? On this side of the Atlantic what are the indigenous paradigms of women's emancipation, which serve women's interests, those of our families, and those of our communities of cultures? I agree with Davies, who asserts that an African feminist perspective "is not antagonistic to African men but it challenges them to be aware of certain salient aspects of women's subjugation which differ from the generalized oppression of all African peoples.... [it] examines African societies for institutions which are of value to women and rejects those which work to their detriment and does not simply import Western women's agendas... [and] looks at traditional and contemporary avenues of choice for women" (*Ngambika* 9, 10). African feminisms inscribe women's significant contributions back into the society.

Ramatoulaye's memory-telling shifts from feeling sorry for herself because of what went wrong with her marriage to another way of looking at marriage in its relationship to family and community: "Aïssatou, si malheureuse que fût l'issue de nos unions, nos maris avaient de la grandeur. Ils avaient mené le combat de leur vie, même si la réussite leur échappait; on ne vient pas facilement à bout des pesanteurs millénaires" (106). ["Aïssatou, no matter how unhappy the outcome of our unions, our husbands were great men. They led the struggle of their lives, even if success eluded their grasp; one does not easily overcome the burdens of a thousand years" (73)]. Ramatoulaye places herself not only in the historical consciousness of postcoloniality but in the global context of women faced with the reverberations of changes and challenges.

African feminisms are linked to those traditional forces that enable contemporary crossings. Madame Bâ has left for us an all-encompassing inspiration:

This book... has so often been described as a "cry from the heart," this cry is coming from the heart of all women everywhere. It is first a cry from the heart of the Senegalese woman, because it talks about the problems of Senegalese women, of Muslim women, of the woman with the constraints of religion which weigh on her as well as other social constraints. But it is also a cry which can symbolize the cry of the woman everywhere.... The cry might be different, but there is still a certain unity... their cry will not be exactly the same as ours—we have not all got the same problems—but there is a fundamental unity in all of our sufferings and in our desire for liberation and in our desire to cut off the chains which date from antiquity. (Harrell-Bond 13)

At this stage of the life course, Ramatoulaye discovers the creative spirit that will engage her in becoming aware of a fundamental unity that globally connects us as mother-women. The tearing apart of sensibilities, or what may appear as the unresolved conflict between tradition and change, can better be regarded as a coming together of the collective and personal consciousness. Ramatoulaye remembers her grandmother's vision of new generations bringing about change: "A génération nouvelle, nouvelle méthode" (113). Advocating the need for women to determine choices as they formulate change, Bâ's central characters do not indiscriminately abandon their ancient properties, nor do they indiscriminately move beyond the boundaries of their own social landscape in appropriating the spirit of the liberated African woman.

New ways of thinking can produce greater resourcefulness for survival, progress, and assurance in those sustaining values. Mariama Bâ illustrates how selected aspects of tradition, through its own vitality, can still be a source of familial strength. Ramatoulaye meticulously determines her role as a Senegalese mother-woman when she begins to formulate her significance for the family and larger community. Ramatoulaye's motivation lies in her search for the balance between traditional values that affirm the past and new feminisms that empower women (those beliefs and practices that will enable women to cease being victims of fear, oppression, and exploitation). The narrative of memory-telling testifies to the redemptive quality of emotional upheaval and loss arising from dispersed values. Ramatoulaye grows spiritually, intellectually, and emotionally and is able to ascend through the reassuring habits that affirm her beliefs (women-friendships, daughter-friendships, and community). By recasting the events that affected her in the past, Ramatoulaye measures her own stability and personal achievements as a Senegalese mother-woman.

Women of good will are ambitious with the ideas and values that will sustain and promote complementarity. Women and men in all stages of the life course can benefit from new forms of complementarity. As progressive women we aim to achieve unity through the diverse ways in which we will express goals for working together. Of course men will benefit even more when women are accorded the respect and honor of achievements through equality. Madame Bâ left us with a unique perspective. She recognized the need for women to challenge certain values that their mothers and grandmothers accepted. At the same time, she is aware of the need for continuity, for values that will continue to sustain new foundations for the mother-women. What are these values? We want to make our personal choices in determining what they are.

Une si longue lettre is an autobiographical consciousness that highlights African feminisms. Mariama Bâ shows how memory-telling creates a write of passage. Through memory-telling we connect and disengage; we empower ourselves. We pass on certain traditions, in order accentuate new methods for the next generation. With such a great letter, Madame Bâ has crossed bridges and left words of good will for women and men everywhere to gain ascendancy.

CHAPTER FIVE

From a Lineage of Southern Women: She Has Left Us Empty and Full of Her

> My mother loved my father
> I write this as an absolute
> in this my thirtieth year
> the year to discard absolutes
>   —Lorna Goodison, "For My Mother
>   (May I Inherit Half Her Strength)"

> I love you my grandma,
> as you can see.
> I love you. Even though you
> are spiritually with me,
> I love you as much as I would if you
> were physically with me.
> I love you my grandma
> as you can see.
>   —Alexandria Reyes, "For My Grandma"

Our diversities, our ways of knowing and mothering continue. There are no conclusions—the dialogues continue. Autobiographical memory and ways of thinking have influenced the presentation of this study and narrative.

In my introduction, I discussed salient issues on mothering across cultures. We have the roles of representation and transformation that enable the foundations of our future. The women writers that I have presented here testify directly and indirectly to the significance of the postcolonial moment—history, gender awareness, class, and the diversity of cultures. The moment celebrates our ethnicities. From Mary Magdalene's slave narrative to personal narratives and fiction by some of today's women writers of color, I have attempted to present a multi-voiced narrative informed by our histories, our writings, and our ideas of memory and culture.

As I began mentally constructing this conclusion, I had the idea that I wanted to move beyond an analytically driven or conceptually grounded closure because many of these ideas are not terminal in my professional or personal praxis. This is not necessarily a contested terrain. I want the space to move beyond the tradition of critical analysis of marginal voices in the written context of autobiographical memory. I would like to engage the conclusion of the narrative, if not of the ideas, in a different way; I would like to tell a story that is particular, even if it is not spectacular, a story that could be found in any hamlet.

My story begins as a praxis within an oral tradition of "testifyin'," which arose from the coming together of the two New World cultures (African American and Latino) that gave birth to me and shape my life and my worldview. That shaping of my life through testifyin' and *testimonio* is meant to be squeezed in between that of my own mother's exceptional being that came from a lineage of southern black women. In his essay "The Margin at the Center: On *Testimonio*," John Beverley affirms that "one common formal variation on the classic first-person singular *testimonio* is the polyphonic *testimonio,* made up of accounts by different participants in the same event" (96). What do I mean by testifyin' and *testimonio*?

Through the years, I have taught Zora Neale Hurston's *Their Eyes Were Watching God* to university students. Inevitably something new has taken flight from the pages for me—the word, phrase, or figurative meaning was always in the text, but I had not been aware of its presence or the certain reading that could be applied. *Their Eyes* is Hurston's powerful litany on life and a certain kind of black womanhood. Nanny's oft-quoted conviction to her granddaughter Janie is familiar: "de nigger woman is de mule uh de world so fur as Ah can see" (14). Janie's journey will challenge the grandmother's belief. Janie, as a young girl however, cries after she hears Nanny's needfulness because she has to forfeit searching out the horizon she believes is waiting. Instead, she does Nanny's bidding, and marries Logan Killicks. But Nanny also tells Janie, with as much passion that her other words of wisdom convey,

You know, honey, us colored folks is branches without roots and that
makes things come round in queer ways. You in particular. Ah was born
back due in slavery so it wasn't for me to fulfill my dreams of whut a
woman oughta be and to do. Dat's one of de hold-backs of slavery. But
nothing can't stop you from wishin'. You can't beat nobody down so low
till you can rob 'em of they will. . . . But all de same Ah said thank God,
Ah got another chance. Ah wanted to preach a great sermon about
colored women sittin' on high, but they wasn't no pulpit for me. . . .
Freedom found me wid a baby daughter in mah arms, so Ah said Ah'd
take a broom and a cook-pot and throw up a highway through de
wilderness for her. She would expound what Ah felt. But somehow she
got lost offa de highway and next thing Ah knowed here you was in de
world. So whilst Ah was tendin' you of nights Ah said Ah'd save de text
for you. (15–16)

Such is Nanny's sermon of love to her granddaughter. The sermon, coming out of the African American oral tradition, converges with Hurston's
text (Janie's storytelling) to underscore what Hurston constructed out
of her own experience of private and public passions. Sermons carry
power and empowerment (internal energy) because they connect the
listener to the sacred myth by way of speech. Sermon and text. More
significant for her than seeing the black woman's position as the mule
of the world, Nanny remembers that she once had the potential to reach
beyond the burden of slavery's legacy. She implies that, at some point in
her life after Emancipation, she had wanted to be an educator, to help
other "colored" women empower their lives. She did not fulfill the dream
of becoming an orator or writer; she did not create a pulpit of her own.
And so Nanny had hoped that her daughter Leafy would *live* the dreams
she had dreamed. That did not happen. Nanny sees her third chance in
Janie. Rather than viewing Nanny as an obstacle on Janie's horizon, we
can view Janie as expounding on Nanny's ambition "to preach the great
sermon to colored women." Janie does not only hear the sermon, but
she is empowered by it and is able to create the text (her own narrative)
and sermon (the telling of the narrative to Pheoby). She has the power
of both sermon and text—long after Nanny has passed on. Her marriage to Killicks merely delays the fulfillment of Nanny's dream until
Janie is finally able to pull "in her horizon like a great fish-net." Nanny's
speech is testifying—oral *testimonio* based on the economic ramifications of race, class, and gender. She voices her passionate hope that Janie

will achieve what she, Nanny, could not accomplish. Consistent with African American testifyin' that has evolved out of the church and the religious sermon, Nanny "calls on the Lord" to help her with the mothering of Janie. But Hurston takes a bold step and brings into focus the intersecting forces of gender and race through testifying: Nanny knows that, because of racism from outside of African American culture and in spite of sexism within African American culture, Janie, as a black woman, would inevitably need the resilience of the institution of marriage as an economic and social bounty.[1]

While testifying is firmly established in an African American context of church and orality, *testimonio* is grounded in Latin American and Caribbean traditions that involve the oration of the life and bearing witness to social and economic change through partisan politics. According to John Beverley, in *testimonio* it is the "intentionality of the narrator that is paramount. The situation of narration in *testimonio* has to involve an urgency to communicate, a problem of repression, poverty, subalternity, imprisonment, struggle for survival, implicated in the act of narration itself.... [T]estimonio is concerned not so much with the life of a 'problematic hero' as with a problematic collective social situation in which the narrator lives" (94). While African American testifying may be grounded in the tradition of the religious sermon, *testimonio* is located in the political domain of urgent social transformation. Testifying and *testimonio* function as texts that create the power of the spoken word and power within the written words of the people. Hurston intersects the dynamics of orality with the empowerment of writing—voice and documentation. At the end of *Their Eyes*, Janie has moved to a higher philosophical level in understanding life through testifying (to Pheoby) by way of Hurston's *testimonio* (the narrative itself).

Many readers focus on the fact that Janie rejects her grandmother's efforts at providing her with learnings, but in fact, Janie acquires the empowerment of public speech and personal transformation that Nanny herself had hoped for. Janie captures Nanny's dreams, lives them, and eventually returns home to live on the "nothing else" of memories. *Their Eyes Were Watching God* is Hurston's timeless gift to us from her own pulpit on high.[2]

Testimonio, although essentially a written document (in various forms), intersects with the power of testifying—the spoken word. *Testimonio* and testifyin' are located at the centers of two New World cultures: African American and Latino American. It is from these centers that I return to the power of memory.

Crazy and Saintly

Alice Walker writes about her "mothers' gardens" and about southern women as the "crazy saints" who could not realize their full potential as creators. Very much like those mother-women who had their personal and public survival strategies, ways to thrive, and pathways that led to triumphs, my own mother was forced to defy adversities to create fulfillment through her and around her. Indeed, the crazy saints, the kitchen bards, the mules of the world—all knew that they had to triumph by going beyond the habits of survival in order to celebrate and expound on life. Different histories but connected lineages that left many of us both empty and full of these mother-women.

In these chapters, I have attempted to introduce ideas about the diversity of the mother-women in New World cultures and in the context of a transitional modern African society. I want to reclaim the fortitude of women of African descent in context and through some of their texts. Toni Morrison explains to Bettye J. Parker that "[b]lack women seem able to combine the nest and the adventure. They don't see conflicts in certain areas as do white women. They are both safe harbor and ship; they are both inn and trail. We black women do both. We don't find these places, these roles, mutually exclusive. That's one of the differences" (251). The borderlines of scholarship and autobiography challenge the ways in which I can illustrate my own sentiments: I did not know how exceptional my mother was until I got older, and now she's no longer physically with me. She has left me empty and full of her (to echo Dionne Brand). My mother used to talk about the "olden days," but what she was really talking about was the *olden ways of kinship,* and she emphasized their importance to her time and place.

Olden kinship includes memories that return to the archaeological site. The return provides access to meaning and allows certain truths to surface. My mother's memories and ways of being were very much connected to that part of Mecklenburg County in Virginia where the James River overflows—where the river remembers, never forgetting its source. Sometimes the rememory process is arduous, at other times the process involves the source of events that are clothed in time and not easy to remember.

In My Mother's House There Were Many Mansions. . . .

The years have passed now but it's seems like only yesterday when my mother was laid to rest. When my mother died, I didn't dream about her. I believe that grief clouded any dreams that I could have seen. My mother had always wanted to retire to where she'd grown up in the south and have her own home. She somehow never went back to live in the southern town of her youth. After a while she stopped wanting to go, but the house and home remained in her dreams. A few weeks after her death, one of my cousins telephoned me and said in an upbeat voice, "Hey girl, guess what?! I dreamed about Auntie Bettie last night. She was so beautiful and happy. She said to me, 'I got my mansion, and I'm so happy!'" Well, first I was jealous that my cousin had dreamed about my mother soon after the funeral and I had not. Why did she have the dream and not me? We grew up in a culture where dreams were read and believed. So I believed in her dream and I felt it to be rather profound considering how my mother had yearned to return to Virginia and build her "mansion." I believed that the dream spoke of other mansions to be lived in.

Our mother is not buried in the forgotten Virginia town she loved but in a secluded and lovely cemetery in a village town along Long Island Sound in New York. This is where she first arrived as a young girl in the 1930s when she was a part of the great movement of black families leaving the South for dreams in the North. The cemetery is not near me or the rest of my siblings, but it is near the remaining women-cousins of her generation who also came up from the South—and if she had known that this quiet and beautiful spot would be her final resting place, it would have been another comfort to her. In fact, upon leaving the church where she had been a member back in the thirties, the hearse, instead of going straight to the burial site, slowly took the funeral entourage around and through the town to the cemetery—her last journey with us. We drove past the elementary and high schools that she had attended as a girl-child recently arrived from the South, the once all-white churches, the Knights of Columbus hall, the quaint stores, the lovely homes and gardens of the white people who had both embraced her and fought her—all her memories and my images of her memories as she used to tell them to me.

My sister and I sat at the kitchen table going through the insurance papers that we had to have before the funeral arrangements could be made. Our beloved mother was gone. It was harder than hard. It just didn't seem possible. A most beloved parent. The women—we're the ones who attempt clarity and do the business of crisis and the perform the protocol of loss—not much time for the commitment to grieving now. It was a holiday—Memorial Day weekend. Ironic. From then on, I knew the Memorial Day weekends to come would be ones of personal mourning and mother remembrances.

She was the daughter of Virginia farmers who could trace their maternal lineage in Virginia to the eighteenth-century. They would be called African Virginians. (The paternal side of her lineage had come from Jamaica in the West Indies.) This we knew from the old handwritten ledgers in the county courthouse. The ancestors were first listed as property in the ledgers, along with the land, farm animals, furniture, and other material possessions of the generations of people who had owned them. The owners had sailed to the Colonies from Scotland and England. They owned thousands and thousands of acres of farmland in this very fertile area of the colony. But that is their story.

As the centuries changed and freedom came, our lineage was eventually able to own some of the land that the earlier ancestors could only slave on.

The land was inviting and fertile. But too soon the tobacco acreage on the farm didn't produce enough. The family was forced to become sharecroppers next to the land they owned in Mecklenburg County. The father hated sharecropping after returning from World War I; he couldn't make a living from it, and it was demeaning. He left for a few years, living and working up north, and then returned. Finally, the mother of the family decided to leave the South. The father followed a few years later with their four young children, of whom my mother was the oldest. As they packed a few suitcases and began the search with hope for new possibilities, they became part of the great migration of African Americans during the Depression.

My grandmother was tall, feisty, proud, self-educated, an ordained Baptist minister, a short story writer, farmer, seamstress, and a log-hauling and truck-driving southern woman. She was from the Virginia family of Burwells. They said that the slave owner had one last girl-child with one of his slaves just before Emancipation, and she would give birth to my grandmother.

My grandmother would later return to her land and have the gift of working on her own farm. She also had the gift of taking care of other people's children when they couldn't feed them or when they didn't want to feed them or when the mothers had been killed by the fathers or when the mothers knew that "Miz Cora will take care of my chilrens' for a spell till things get better" or when the children simply wandered onto the farm because they'd heard they would be fed and cared for and ended up staying. There were the young girls who came because they were "in the family way" or because they were sexually abused by their stepfathers. She accepted them as well. So she adopted or was legal guardian to more than twenty-six of them. During my childhood, I came to know some of the children and youths, and we'd play together during the summers. I'd go berry picking with them and climb peach trees and eat cucumbers out of the garden and never think of their poverty or the reasons why their fathers had made them motherless or why their mothers had abandoned them to the charity of my grandmother, who always had room for one more. There had been thirteen different families of babies, children, and youth. That was the kind of woman that produced my mother.

I had never wanted to talk about dying. About death itself. Much too painful to even imagine my worlds without her world, my life. She knew, however, when the time was coming for her, as so many elderly women of color do. Those who know possess that ancient spiritual essence that enables them to communicate with those who have already passed on to other worlds. A few weeks before her passing, her aunt, my great-aunt of eighty-nine years, deaf and blind, saw the death in one of her dreams. She said to me, "I saw your grandmother [my mother's mother] come to a door, there was lot of light, and she stretched out her hands to your mother. She was smiling." And my great-aunt cried into the muffled years of her own memories.

Yes, I am convinced of this ancient spiritual essence that many olden women seem to possess; a spirituality that guides them as they move closer to their own mother-ancestors—who wait for them. But of course this connection is not limited to women of African ancestry; women of other cultures can possess this power of communication. It is one of the gifts that women claim as technicians of the unseen.

We worked through the immediacy of funeral arrangements that night in my mother's home, an urban apartment in a modern high-rise. More spiritual than religious, she had not been an active member of any church for many years. Would the current Baptist minister in the little church where she had been a member when she first came north agree to do the service? We made the necessary calls. But of course the funeral can be held there, said my uncle, who was a deacon of the church.

The Baptist minister wanted to know the service we were planning. We asked if he would he accept an interfaith program.

"He won't know the difference," I told my sister. "Just give him the titles of the Catholic, and Baptist prayers. I don't know if Mr. M. will say anything from the Talmud. We'll leave a space for him in case he's able to come. He's so old now, his heart probably couldn't take this loss. I think he's too upset to come."

The eighty-something Mr. M. was too filled with grief to attend the funeral. He was our mother's companion. Of course, both always told us that "we're only neighbors!" In naiveté, we believed it. I would call my mother long distance every day, either before the six-o'clock TV news or after it finished. Sometimes, however, my timing was off. I would get annoyed when she wouldn't talk to me and would tell me she'd call back after Peter Jennings finished . . . or after Mr. M. had left for the evening. Why did he always have to be there? I wondered in more annoyance. Why doesn't she tell him to leave so that she can talk to me? Why is she serving him tea? Why doesn't he leave? Why is she making another cheesecake for him? Why doesn't he go back to his own kitchen where it's kosher? Why is he always there? Why is she baking a delicious carrot cake for him—again? Why doesn't she save the time for me?

He was her companion. This Jewish man loved her, and he had helped her when she could no longer do much of the housework. He would do it for her; he would grocery shop for her, and so he was always there. And when I found out, I was very grateful to him for helping her and for the companionship he had shared with her. He told me in his raspy old voice that he had asked her to marry him.

"You see, I asked my children first. I didn't want any problems there.

I've been living long enough to know that you can't build happiness on somebody else's unhappiness," he said.

"So, what did they say?" I asked.

"My son and daughter told me to go ahead! But when I asked your mother for her hand, she said no!" And then he paused with sadness.

"But your mother was a queen," he went on to say. "We Jews have a name for this kind of woman and mother—the highest honor, it is *balabusta* in Yiddish."

And so, he decided to plant a tree for her in Israel, a tree that would grow in my mother's name. My mother's spirit can truly be in so many places.

> There is a place where women are buried... where the daughter is never fully a woman until her mother has passed on before her....
> There is always a place where, if you listen closely in the night, you will hear your mother telling a story...
> —Edwidge Danticat, *Breath, Eyes, Memory*

I had never imagined this place without her presence. I had not yet fathomed the reality that she would never return from the hospital. I would look out the window—a view of the city from the fourteenth floor. It seemed as if she would come back. No, she won't be coming back. She had even readied the insurance papers for us—her will had been made years ago and changed and written again. She had told us where everything could be found—she'd labeled everything. A final Christmas present for her only granddaughter—labeled. Gifts—labeled. I also found something else, and as I curiously began reading it, my whole being simultaneously folded up and fell apart. "Look!" I said to my sister. "She has even written her own obituary for us! When did she do this?" My sister took the yellow legal pad from me. The clear, recent handwriting of our mother filled the pages.

During my high school years, I chose nursing for my career. I prepared myself with an academic course with the intention of attending college and the training for being a registered nurse. Now I desire to take the next best step and try to become a practical nurse.... It qualifies me to better my condition and give better service to others. My service is widely needed, as there seems to be great demand for nurses in hospitals, nursing homes, nurseries, and private homes. With my previous experience in the nursing

department I have acquired great knowledge in dealing with people of all
natures and performing the aide's duties. If I become a trained nurse, I
shall endeavor to be one of the best. Nursing is my greatest interest. It gives
me much pleasure when I can comfort a sick person.

In her own hand, from her text, she wanted us to know all the important dates and hurdles of her life we may have forgotten—or never knew.
She had documented for us the dates of the little rituals and events in
her life: her correct birth date on January 1, 1919, in a Virginia hamlet
that the James River had long ago swallowed up. It had snowed the
night she was born. The midwife, Aunt Sally, had come though. Her father, our grandfather, was in France fighting in the War.

I once told her, "The world celebrates your birthday, Mom."

"No, they don't. Most everyone is drunk on my birthday, they only
want to celebrate the night before. I'm usually sad on my birthday. . . . I
don't know why."

We continued to read that she attended the segregated school not
too far away from the old house in which she grew up.

"Thyne Institute produced many black teachers in those days. When
you told someone you went to Thyne, they knew that you had a real education! But many times I had to stay home and take care of your aunt
and uncle. Irene was getting blind and couldn't go to school."

"Mom, what happened to Aunt Irene's eyes?"

"I think it was that somebody was very jealous of Mama and poisoned
Irene. She at first had measles. Back then we didn't have injections. She
never fully recovered. But then I remember once when she was just a
baby and I had been left to take care of her. I was all alone and afraid in
the house. Mama used to get mad at me when I would go outside and
holler for her to come back to the house. She would sometimes be on
the farm working somewhere. Anyhow, on this night I was alone with
your aunt Irene and your uncle Paul and it was getting very dark. A
woman whom I had never seen before came to the house—a gypsy
woman with very beautiful long black hair. I didn't know what she wanted
and she looked at Irene and said what a beautiful baby she was. She put
her hands all over Irene's face. Then she left. I told Mama when she
came home that night. She was angry that I had let the woman in the
house. But she had been gone all day and I was scared and I wanted
company. It was after that that Irene became blind—she was so helpless. . . ."

Many times our mother would tell us that, "Mama was usually away working—she liked being on the road working, or traveling up to Pennsylvania to find work. So I had to be home taking care of the children with Papa. . . . I vowed not to leave you children home alone like Mama used to leave us."

In 1929 she was ten years old. She grew up knowing what it felt like to be left alone at home with her brothers and sister. On December 8, 1929, she wrote:

Jeffress, Virginia
My dear Mother,
Just a few lines to let you hear from me. I am well at this time and hope you are the same momma. I wrote you this letter some time ago. You don't never say nothing about coming home. See if you can come by the 18 of December. We are going to have a Christmas tree and I want you to come home and help me clean up for Christmas. I have so much to do. I go to school all week long and when saturday comes I wash and iron. Come home as quick as you can because Christmas is coming on fast and I want you to hurry and come home momma. The teacher house got burned down Friday and she didn't teach but half a day. Be sure to let me know when you coming home don't forget. We all send love. From you daughter Bettie D. Shields. Write soon and let me hear from you.[3]

Because of being left alone our mother was determined that that aspect of her childhood would not be repeated with us. Our lives would be different. We would not have to come home after school to an empty house or stay alone because she wanted to work. Things would be different for us.

Our mother often told stories of her life in the segregated town of Clarksville, Virginia. Segregation produced not only violence but absurdity in the lives of blacks and whites. My mother could not be hired for civil service work after graduating from high school because of segregation. The white postmaster wished he could hire her because of her high school diploma and her distinguished handwriting. He would whine in his Virginia drawl, "I declare you got a pretty handwritin', I shur wish I could hire you heah. But I can't hire no colored gal." Every time he saw her when she went back to visit he would tell her this![4]

My mother stayed in high school and celebrated earning her high school diploma in 1940. She was extremely proud—in her quiet way—of that diploma. For a black woman to have actually completed high school in four years in those days was a special achievement. As it was to many black people of her generation, education was the cornerstone of racial progress and dignity. In the senior class yearbook, *The Trawler,* they would write that she is: "Domestic . . . artistic . . . capable . . . soft spoken . . . rarely explosive . . . Damecon Club member." Her motto was: "A soft voice turneth away wrath."

As I read her *testimonio* of collected memories, I envisioned all her struggles—at least the ones that I knew about—and her stories of her Virginia girlhood, her northern triumphs, her challenges in being married to a foreigner whose language she did not learn, all wrapped up with the little treasures of progress, which in those days of racism and sexism were like mountains that had been leaped or tossed aside. She went on to reminisce about attending Goldwater School of Nursing in New York City (how many stories I'd heard about her experiences as a psychiatric nurse in a state hospital!), her short venture at a business school, but most of all, she wrote about her love of being a mother and for her five children and about the ambitions that were cut short:

> *Misfortune overtook me. Since graduating from high school in 1940 I have obtained different jobs plus raising a family. Many regrets have confronted me due to the fact that opportunity to carry out my desired nursing career was neglected. Little satisfaction has been achieved while employed in factory jobs and in hospitals as an aide. Working with the sick and the aged, I would be more satisfied with being skilled in this line of duty by becoming a nurse.*

Her life, however, was empowered through the will not to give up just because things get a little hard. Education was the avenue to different kinds of achievement and success, she told us. All five of us would graduate from college.

Obtaining her education was not as easy for her. How many times did I hear the story about how she and "brother Joe, we had to fight to go to Babylon High School. I had to fight for and protect Joe since he was younger than I. The white boys would wait in ambush for us on the way to school—we had to walk to school, you know. They didn't want us there . . . getting an education. I would put rocks in my lunch pail, and when they came out to attack us, I would yell to Joe to run and start throwing the rocks at the boys. Whenever a boy was hit very badly with a rock and bled, I would be called to the principal's office. Joe turned to amateur boxing. But finally, Joe, he couldn't take it anymore . . . he dropped out of high school and went into the army." My uncle Joe, whom I only knew from the handed-down stories, was killed in the army, even before he went overseas to fight in World War II. He was handsome, carefree, the spoiled baby of the family, an invulnerable prizefighter, a boxer until the letter from the War Department of the United States of America arrived:

> The Adjutant General's Office
> July 16, 1942
> The report of the board of officers which investigated the death of Private Joseph Shields showed that he died June 9, 1942. Shortly after supper that evening, he had an argument with another soldier concerning some cigarettes. The point of contention was apparently forgotten after a few remarks were made by both parties. However, a short while later the other soldier approached . . . and after making a few remarks concerning the cigarettes drew an opened knife out of his pocket and without warning cut Private Shields in the neck, severing the internal carotid artery and the internal jugular vein. He was immediately rushed to the station hospital where he died a few minutes later after all efforts to stop the hemorrhage failed.

Many times I heard my mother say this about Uncle Joe's murder: "Because of that, when your uncle Paul had to go war, I kept him supplied with enough cigarettes. We all kept him supplied with enough of whatever he needed and wanted—because of what had happened to Joe." Through memory-telling of her brother, my mother could heal and be healed, and through her own transformation she could then pass on the story of the brother who was killed "all for a pack of cigarettes."

There is an African belief that the dead are not gone until they are no longer remembered. *And he doesn't die until we, the living, don't remember his name anymore.* My mother loved her brother and that love was one of her spiritual absolutes. She never visited his gravesite. She made excuses about not being able to find the site in the national cemetery or that it was too far away. Those were excuses and the cemetery was a site that she did not want to resuscitate. Memory-telling about the brother did not resonate at that particular logisitical place of memory, the cemetery. It was more important that others in the family understood how his memory had to have a relationship with them. Memory-telling would reveal how central the "politics of memory" is to configuring identity and cultural values through oral and intimate narratives.

The time became twenty-five years since those high school days and war years. She moved away. Married. Five children. Private and public careers. All-consuming. All-encompassing.

A letter came one day inviting her to the reunion of her high school graduation class. They had found her address and wanted her to come. She was hesitant, nervous, and afraid. Why did they invite her? She had been one of two blacks in that graduating class—the other one, a black male, did not associate with her because "his family was part Indian and thought they were better than us—they said we came from blip." *Blip* meant you were from an insignificant, mean place in the South. All the memories came rushing back for her: she had had no true friends during those four years. With whom would she sit? What would they talk about? Some of them had become wealthy professionals and even national names. The late radio and TV commentator William B. Williams had been in her graduating class.

Tapping into her courage and pride, she went to the Babylon High School reunion for the class of 1940. It was a beautiful night. Summer. Stars. Old memories. Hugs. Kisses, even. The Most Popular. The Most Handsome. The Most Likely to Succeed. And the one who had the soft voice, because a soft answer turns away anger.

"I can't believe that the very boys who I had to fight and those white girls who never said anything to me only to call me names, now hugged me and each one wanted me to sit at his table. I sat at the class president's table with the girl who had been voted most beautiful and likely to succeed. They acted as if none of what had happened had happened. Did they mean it? I don't know. Maybe. Times are changing. But I had a good time! We even danced! And the food was good!

She was quiet and soft-spoken in public. That was her Thyne upbringing. But with us she talked and was lively and could offer "motherwit" whenever we needed it. Some of our talks would go into the very late hours of the night as I watched her sew or bake a glorious downhome cake or do a marvelous French pastry. During these times I learned about some of the things that she did not tell everybody. How did it come about that, after graduating from high school, she had applied to Purdue University in Indiana and had been accepted?

"What?! You went to Purdue? Are you serious? REALLY?"

"I did."

"But you never told me."

Silence. And then:

"I went out there to start school in the fall of that year. . . . I had been accepted. I couldn't stay there—there was no place for me to live. We weren't allowed to live in the dorms. No family. I missed Mama. I got back on the train to New York."

She did not talk about the humiliation and disappointment she must have felt when the white university first had accepted her, and then rejected her when she arrived because she was—a Negro. Nobody welcomed her. As she told me only pieces of the story, I filled in the other parts. Her pain and sadness of long ago became my pain and anger. A black woman in the forties at a Midwestern university. Not totally unheard of but certainly a challenging, if not lonely, feat. I recognized the many ways in which she, too, had jumped at the sun. Our mother existed because her family existed, and because they were, she was. "There was no family out there for me. I knew I couldn't stay even as I thought I could."

I remembered the telling of the Purdue incident. I thought how, forty years later, her sacrifices and fortitude enabled me to make the trek out to a predominantly white, Midwestern university for a degree. Because of the civil rights struggles, I had a place to live—anywhere I could afford. And if anyone denied me that right, I would get a civil rights lawyer, a women's rights lawyer, a housing lawyer, the university attorney, the Human Rights Commission, the Women's Resource and Action Center, and so on and so on. These were the support systems my generation would have. In Iowa City, I met two elderly black women who housed black students when the University of Iowa also didn't permit students of color to live on campus. I owe my survival and success in Iowa not only to the system of "new freedoms" but to our mother's insistence on our getting our education to the fullest, regardless of her fear of "no family" in Purdue. Certainly her gender-oriented decision to leave Purdue did not at all alter her belief and confidence in eventually obtaining an education for herself and for the children she would bring into the world. Her relentless work put confidence into me. It would be her relentless work that would allow all of us to have a completely different kind of life. Her relentless work would provide me with the freedom and financial support to travel, writing back to her from Europe, the Middle East, or Africa about how much I loved her, even though I had to be elsewhere.

As we searched and sifted papers that week following our mother's funeral, I saw the essence of my mother's spiritual and emotional prosperity. We found birthday, Christmas, Mother's Day cards—all kinds of holiday cards—that our own friends had sent to "Mom" throughout the years. She had saved the very pretty ones in a ribbon-tied box. Our mother also had been the other mother.

May 8, 1983
New York City

Dear Friends,

Thank you for the beautiful Mother's Day card. It was a great surprise and the most outstanding card on my Mother's Day card display table.... The picture of the singing birds and the blooming flowers gave notes of love, faith and hope. It is nice to know that others care especially on this special day for Mothers.

I am so proud to be a Mother. Not only did all my children send greetings and gifts, but many friends far and neighbors near remembered me. The phone call rang out from across the country with love and greetings. I love each one of you. Truly this was prosperity on Mother's Day.

Love,
Bettie D. Reyes

My mother took care of her own children even as she mothered so many others. Because of our Latino father, of whom the southern relatives would say, "that Spanish Negro who don't speak good English," our growing up was in a bicultural family of Spanish- and English-speaking cousins and aunts and uncles. There always a welcoming mat at "Auntie Bettie's." When we got older and went to college, our African, Caribbean, and Latino friends recognized this mother-woman as an other mother with whom they could securely find a warm welcome.

One day when I was still in college and living at home, I answered a telephone call and was surprised to hear the voice of a former South American boyfriend. I righteously wondered why he was calling, since we were no longer seeing one another. He replied, "I'm not calling to talk to you, I would like to speak to *Mom*, I want to know how *she* is doing!" During our college years, for many of our friends who were foreign students away from home, our home was special because of our mother. For her, there was the unspoken need to sustain the way of the family, of the olden kinship of tradition through practicing and celebrating the sustaining values.

"How could I ever repay you for what you have sacrificed for us?" we would often ask her.

"You all could never *repay* me! The only way you could pay me back is to have children of your own."

I used to think that when she told us this, she meant that we had to have children who would give us grief, disappointments, and hardship; that she wanted us to feel what she had endured by having five children of her own as well as taking care of other mothers' children when they could not. Do I have to sacrifice like that? No, that was not what she meant. It took me a long time to "grow up" and finally understand what she was telling us, that by having our own children we would, as parents, learn compassion—not sacrifice, but sharing what we gained through her sacrifices. We could only put into practice the values she had instilled in us by having children of our own. Having a wanted child brings enlightenment, compassion, and hope—despite the ever-present adversities that confront us. There would be the feeling that "I want things to be better for my child—for better tomorrows." Her *testimonio* continued:

> My leisure hours are spent mostly reading, arts and crafts—that is usually spent with the children. I believe in talking to them and being with them— we all come together for dinner at night. When I listen to their stories of the day, I not only listen to them but I can correct their grammar and there is always a teaching opportunity. A learning time. When they were young I would read to them; now we have all kinds of discussions. I am foremost, a mother of which I very much enjoy being and doing.

Because of her belief in the olden kinship that had sustained her people, she always told us the importance of staying together as a family. There were sibling squabbles among the five of us, each vying for her special attention—even when we became adults!—but she wanted us to be close to each other and find for ourselves another center among us after she was gone. "When I am gone, my spirit will be able to be with all of you at the same time."

My mother had a belief in self that was larger than anyone's disbelief. She had a strong belief in self, regardless. Whatever I have to endure is not nearly so painful and dehumanizing as what my mother and her foremothers have undergone. And so now, when my own thirteen-year-old daughter cries and complains only because "piano practice is too hard," or whenever I am overwhelmed by life, I begin remembering all over again of how my mother, walking miles to school with Uncle Joe, had to carry fighting rocks in her lunch pail because the white kids did not want her to go to school with them. I have told my daughter the story over and over again:

"It's because of your grandmother and so many others before her that you don't have to fight to go to school; she had to fill her lunch pail with fighting rocks. She had to fight in order to attend school. Whenever it gets to what you think is too hard, young lady, remember you are here with this opportunity to go to any school we want you to attend—and you are going to the best of schools—because of her."

"But some things are hard, mom."

"*Mi querida,* my little lamb, I don't want to hear that word 'hard.' Your grandma's going to school put me where I am now in order to provide for you—to make a better world for you."

Women-centered memory-telling is linked to metaphorical and conceptual sites and to the ways in which black women facilitate the representations of oral narratives in the context of multiethnic African American traditions and experiences. Karen Fields succinctly tells us, "In filling blanks mistakenly, memory collaborates with forces separate from actual past events. . . . In these collaborations . . . memory acquires well-noted imperfections. We seek to understand these imperfections systematically . . . if we are scholars who use memory as a source" (150). Undoubtedly scholars as well as writers actively participate in the memory source.

In Marcia Douglas's exquisite novel *Madame Fate,* the central character, Bella, is a kin-owl, a shapeshifter who has the power to hear back and forth through the centuries of black New World and West Indian island history. As a kin-owl who is also a long-memoried woman, Bella negotiates her way through history and with other women by listening to a calabash as you would listen to the insides of a seashell to hear the rushing of the sea:

> The other thing I enjoy is the whisper in seashell and dry coconut husk. If you put these to your ear, you hear whoosh, whoosh, whoosh, like someone calling real soft from way back, or way forward. Whoosh, whoosh, whoosh. . . . [T]his calabash is special-special. (10)

Bella resides in the Garden, an asylum for elderly women who are supposed to be mentally ill. Bella, however, is not mad as she courses through history with her magical power or rememory. "Through the process of memory," Marcia Douglas affirms, "we reclaim/retrieve ourselves and tell our story. The process of telling our story—having our say—is healing. . . . Something magical happens when we tell our stories."[5] My mother was a long-memoried woman who endeared relationships.[6] As a product of the racialized South she knew that family was the fabric of everyday "inside" culture. All the pieces in the culture were woven together by this fabric of family and relationships. When the larger outside society failed—and this was inevitable because of America's historical legacies—family, regardless of its imperfections, was the ultimate support, retreat, and refuge.

My mother's memory-telling often held thousands of years in one moment. I still hear her tongue-language and remember her fears of the outside world despite her strengths gathered from the inside worlds. Like Bella in *Madame Fate,* she calls real soft from way back, helping me to move way forward. I'd like to connect back, rather than cast off, and pay homage to the inheritance of my mother's purpose and endurance, and may I become a long-memoried woman through memory-telling.

APPENDIX A

Legacies of Margaret Garner

In 1856 Frederick Douglass, orator, statesman, former slave, and abolitionist, wrote that the Margaret Garner incident would become a legacy for painters and poets: "The poet will gather inspiration from this offering of blood to the goddess of Freedom; History will hand down her name to the last generation. Yes, MARGARET, THE SLAVE MOTHER, will furnish an inspiring theme for the painter's pencil, and the poet's song." Although Margaret Garner died in slavery and did not attain the freedom that she so desperately wanted, she, indeed, has been remembered in nineteenth- and twentieth-century art. In the twentieth century, Toni Morrison's novel Beloved *would inspire Oprah Winfrey to produce the film of the same name. These two creative works, as well as the "Garner" poems of the nineteenth century, are tributes to Margaret Garner's fortitude and struggle for freedom. What is the role of the artist in relation to social change, consciousness, and often unpalatable truths? Many of us are fascinated with how the artist's palate may convey prophetic "truths" about our human passions and the human condition.*

THE BEAUTIES OF SLAVERY—
A SLAVE CHILD KILLED BY ITS MOTHER

We give elsewhere in our columns, a full report of the particulars of the dreadful tragedy in Cincinnati, which resulted in the death of a slave child by the hands of its mother. It seems that she was a party of eight slaves, who had escaped from Kentucky. The brave fugitives were pursued soon after their departure, and captured after the most desperate resistance. The frantic mother, finding that she and her little ones would be captured, determined that they should never return to the house of bondage, and with a butcher knife commenced the work of death. She succeeded in killing but one of the children, though she states it was her intention to kill them all, and then herself, preferring DEATH to Slavery. And now, while in prison she constantly avows that she will never more be a slave, but will take her own life whenever an opportunity presents itself. Her husband and parents also declared that they would rather die, than be replunged into the burning hell of Slavery.

What a commentary upon the "blessed" realities of American Slavery, Republican Despotism, Fourth-of-July Democracy! A slave mother, on the soil of the "Free" States, hunted like the wolf, and rescuing her little ones from the grasp of her pursuers, by delivering them into the jaws of Death, preferring to see them weltering in their hearts' blood, rather than to see them slaves! And this is the "land of the free, and home of the brave!"

What a terrible protest have we here against the infernal enactment, which allows the hunting of a poor and defenseless mother with her little babies, whom she prefers seeing locked in the arms of Death, than in the clutches of the tyrants of Free and Democratic America! The act of this despairing slave mother, is vastly more expressive than tongue can tell of the wrongs, and cruelties, and miseries of Slavery. How perfectly happy and contented the slaves must be in their "normal", "Heaven-appointed" condition! Where is Rev. NEHEMIAH ADAMS, of "South Side" notoriety? Here is a fine opportunity for gazing upon a North Side picture of the "Patriarchal Institution." Let him gaze upon it, until his eyes are red with weeping, and heart o'er flows with penitence. And then let him gather every number of his South Side view, and burn them at the base of Bunker Hill.

The name of this brave slave mother, the heroic act which she performed, and all the circumstances connected with it, will never be forgotten. History tells us of a Roman maiden who was sacrificed by her father in order to preserve her chastity. The deed has been immortalized in verse; music, painting, history, oratory, the drama, all, all, have kept the ashes of the Roman Father, glowing as it were in eternal beauty. And so shall the name of this heroic slave mother never die. The "wide,

wide, world" will do her homage. The poet will gather inspiration from this offering of blood to the goddess of Freedom; History will hand down her name to the last generation. Yes, MARGARET, THE SLAVE MOTHER, will furnish an inspiring theme for the painter's pencil, and the poet's song. She will not be viewed as a *murderess* but as a heroine, who loved her little babies too well, to behold them slaves, and therefore, fled for refuge to the grave—for "*there is the servant free from his master, and the voice of the oppressor is heard no more.*"

Sleep on Child of the Slave Mother! No blood hound will 'er be upon thy track. Thou art free! Sleep on! The cruel task-master cannot reach in thy secure abode. There are no whips or chains or slaveholders in the place where thy spirit dwelleth. The voice of thy blood crieth unto Heaven from the ground. Sleep on! Retribution is on the wing.

From the *Anti-Slavery Bugle* February 23, 1856

Throughout the early spring and summer of 1856 poems, speeches, and parodies about Margaret Garner and the fugitive slave case continued to appear in contemporary newspapers. Lucy Stone Blackwell visited Garner while she was in jail, and the Reverend P. C. Bassett of the Fairmont Theological Seminary publicized the interview he had with Margaret Garner.

THE SLAVE TRAGEDY AT CINCINNATI
BY MRS. MARY A. LIVERMORE

Bright the Sabbath sun shining through the clear and frost air
Solemnly the bells are calling to the house of praise and prayer;
And, with hearts devout and holy, thither many wend their way,
To renew to God their pledges—but I cannot go to-day.

For my soul is sick and maddened with that fearful tale of woe,
Which has blanched the cheeks of mothers to the whiteness of the snow;
And my thoughts are wandering ever where the prison walls surrond
The parents and their children, in hopeless bondage bound.

Oh, thou mother, maddened, frenzied, when the hunter's toils ensnared
Thee and thy brood of nestlings, till thy anguished spirit dared
Send to God, uncalled, one darling life that round thine own did twine
Worthy of a Spartan mother was that fearful deed of thine!

Worthy of a Roman father, who sheathed deep his flashing knife
In the bosom of Virginia, in the current of her life!
Who, rather than his beauteous child should live a tyrant's slave,
Opened the way to freedom through the portals of the grave!

Well I know no stronger yearning than a mother's love can be—
I could do and dare forever for the babe upon my knee!
And I feel no deeper sorrow could the light of life eclipse,
Than to see death's shadows settle on its brow and faded lips.

Yet (oh, God of Heaven, forgive me!), baby sitting on my knee,
I could close thy blue eyes calmly, smiling now so sweet on me!
Ay, *my* hand could ope the casket, and thy precious soul set free;
Better for thee death and Heaven than a life of slavery!

And before the Judge Eternal, this should be my anguished plea:
"They would rob my child of Manhood; so, uncalled, I sent it Thee!
"Hope and Love, and Joy, and Knowledge, and her every right they
      crave;
"So I gave her what they left her—her inheritance—the grave!"

And the Lord would judge between us, oh ye men of stony heart!
Even 'gainst the strong and might, for the weak He taketh part;
Think ye, hunters of His children, bowed beneath your iron rod,
With your heel upon their heart-pulse, this ye do unto your God!

But the day of vengeance cometh—He will set his people free,
Though He lead them, like his Israel, through a red and bloody sea;
For the tears and gore of bondmen, staining deep the frighted sod,
And the wailing cry of millions riseth daily up to God!

From the *National Anti-Slavery Standard* February 16, 1856

A VISIT TO THE SLAVE MOTHER WHO KILLED HER CHILD

Last Sabbath, after preaching in the city prison, Cincinnati, through the kindness of the Deputy Sheriff, I was permitted to visit the apartment of that unfortunate woman, concerning whom there has been so much excitement during the last two weeks.

I found her with an infant in her arms only a few months old, and observed that it had a large bump on its forehead. I inquired the cause of the injury. She proceeded to give a detailed account of her attempt to kill her children.

She said that when the officers and the slave-hunters came to the house in which they were concealed, she caught a shovel and struck two of her children on the head, and then took a knife and cut the throat of the third, and tried to kill the other—that if they had given her time, she would have killed them all—that with regard to herself she cared but little; but she was unwilling to have her children suffer as she had done.

I inquired if she were not excited almost to madness when she committed the act? No, she replied, I was cool as I now am; and would much rather kill them at once, and thus end their sufferings, than have them taken back to slavery and be murdered by piece-meal. She then told the story of her wrongs. She spoke of her days of suffering, of her nights of unmitigated toil, while the bitter tears coursed their way down her cheeks, and fell in the face of the innocent child as it looked smiling up, little conscious of the danger and probable sufferings that awaited it.

As I listened to the facts, and witnessed the agony depicted in her countenance, I could not but exclaim, O how terrible is irresponsible power, when exercised over intelligent beings! She alludes to the child killed as being free from all trouble and sorrow, with a degree of satis-

faction that almost chills the blood in one's veins. Yet she evidently possesses all the passionate tenderness of a mother's love. She is about twenty-
five years of age, and apparently possesses an average amount of kindness,
with a vigorous intellect, and much energy of character.

The two men and the oldest children were in another apartment, but
her mother-in-law was in the same room. She says she is the mother of
eight children. Most of whom have been separated from her; that her
husband was once separated from her twenty-five years, during which
time she did not see him; that could she have prevented it, she would
never have permitted him to return, as she did not wish him to witness
her sufferings, or be exposed to the brutal treatment that he would receive.

She states that she has been a faithful servant, and in her old age she
would not have attempted to obtain her liberty; but as she became feeble,
and less capable of performing labour, her master became more and
more exacting and brutal in his treatment, until she could stand it no
longer; that the effort could only result in death, at most—she therefore
made the attempt.

She witnessed the killing of the child, but said that she neither encouraged nor discouraged her daughter-in-law—for under similar circumstances she should probably have done the same. The old woman is
from sixty to seventy years of age; has been a professor of religion about
twenty years, and speaks with much feeling of the time when she shall
be delivered from the power of the oppressor, and dwell with the Sav-
iour, "where the wicked shall cease from tumbling, and the weary are at
rest."

These slaves (as far as I am informed) have resided all their lives within
sixteen miles of Cincinnati. We are frequently told that Kentucky slavery is very innocent. If these are its fruits where it exists in a mild form,
will someone tell us what we may expect from its more objectionable
features? But comments are unnecessary.

From the *National Anti-Slavery Standard* March 15, 1856

When Margaret Garner was taken back to Kentucky, her owner, Mr. Gaines, immediately sold her and the family "down the river." The oral accounts said that she died of tuberculosis, and her husband, it is said, wrote to Lucy Stone Blackwell that "she has finally escaped." The Garner fugitive slave case was "laid to rest" by the press.

THE CINCINNATI TRAGEDY

Still another act of the extraordinary slave drama at Cincinnati has passed during the last week. Governor Chase of course promptly issued his requisition, and sent it by a trusty officer to the Governor of Kentucky, calling for the rendition of the alleged slaves to be tried on an indictment for murder. To the surprise of many, the Governor of Kentucky made no objection to the issuing of the proper warrant, only asking time till the next day to see that the papers were all right. The next day he issued his warrant, but when the officer went to the place where the woman had been kept, professedly on purpose to meet this requisition, the "evangelical" Mr. Gaines had suddenly removed *her [sic]* to Louisville and there shipped her as one of a cargo of human chattels, Kentucky's staple product, down the river to find a market in Arkansas or Louisiana. Whether Gaines broke his word to the Governor, or whether the Governor took a day to examine the papers, in order to give time for this magnanimous manoeuvre, we have not now the evidence necessary to determine. At any rate, that delay served the purpose, for the steamboat had only been gone two hours when the Ohio officer arrived at Louisville. Of course, pursuit was impossible.

The scene now shifts to the steamboat *Henry Lewis,* on which Margaret and her infant child are borne down the Ohio river, in company with four other unhappy Native American Kentuckians, all ironed together in couples, among whom are four others chained by this pious Mr. Gaines, who ran away during the Cincinnati trial, but were overtaken and recaptured before they reached the river. It is the dead of night. Suddenly there is a terrible crash, the boat has come in collision with another, the *Hungarian,* her timbers are crushed like an eggshell. The *Cincinnati Commercial* of March 11, tells the issue:

"Margaret had her child—the infant that she hit on the head with the shovel when arrested here—in her arms, but by the shock of the boat that came to the assistance of the *Lewis* (as one story goes) she was thrown into the river with her child and a white woman who was one of the steerage passengers, and was standing by her at the moment.

"The woman and the child were drowned, but a black man, the cook on the *Lewis*, sprung into the river and saved Margaret, who it is said displayed frantic joy when told that her child was drowned, and said she would never reach alive Gaines's Landing in Arkansas, the point for which she was shipped.

"The last that was seen of Peggy, she was on the *Hungarian*, crouching like a wild animal, near the stove, with a blanket wrapped around her. Our readers will, we presume, be struck with the dramatic features of the fugitive slave case, and that it progresses like a plot, wrought by some master of tragedy. First, there was the flight—the crossing of the frozen river in the twilight of morning, the place of fancied security, the surprise by the officers, the fight with them, the murder of the child, the arrest, the scenes about the court room and in the jail, the long suspense, the return to Kentucky, the removal to Frankfort, the separation there, the approach of the messenger with the requisition for Peggy, her removal to Louisville, the pursuit of the messenger, the boat on which she was to have been taken South leaving two hours ahead of Cooper with the writ from Governor Morehead—then the speedy catastrophe on the steamer, the drowning of the babe of the heroine, and her own rescue, as if yet saved for some more fearful and startling act of the tragedy; and lastly the curtain falls, leaving her wet and dismal, on a boat bound South, perfectly careless as to her own fate, only determined never to set foot on the soil of Arkansas. There is something fearfully tragic about this, which must occur to every mind, and we shall look with much interest for information of the catastrophe which will complete the dramatic unity of the affair."

From the *American Baptist*, Utica, Thursday, March 27, 1856

In 1867, the American painter Thomas Noble was commissioned by Harlow Roys of New York to do a painting. Noble's artist's creation of the Garner incident is often used in secondary history texts. Noble's painting was photographed and a copy of the wood engraving was published in Harper's Weekly *along with a story entitled, "The Modern Medea." Garner's story was not the modern Medea. Toni Morrison says, "This is not Medea who kills her children because she's mad at some dude, and she's going to get back at him. Here is something that is huge and very intimate." By 1867, Garner's story is presented as melodramatic and transformed into the imagery of the helpless and tragic mother who, "after her capture she sank into speechless stupor, and while being returned to slavery eluded the watchfulness of her guard and plunged into the Ohio River." Noble's painting creates an aesthetic tension between the image of Garner as the very angry, middle-aged, black mother (as opposed to mulatta) and the astonished "gentleman" slave catchers who have rushed into the room. Juxtaposed between the two sets of drama are the slain boy child and two boys clinging to the enraged mother's skirts for mercy. The face of the mother is angry, and she points to the slain boy as if "presenting" his death to the slave catchers as they rush into the room.*

THE MODERN MEDEA

Among the most interesting of the pictures at the Academy of Design is that which we reproduce on page 308. The artist, Thomas Noble, has illustrated one of the horrors of the institution of Slavery as it formerly existed, and produced a vigorous and interesting work, although it is on a repulsive subject. The painting is not a mere fanciful sketch; it is really historical, being the true story of a slave woman named Margaret Garner, who with her children, escaped several years ago from Slavery in Kentucky to Ohio. The Fugitive Slave Law was then in existence, and her master pursued her. She secreted herself in the house of some of her people, and with their help for some time evaded pursuit. At last her hiding-place was discovered. She defended herself from the attacks of her master and the officers of the law, but was driven from one room of the house to another and finally hemmed in and surrounded. The door of the apartment in which she had taken refuge was broken open, and the pursuers entered to behold the horrible scene which the artist has so powerfully depicted. Margaret Garner, with a far nobler jealousy than that which actuated the mythical Medea, finding her children were about to be given up to the slavery she had endured, seized a knife and took the lives of two of them. Before she could slay the others she was seized by her horror-stricken but heartless pursuers. After her capture she sank into speechless stupor, and while being returned to slavery eluded the watchfulness of her guard and plunged into the Ohio River and found freedom there.

From *Harper's Weekly* May 18, 1867

In her 1892 novel, Iola Leroy or Shadows Uplifted, *Frances E. W. Harper incorporates the Garner fugitive slave incident in one of the characters' discussions on slavery:*

> "No; I don't think these Abolitionists have any right to meddle in our affairs. . . . My father says the slaves would be very well contented if no one put wrong notions in their heads."
>
> "I don't know," was the response of her friend, "but I do not think that that slave mother who took her four children, crossed the Ohio River on the ice, killed one of the children and attempted the lives of the other two, was a contented slave." (98)

Harper uses a strategy of ideological interplay with history and the literary imagination by citing the Garner incident. It is a strategy that forces her nineteenth-century audience to become engaged in the era's social injustices against black women.

The Garner story would continue to be remembered in and out of history. On February 17, 1979, the Cincinnati Enquirer *had a peculiar headline and lead story:*

TALE OF HORROR
NEGRO MOTHER CUTS CHILD'S THROAT

Cincinnati was thrown into much excitement yesterday by the information that a party of slaves had made a stampede from Kentucky to this side of the river . . .

Slaves stampede? Negro (!) mother cuts child's throat? Your eyes quickly and maybe even desperately searched for an explanation—and you found it. The news article following that headline was about the 1856 Garner family and their fugitive journey. The year is 1979 but the Enquirer *reprints the headlines of a sensational news story that had taken place in Cincinnati one hundred twenty-three years previously: Margaret Garner's killing of her child. With Alex Haley's remarkable story,* Roots *on national television, the newspaper reminded readers that Cincinnati had "played a part in the tortuous road toward abolition" and that "the 1856 capture of fugitive slave Margaret Garner is a stark reminder."*

APPENDIX B

From *Periodical Accounts Relating to the Missions of the Church of the United Brethren Established among the Heathen* XIII: 486–87. 1739

Der erweckten Negros in St. Thomas schreiben an Ihro Maiest. den Konig in Dannemarck.

—An. 1739.

Groote Koninginne

Die tyd mi a wes na Poppo op Africa, doen mi a dint die Heer Mau, nu kome na blanco land, mi no wilt gu din de Heere. Mi no ha di grond vor tú dien die Heere; mi ben bedrœv na min herte, voor dat Negrinne no kan dien die Heere Jesus in Thomas, die Blanke no wil dien die Heere. Lat so as sili wil, maar soo de povre swarte Brœders en susters wil dien de Heer Jesus, so mœt zilli dœn, as si bin maron volk. As Neacanda belyv, gy mœtbidde de Heere Jesus voor ons, en bidd ook A Niba, voor la stan Bas Martinus prek de Heere woord, voor ons mœ leer voor kenn de Heere, en voor Doop ons Negers, op Naam des Vaders, Sons en Hilig Geest. Die Heer bewaar sinder, en seegene sinder, son en dochtersen, heel Familie, en mi sal bid den Heer Jesus voor sinder.

    Ob naam van over Tweehondert en
    Vyftig Negerssen Zrouwen, die
    den Heere Jesus beminnen,
    geschreven door.
        Marotta
        nú
        Madlena *van Poppo uyt Africa*

Great Queen

When I was in Poppo [sic] in Africa, I served the Lord Mau. Now that I come to the white people's Land, I do not want to serve that Lord anymore. I do not have reason to serve that Lord. My heart is saddened because Negro women cannot serve the Lord Jesus on St. Thomas. The whites do not want to serve the Lord. Let it be as they want; when the poor black Brethren and sisters want to serve the Lord, they are treated as Maroons. Please Neacand [Queen], you have to pray to the Lord Jesus for us and also pray to the [King] to let Bas Martinus remain and preach the word of the Lord, because we have to learn to know the Lord before we negroes [can be] baptized in the name of the Father, the Son, and the Holy Ghost. May the Lord save them and bless them, your son and daughter, the whole Family, and I will pray to the Lord Jesus for them.

In the name of over two hundred and fifty negro women who love the Lord Jesus, written by

Marotta, now Madlena *[sic]* from Poppo *[sic]* in Africa

Notes

Introduction

1. I concur with Gwendolyn Etter-Lewis who writes, "As a woman of color I find that I can no longer use a writing style that alienates me from my community. Therefore, I choose to use inclusive terms like 'we' instead of distancing/generic words like 'they,'" in Gwendolyn Etter-Lewis and Michele Foster, eds., *Unrelated Kin: Race and Gender in Women's Personal Narratives*, 11.

2. These ideas may be further explored in *The Promise of World Peace*, an analysis of the quest for peace by the Universal House of Justice.

3. As first teachers we do not alienate the role of fathers and other male kin in the development of parenting and educating the next generation. The roles are complementary to and for each other.

4. Progressing into the twenty-first century, we can realize how the word "race" is also inadequate. Although I use this term in its traditional meaning, I do not advocate its socially constructed and problematic meaning. Contemporary scientists and social scientists attest to the social construction of race, which makes the term fluid, subjective, with the propensity to change meaning relative to the whims of human behavior and thinking. Therefore, the one "race" is that of humanity—Homo sapiens. In his ground-breaking book, *The Emperor's New Clothes: Biological Theories of Race at the Millennium*, Joseph L. Graves Jr. demonstrates that science does not identify race in the human species. Graves argues that racism, however, persists because twentieth-century scientists have not adequately participated in the discourse of eliminating racism. See also Paul Gilroy's book *Against Race: Imagining Political Culture beyond the Color Line*.

5. As one of the editors of a special issue on "Postcolonial, Emergent, and Indigenous Feminisms," I have expanded on this notion in *Signs: Journal of Women in Culture and Society*. See Angelita Reyes et al., "Editorial."

6. Rosenberg says that "expressing the experience of caregiving in ungendered language poses a problem.... [A] young man, in trying to articulate his experi-

ence in caring for his lover with AIDS, found that: 'the closest model with which to compare my seven months with Paul is the experience of mothering.... By this analogy I mean the cluster of activities, characteristics, and emotions associated with the social role of motherhood'" (54).

7. Quoted from Deborah Gray White's book *Ar'n't I a Woman? Female Slaves in the Plantation South* (14).

8. Patricia Hill Collins also uses the term "othermothers" in her discussion of African American women and motherhood in *Black Feminist Thought: Knowledge, Consciousness, and the Politics of Empowerment.* "Black motherhood as an institution is both dynamic and dialectical.... [M]otherhood can serve as a site where Black women express and learn the power of self-definition... and a belief in Black women's empowerment" (118).

9. See Honor Ford Smith, *Lionheart Gal: Life Stories of Jamaican Women,* in which members of the Sistren Theatre Collective discuss biological mothers and "other mothers" who have influenced their lives. Significantly, the book is dedicated "[t]o the daughters and mothers of all the Caribbean and the vision their struggles will set free." Many of the stories in this collection show how Jamaican women in particular and women in general, as Ford writes, "must beware of notions of 'naturalness' [that women are by nature eternally forgiving, physically weak, dependent on men, bearers of children, etc.] as far as womanhood is concerned. There is no such thing" (xxi).

10. One of my aunts from Honduras loved children but was never able to have any of her own. She was the only one among eight sisters who could not have children, which was a tremendous disappointment for her even though she had become a comadre in the extended family. The years passed: I grew up and moved away, and my aunt retired to Honduras. I took my own daughter to Honduras and introduced her to this special aunt whom she'd never met. Having forgotten cultural etiquette after being away too long, I mistakenly said, "This is your tía!" My aunt looked at me with annoyance and quickly corrected me by saying in Spanish to my daughter, "No, I'm your *abuelita* (grandma)!" I could still refer to her as "auntie" but my daughter, the next generation, should not call her aunt. My other aunts who had children could still be called "tía" or "auntie" by my daughter. (Out of respect for generational difference, my cousin's children could call me "tía.")

11. The journal of the Association of Caribbean Women Writers and Scholars is titled *MaComère.* Helen Pyne Timothy explains that, "The word *macomère* is widely used by women in the Caribbean to mean 'my child's godmother'; 'my best friend and close female confidante'... the woman who, by virtue of the depth of her friendship, has rights and privileges over my child and whom I see as surrogate mother.... the name ... clearly expresses the intimate relations which women in the Caribbean share," *MaComère* 2 (1999): i.

12. Historian Douglas L. Wilson discovered a letter written by Thomas Jefferson in 1796 that suggests Jefferson may have wanted legislation in his state of Virginia to allow the education of slaves. "Because of the lack of documents surrounding his views on the issue, scholars presumed Jefferson didn't feel strongly about educating slaves, even though many of his personal slaves could read and write." *The Chronicle of Higher Education* (13 March 1998): 10.

13. For example, a fascinating story of how African American quilts probably were used as secret codes that helped slaves to escape via the Underground Railroad is explored in *Hidden in Plain View: The Secret Story of Quilts and the Underground Railroad,* by Jacqueline Tobin and Raymond G. Dobard.

14. Gwendolyn Etter-Lewis's term succinctly highlights the concept that there can be unity in diversity among women despite their diverse ethnic histories and cultures. Indeed, she writes that "cross-cultural interactions, even between women, are problematic and complex, but potentially transforming" (*Unrelated Kin* 6).

15. For the extensive study of the Code, see *Le Code Noir* by Louis Sala-Molins.

1. Taking Flight and Taking Foot

1. From "Ibo Landing" by Craig Dominey. Although the spelling varies from "Igbo" to "Ibo," I will use the contemporary accepted spelling of "Igbo" but maintain the spelling (Ibo) that is used in the citations.

2. Dany Bébel-Gisler, *Léonora: L'Histoire enfouie de la Guadeloupe,* 8–9 and the English translation is from *Leonora: The Buried Story of Guadeloupe,* 2. Unless otherwise noted, I take responsibility for subsequent translations. However, I would like to thank everyone who assisted and offered suggestions in the collective project.

3. "To this very day, no marker or shrine celebrates the site where the indomitable Ibo are said to have disembarked. In fact, Gullahs and Geechees can only look at the site from a distance, since it has been fenced off as private property. The owner's failure to cooperate and other disputes concerning the landing have prevented a marker even being placed at the road outside the property line where the landing is thought to exist," cited in *The Legacy of Ibo Landing: Gullah Roots of African American Culture,* ed. Marquetta L. Goodwine, p. 6.

4. Michael Craton, *Searching for the Invisible Man: Slaves and Plantation Life in Jamaica.*

5. In Afro-Cuban mythology, dundunbanza is an evil spirit: "Dundunbanza, who has sent you? Dundunbanza, I can vex you now!" Sierra Maestra. *¡dundunbanza!* World Circuit compact disc WCD041AM. Quoted here with permission.

6. Mary C. Karasch discusses at length the role of suicides among Brazilian slaves during the nineteenth century in *Slave Life in Rio de Janeiro: 1808–1850.* She provides contemporary reports, travelers' accounts, and government documents (316–20) to illustrate the extent to which slaves in Rio de Janeiro committed suicide. Karasch superficially argues that "nostalgia" was one of the common reasons for suicide. Claiming nostalgia and jealousy as reasons for suicide among New World slaves is a romanticist attitude towards the sufferer. Although it remains difficult to establish the perspectives of the slaves themselves about death by suicide, to say that nostalgia for Africa was the fundamental reason for suicide diminishes the severity of their captivity and the magnitude of their resistance. As captives, they were people who resisted slavery. Despite some of her arguments, I highly recommend Karasch's text because it has an extensive bibliography on the subject of nineteenth-century slave suicide in Brazil.

7. For some readings and documentation on slave suicides during New World slavery, see the following: María Poumier Taquechel, "El Suicidio esclava en Cuba en

los Años 1840"; Manuel Moreno Fraginals, *El Ingenio: el complejo económico social cubano del azúcar;* Victor Schoelcher, *Des colonies françaises: abolition immédiate de l'esclavage;* and José Alípio Goulart, *Da fuga ao suicídio.*

8. I use this term from James C. Scott's book, *Domination and the Arts of Resistance: Hidden Transcripts,* in which he theorizes about dominant ideology and the "infrapolitics of the powerless." Resistance among powerless groups has not always been recognized because of the "hidden transcripts" that express resistance and the covert ways in which resistance is created and maintained. The "performance" of suicide takes place on-stage, while the "discourse" of flying occurs off-stage. The subordinates (the slaves) have the power to create a mediated tension between the hidden text and the public context.

9. In Edward Brathwaite's, *The Arrivants: A New World Trilogy,* the first Africans forced to the New World as slaves are the "arrivants."

10. For additional reading on salt taboos, see Margaret L. Arnott, *Gastronomy: The Anthropology of Food and Food Habits.*

11. Although external sources for salt are now available in the Sahara desert, in places such as Niger and Chad salt continues to be an important local trading commodity that is mined and transported. Mercedes trucks caravan along with the ancient and inexpensive ships of the desert, camels, to and from remote villages. A *National Geographic* team recently explored the Sahara where "high-quality salt sells at a premium" and where, among the Tuareg, "salt is life" (Donovan Webster, "Journey to the Heart of the Sahara," p. 13, 17).

12. In this instance I'm remembering an African ontological belief that has transatlantic philosophical groundings: the individual is not separable from the community and family, and in this tradition the individual believes that, "I am because we are; and since we are, therefore I am."

13. I use the term "collective" rather than "mass" because of the latter term's contemporary negative association with extremist religious cults. The Matouba incident is similar to the collective suicide that occurred in 73 A.D. at Masada in the Judean desert, where suicide was decided upon and carried out systematically. When they realized that they would be defeated in their resistance against the Romans, the group of Jews, commanded by Eleazar ben Yair, decided upon suicide and kinship homicide. Legend has it that there were survivors who told what had happened.

14. For additional readings that refer to beliefs on suicide in African societies see Ronald Cohen, *Dominance and Defiance: A Study of Marital Instability in an Islamic African Society;* Wilhelm Junker, *Travels in Africa during the Years 1882–1886;* Paul and Laura Bohannan, *A Source Book on Tiv Religion;* Ladislav Holy, *Gender and Ritual in an Islamic Society: The Berti of Darfur;* and E. E. Evans-Pritchard, *Witchcraft, Oracles and Magic Among the Azande.*

15. Detailed information on this Cuban uprising is located in *Representación extendida por Don Diego Miguel de Moya y firmada por casi todos los dueños de ingenios de la jurisdicción en enero 19 de 1790.* ANC, Real Consulado, 150/7405, quoted in *El Ingenio* (117).

16. A similar scene begins Earl Lovelace's novel *Salt* (1996), where the slave, Guinea John, returns to Africa by taking flight from a cliff overlooking the ocean in the West Indies. His descendants have to "suck salt" (endure hardships) because they have eaten salt and cannot fly.

17. Zora Neal Hurston's profound novel, *Their Eyes Were Watching God* resonates this compelling reality of gender warmth through Janie's relationship with Tea Cake. In Sherley Anne Williams's novel, *Dessa Rose,* gender warmth is depicted through Dessa's relationship with and memory of Kaine.

18. Discrepancies surround the age of the daughter that Margaret Garner killed. In 1864, S. P. Chase, governor of Ohio when the Garner homicide occurred, wrote that the child, Mary, was ten years old (Ripley 172). In an 1859 speech, Black abolitionist Sarah Remond refers to the murdered daughter as being Garner's first born (Ripley 437–38). Consistent with nineteenth-century minimal regard for children in journalism (slave or not), little attention was given concerning the accuracy of the murdered child's name or age.

19. Here, the term mulatta is used to designate a fair-complexioned woman of African ancestry and will include the terms octoroon and quadroon. See Verena Martinez-Alier's *Marriage, Class and Colour in Nineteenth-Century Cuba,* where the author analyzes the implications of racial and social discrimination based on legal skin color classifications. In nineteenth-century Cuba, as in other areas of the Caribbean, social classification was defined exclusively by the European phenotype of beauty and skin color.

20. The account of the Garner incident presented here is taken from the following sources: Levi Coffin, *Reminiscences of Levi Coffin* (Coffin may have taken much of his information from contemporary newspaper sources); Samuel May, *The Fugitive Slave Law and Its Victims;* Julius Yanuck, "The Garner Fugitive Slave Case;" *The British Friend; Cincinnati Commercial, Cincinnati Daily Enquirer, Cincinnati Daily Gazette, Cincinnati Times, Louisville Courier; The Glasgow Courier; Glasgow Chronicle;* Glasgow Emancipation Society Minute Books; *The Liberator; National Anti-Slavery Standard; The Provincial Freeman;* and *The American Baptist.* In most instances, the newspapers used the same sources and had the same reports. Where one account was used by a particular source I include the specific citation. For additional information please see the complete bibliography.

21. From "The Case of the Garner Fugitive Slave Family" (*The Pacific Appeal,* 1 November 1862).

22. A typical attitude is expressed in Johann David Schoepf's *Travels in the Confederacy,* where he writes that "in almost every house there are negresses, slaves, who count it an honor to bring a mulatto into the world" (1:101).

23. Fancy girls were maintained exclusively for the sexual pleasures of wealthy planters. For additional discussions on nineteenth-century fancy girls and the fancy trade, see Frederic Bancroft (217–18, 328–34), Eugene D. Genovese (416–18), and Deborah Gray White (27–61).

24. In the French-speaking Caribbean, a category of mixed-race women is referred to as *chappé* (from the verb *échapper,* which means "to escape"). The implication is that these women have escaped from being black.

2. Surrogate Mothering

1. Personal communication. July 1988, Moore Town, Jamaica. Subsequent references refer to this fieldwork. I thank the Maroon descendants of Moor Town for all their assistance.

2. During periods between 1988 and 1993, I conducted field and archival research in Moor Town, Jamaica, at the National Library of Jamaica, and at the West India Collection at the University of the West Indies, Mona, Jamaica. Research for fieldwork in Jamaica was funded, in part, by a grant from the National Endowment for the Humanities. Again I am most appreciative of the staffs at these archives who generously helped with this work. I wish to thank Mary Lou Emery for her comments and suggestions regarding parts of this essay during my residence at the University of Iowa as a Rockefeller Humanities Scholar.

3. *Journals of the Assembly of Jamacia*, vol 3, 1733, p. 121.

4. Jamaica Archives. Land Patent Office (Nanny Land Patent, vol 22, folio 15B, 1741). Spanish Town, Jamaica.

5. The film version of *Wide Sargasso Sea* was released in 1993. Directed by John Duigan, Fine Line Features. 100 mins.

6. I don't refer to this character as Rochester even though it may be convenient to call him that considering Rhys's literary references to Charlotte Brontë's *Jane Eyre*. By calling him Rochester I would give a name to a character Rhys intended to be nameless.

7. *Jean Rhys's Historical Imagination: Reading and Writing the Creole* by Veronica Marie Gregg and *Jean Rhys at "World's End": Novels of Colonial and Sexual Exile* by Mary Lou Emery are exemplary texts that explore the fluidity of Jean Rhys's transcultural and transnational West Indian consciousness.

3. Refusing to Live on Scent

1. The narrative is a fictional memoir as a witness to history. It could have belonged to Mary Magdalene of St. Thomas, a Moravian African slave who communicated with the Queen of Denmark in 1739. It is written in the style of the eighteenth-century Moravian religious vernacular which I gleaned from the periodicals of the United Brethren. At that time in the Danish West Indies, the written language could have been German, Dutch, or Danish Creole. The original letter is in Creole Dutch—what was known as Danish Creole as I explain in the text. A "single sister" (an unmarried Moravian woman) most likely would have been with Mary Magdalene as she wrote her narrative. Narratives and letters were published in Moravian periodicals and circulated to their communities in Indonesia, South Africa, North America, the West Indies, and Europe. For additional information on Moravian missionary texts and writings, see C. G. A. Oldendorp, *History of the Mission of the Evangelical Brethren on the Caribbean Islands of St. Thomas, St. Croix, and St. John*, and John Holmes, *Historical Sketches of the Missions of the United Brethren*. See Appendix B for the narrative that was signed by Mary Magdalene. See also Jon J. Sensbach's *A Separate Caanan*, an illuminating study of "Afro-Moravians" in North Carolina during the late eighteenth and early nineteenth centuries. I would like to express my gratitude to my longtime friend and colleague Angelo Costanzo who first shared with me the references leading to the African Moravian writings.

2. From 1730–1746, Christian VI (1699–1746) was the Danish king. He was married to Sofie Magdalene of Brandenburg-Kulmbach-Bayreuth (1700–1770). Perhaps Mary Magdalene knew that the Danish queen shared her name.

3. For an excellent and detailed historical account of the Danish colonial presence in the Caribbean, see Neville A. T. Hall's *Slave Society in the Danish West Indies: St. Thomas, St. John, and St. Croix.*

4. The narrative is important because it demonstrates an interesting and rarely recorded occurrence among early African slaves in the Americas. In the United Brethren communities, many slaves who converted became literate under the auspices of the missionaries. Some were manumitted and were allowed to legally marry Europeans. Some of the African Moravians traveled to Europe and Africa as missionaries.

5. See Geoffrey Parrinder, *African Mythology*, 23. In *Flash of the Spirit*, Robert Farris Thompson writes, "the highest deity of the Fon, Mawu-Lisa, combines female (Mawu) and male (Lisa) valences.... Their union represents a Fon ideal" (176).

6. In Maryse Condé's short story "Three Women in Manhattan," one of the characters reminisces how writing is like a "secret and remarkable alchemy.... What magic! These series of arabesques symbolized a thought, communicated an element of the imaginary which, through them, was more penetrating than reality" (59).

7. Another woman, Magdalene Beulah Brockden (1731–1820), was also born in Popo and was taken as a slave to Bethlehem, Pennsylvania. From her memoir, we learn about her life as a slave. She wrote that, as a young girl, she had no interest in seeking freedom in the religious community (the United Brethren in Bethlehem) her master wanted to send her to. She wrote, "I had no desire to do so, I asked him [her owner] rather to sell me to someone else, for at that time I still loved the world and desired to enjoy it fully" (from Katherine M. Faull, *Moravian Women's Memoirs: Their Related Lives, 1750–1820*, 78). I reiterate how important it is to find these pieces of artifacts that provide the perspectives of the individuals themselves, not because literacy proves their humanity, but because it demonstrates to us their tenacity for finding ways to affirm life. Magdalene of St. Thomas's narrative predates Magdalene Beulah Brockden's by sixteen years. Their lives are related not only through their position as slave women in the New World but also through their beliefs as Moravians, through their ironic *status* as literate slaves and ultimately through their birth origins in Popo, West Africa. It is my pleasure to thank Katherine Faull for discussing with me the extensive research on Magdalene Beulah Brockden that she conducted at the Moravian Archives in Bethlehem, Pennsylvania (telephone communication on 15 May 1998). We both are fascinated with the similarities between the two Magdalenes. African Moravian women were commonly renamed Mary Magdalene when they were baptized in the church. In the New Testament "Mary of Magdala" is "converted from a life of wantonness... to the contemplative friend of God" (Cunningham, 40).

8. Other levels of freedom affect gender and its relationship to literacy in this context. Because they could read and write, many slaves were able to escape into legal freedom. Freedom was both a concept (ideology) and a sought after logistical reality (escape). Being able to write, however, was not just a matter of schooling; it also encoded citizenship in humanity. In her escape to freedom, the disguised Ellen Craft (see chapter 1) could pass for white as a southern gentleman traveling with his slave valet (her dark-complexioned husband). But gentlemen can write, and Ellen

could not. The Crafts had to find a convincing reason for Ellen's "handicap." The Crafts knew that their ruse could only work if they could hide the fact that she could not write. They conquered the problem by bandaging her writing hand and pretending that it had been temporarily disabled. Through the illusion of writing, they escape. During slavery, writing would remain a significant asset for maintaining the ideology of freedom. After the abolition of slavery and continuing into the twentieth century, freedom and literacy would convey issues of civil rights, voting, and equal opportunity within the nation and human rights within the solidarity of disenfranchised peoples of the world. The twenty-first century begins with African Americans questioning and challenging the meaning of freedom as they revisit history through issues of reparation. See Randall Robinson's *The Debt: What America Owes to Blacks*.

9. In "The Path of the Leopard: Motherhood and Majesty in Early Danhome," Suzanne Preston Blier offers further insight into an ethnographic construct of memory and history among the Fon of the ancient West African kingdom of Abomey: "History was of critical importance in ancient Danhome.... Adding to this sense of the primacy of history, there is a tradition in [Dahomey, or the present-day Republic of Benin] of memorializing key figures of the past through named place-holders, that is persons... who assume the names, identities, homes and histories of an individual from an earlier era, promoting through this means the memories of those of the past into the present" (391).

10. Jean Bernabé, Patrick Chamoiseau, and Raphaël Confiant, *Éloge de la créolité*; and *Lettres créoles: tracées antillaises et continentales de la littérature: Haiti, Guadeloupe, Martinique, Guyane, 1635–1975* by Patrick Chamoiseau and Raphaël Confiant.

11. In their essay "Shadowboxing in the Mangrove," Richard Price and Sally Price present an interesting discussion about *créolité* and its contemporary context and social text. They discuss how contemporary francophone women writers are "silenced and erased" by the dominating male *créolists*, not only in their (the male critics) theorizing about *créolité*, but in practical erasure as well. Decidedly, such gross omission "impoverishes... interpretations of both the Antillean past and present" (19).

12. In her essay "Les femmes au travail dans *Lettres á une noire*," Annabelle Rea explores the importance of fiction as autobiographical voice in Françoise Ega's novel *Lettres á une noire*, in which Caribbean women of color working as domestics in France empower themselves through self-definition that is expressed through writing.

13. "Learnings" are enabling lessons of experience that allow reflection and provide meaningful guidance.

14. The English title of the novel is *The Bridge of Beyond*, which places emphasis on the mysticism of place (isolation) rather than on the memory sites of adversity and nourishment (rain and wind as an extended metaphor). From here on the text will be referred to as *Pluie et vent* with subsequent page references cited in the text and corresponding page numbers of the English edition, *The Bridge of Beyond*.

15. Maryse Condé, *La parole des femmes*, 15.

16. Christiane Ndiaye, *Danses de la Parole*, 22. For further discussions on the empowering aspects of language and character in *Pluie et vent*, see also Kathleen Gyssels's essay "Dans la toile d'araignée: Conversations entre maître et esclave dans *Pluie et vent sur Télumée Miracle*."

4. Crossing Bridges and Memory-Telling

1. The *signares* were a wealthy class of African-European women who were usually mistresses of Europeans. They juxtaposed glamorous living with the decadence of human suffering that they commodified. Adam Jones points out that "the British called them mulatresses, while Dutch documents usually refer to them as *tapoeyerinnen*" (102), in "Female Slave-Owners on the Gold Coast: Just a Matter of Money?" *Signare Anna, ou Le Voyage aux escales* by Tita Mandeleau is a novel that illustrates the historic roles of these female entrepreneurs.

2. Zora Neale Hurston, *Their Eyes Were Watching God*, 21.

3. This twentieth-century ceremony continued with possibilities for retribution: "The English must bring guns. The Portuguese must bring powder. The Spaniards must bring the small stones which give fire to our fire-sticks" (Herskovits, "Footnote to the History of Negro Slaving" 87). Herskovits also viewed the chant as an oral *mémoire*—a distinct selection of oral literature.

4. Mariama Bâ, *Une si longue lettre* (Dakar: Les Nouvelles Éditions Africaines, 1980) and *So Long a Letter,* trans. Modupé Bodé-Thomas (London: Heinemann, 1989). The title will be abbreviated as *Lettre.* Subsequent page references in the text will refer to the French and English editions.

5. "Let us remember ... all poets and readers of poetry ... because if for decades poetry has no longer been about explaining the world, but about transforming it for the wellbeing of everybody, today we can no longer simply write about everyday life and read poetry, we must turn all movements into poetry" (René Depestre, "Réponse à Aimé Césaire," 61).

6. Page references in the text will be for the French and English editions, respectively.

7. Sylvia Washington Bâ has observed that early publicity for *Une si longue lettre,* on both sides of the Atlantic, often showed a woman's hand holding a pen poised over a sheet of writing paper ("Mariama Bâ and Toni Morrison: Voices Unveiled, Unhushed, and Otherwise Underground," a presentation at the University of Minnesota, 22 September 1999).

8. At her age Ramatoulaye can be perimenopausal or menopausal. In this context I'm using the term menopause to describe the physiological life passage of women and as a metaphor for gender-oriented middle-age empowerment. Comparative medical studies indicate, "The average age of onset of menopause is 50 years (range: 37–56). ... Menopause is completed after one year of amenorrhea, normally by 55 years of age"(Hafez 215). In Western countries the median age of menopause for women is between 49 and 51 years (Gosden 10).

9. Some of the physiological changes that cause hot flashes and other physical discomforts occur more often among women in industrial societies: "The few existing data on menopausal experiences of women in non-Western cultures suggest that menopausal women in Western cultures report more symptoms than women in non-Western cultures. In the cross-cultural literature, the rarity or complete absence of menopausal symptoms in non-Western cultures was thought to be due to the fact that menopause precipitates a positive role change for women in these cultures" (Beyene 127). See also Judith Brown, "Cross-cultural Perspectives on Middle-Aged Women"; Jane B. Lancaster and Barbara J. King, "An Evolutionary

Perspective on Menopause"; and Abdoulaye Bara Diop, *La famille wolof: tradition et changement.* Studies done in other areas of Africa find that women have similar experiences of menopause cross-culturally. For example, in Zimbabwe, "women's experiences of menopause were not regarded as distressing and were interpreted as a normal stage in the life cycle.... Particular cultural beliefs are described which impact on women's understandings and reactions to the menopause" (McMaster et al. 1).

10. In his essay "Postscripts: Mariama Bâ, Epistolarity, Menopause, and Post-coloniality," Keith L. Walker aligns menopause with the political narrative of colonial independence. The Western perspective on menopause is very different from the way non-Western cultures generally view female menopause. Although Walker recognizes that Bâ refuses to allow menopause to "disable" Ramatoulaye, he does not accentuate the fact that non-Western women view menopause differently. In this instance, he imposes the Western model that doesn't accurately describe the non-Western reality.

11. Ruth Perry's *Women, Letters, and the Novel* analyzes the relationship between epistolary writing and women's culture in eighteenth-century England.

12. For example, in Andrée Blouin's autobiography *My Country, Africa,* Blouin's mother is a dubious African woman who indiscriminately clings to European values and ways of being through the Frenchman who fathered her daughter.

13. I interchange the terms female genital mutilation (FGM) and female genital cutting. What term should be used? Mutilation? Circumcision? Infibulation? Clitoridectomy? Cutting? Fauziya Kassindja, an African woman from Togo, maintains that the practice of FGM is "horrific," and thus she fled from her country because she didn't want to be a victim of the surgery. Others refer to the practice as "female surgeries" because this term addresses the different kinds of female cutting that occur globally. "Female cutting" is a euphemism that historicizes and problematizes the reality of the practice, which is both a human rights issue and a women's health issue. With her film *Warrior Marks,* Alice Walker may have adversely affected cross-cultural debates about the practice between African women and women in Western societies, but debate and discussions have been started in the consciousness of the women who are directly affected.

14. During my fieldwork in the Republic of Benin, I met an educated, modern Beninoise who was in her mid-thirties and had never married. She had an affair with a married man and a child resulted from their relationship. This woman was not in an official polygamous relationship with the father of her six-year-old daughter. In fact, they were no longer lovers. Because of the child, however, she would always be the "other woman" and she accepted that relationship because, as she told me, "I had to have a child and having an affair with a married man did not matter." Does his wife know? "She knows [the woman shrugged her shoulders] but what can she do?" She concluded by saying, "I could not [shaking her head gravely], could never go without having a child during my life [she smiled as her young daughter skipped into the room, and she folded the child in her arms]. I had to have a child." This response reflects the still prevalent attitude among women across the cultural and economic spectrum in many African cultures. Note a difference in the context of mothering and tradition: these women are not having children to please a male partner or to continue his lineage. They define mothering as a site of their own valued, self-reliant, and empowering modality.

15. The term "levirate" means "husband's brother." This practice, which occurs among African Muslims as well as among animists and Christians, specifies that a man's widow must marry one of his surviving brothers, usually in order to continue the relationship between their respective lineages and to ensure economic welfare for the widow and children. Despite its lingering continuity, the practice "has been often opposed by Christian churches because it tends to put widows into polygynous marriages, since inheritors often have at least one wife already.... It has also come under attack from colonial and modern marriage laws aimed at promoting the conjugal unit over lineages." (Cattell 75). African women are beginning to reject the practice of widow inheritance because, as a Kenyan woman says, "It is useless, completely useless!... We are all working hard and all surviving. So inheritance is useless" (Cattell 96).

16. Société Africaine de Culture, "La civilisation de la femme dans la tradition Africaine." Abidjan, 3–8 July 1972.

17. According to Judith Brown, who bases her model on the work of Andrei Simic, "Intermediate societies are those in which modernization is occurring, yet many elements of traditional life persist" ("Lives of Middle-Aged Women" 27). See also Barbara G. Myerhoff and Andrei Simic, eds., *Life's Career—Aging: Cultural Variations on Growing Old.*

5. From a Lineage of Southern Women

1. Some Hurston readers focus on her depiction of colorism in African American communities, in which fair complexions are more privileged. Although Janie does not view herself as privileged because of her fair complexion, some of the townspeople do. Hurston portrays colorism as a debilitating prejudice within black communities.

2. For a comprehensive analysis on the sermon and text reading of Hurston's *Their Eyes Were Watching God,* see Nellie McKay's "'Crayon Enlargements of Life': Zora Neale Hurston's *Their Eyes Were Watching God* as Autobiography." For additional reading on *testimonio,* see René Jara and Hernán Vidal, ed., *Testimonio y literatura* and Margaret Randall, *Cuban Women Now.*

3. Shields Family papers. Clarksville, Virginia. Subsequent excerpts are from these papers.

4. I recently learned that one of my female relatives is a U.S. postmaster in Virginia. Such an achievement, when we know about the past, is remarkable and empowering.

5. Personal communication.

6. Grace Nichols's poem "I Is a Long Memoried Woman" celebrates women across the cultures of the African diaspora.

Bibliography

Abrahams, Roger D. *Singing the Master: The Emergence of African American Culture in the Plantation South.* New York: Pantheon Books, 1992.

Achebe, Chinua. *Things Fall Apart.* African Writers Series. London: Heinemann, 1958.

Adisa, Opal Palmer. "She Scrape She Knee: The Theme of My Work." In *Caribbean Women Writers: Essays From the First International Conference,* ed. Selwyn Cudjoe. Wellesley, Mass.: Calaloux Publications, 1990. 145–50.

Adjaye, Joseph K., ed. *Time in the Black Experience.* Westport, Conn.: Greenwood Press, 1994.

Ako, Edward, ed. *On the Road to Guinea: Essays in Black Comparative Literature.* Yaoundé, Cameroon: Yaoundé University, 1992.

Alexander, G. W. *Letters on the Emancipation with a Reply to Objections Made to the Liberation of the Slaves in the Spanish Colonies addressed to Friends on the Continent of Europe.* 1842. New York: Negro Universities Press, 1969.

Alexander, Simone A. James. *Mother Imagery in the Novels of Afro-Caribbean Women.* Columbia: University of Missouri Press, 2001.

Angelou, Maya. *I Know Why the Caged Bird Sings.* New York: Random House, 1969.

———. *Wouldn't Take Nothing for My Journey Now.* New York: Random House, 1993.

Archivo de Cuba Nacional. *Representación extendida por Don Diego Miguel de Moya y firmada por casi todos los dueños de ingenios de la jurisdicción, en enero 19 de 1790. Real Consulado, 150/7405.* La Habana, 1790.

Armah, Ayi Kwei. *Fragments.* Boston: Houghton Mifflin, 1970.

Arnold, A. James. "The Gendering of Créolité: The Erotics of Colonialism." In *Penser la créolité,* ed. Maryse Condé and Madeleine Cottenet-Hage. Paris: Éditions Karthala, 1995. 21–40.

———, ed. *A History of Literature in the Caribbean: Hispanic and Francophone Regions.* Amsterdam: John Benjamins, 1994.

Arnott, Margaret L., ed. *Gastronomy: The Anthropology of Food and Food Habits.* The Hague: Mouton, 1976.

Atwood, Margaret. "Haunted by Their Nightmares." *New York Times Book Review* (13 September 1987): 631–33.

Bâ, Mariama. *Un chant écarlate*. Dakar: Nouvelles Éditions Africaines, 1981.

———. *Une si longue lettre*. Dakar: Nouvelles Éditions Africaines, 1980.

———. *So Long a Letter*. Trans. Modupé Bodé-Thomas. London: Heinemann, 1989.

Bachelard, Gaston. *The Poetics of Space*. Boston: Beacon Press, 1958.

Baker-Fletcher, Karen. "Fierce Love Comes to Haunt." *Commonwealth* 6 (1987): 631–33.

Balutansky, Kathleen M. "Créolité in Question: Caliban in Maryse Condé's *Traverseé de la Mangrove*." In *Penser la créolité*, ed. Maryse Condé and Madeleine Cottenet-Hage. Paris: Éditions Karthala, 1992. 101–11.

Bancroft, Frederic. *Slave Trading in the Old South*. New York: Frederick Ungar, 1931.

Bastide, Roger. *The African Religions of Brazil: Toward a Sociology of the Interpenetration of Civilizations*. Trans. Helen Sebba. Baltimore: Johns Hopkins University Press, 1960.

Beauvue-Fougeyrollas, Claudie. *Les femmes antillaises*. Paris: L'Harmattan, 1979.

Bébel-Gisler, Dany. *Léonora: L'histoire enfouie de la Guadeloupe*. Paris: Editions Seghers, 1985.

———. *Leonora: The Buried Story of Guadeloupe*. Trans. Andrea Leskes. Charlottesville: University of Virginia Press, 1994.

Beckles, Hilary. *Afro-Caribbean Women and Resistance of Slavery in Barbados*. London: Karnak House, 1988.

Beckles, Hilary McD. *Natural Rebels: A Social History of Enslaved Black Women in Barbados*. New Brunswick, N.J.: Rutgers State University Press, 1989.

Bell, Roseann P., Bettye J. Parker, and Beverly Guy-Sheftall, eds. *Sturdy Black Bridges: Visions of Black Women in Literature*. New York: Anchor Books, 1979.

Bell-Scott, Patricia, et al. *Double Stitch: Black Women Write About Mothers and Daughters*. Boston: Beacon Press, 1991.

Benítez-Rojo, Antonio. *The Repeating Island: The Caribbean and the Postmodern Perspective*. Trans. James Maraniss. Durham: Duke University Press, 1992.

Bernabé, Jean. "Le travail de l'écriture chez Simone Schwarz-Bart." *Présence Africaine* 121/122 (1982): 176–79.

Bernabé, Jean, Patrick Chamoiseau, and Raphaël Confiant. *Éloge de la créolité (In Praise of Creoleness)*. Trans. M. B. Taleb-Khyar. Paris: Gallimard, 1993.

Beverley, John. "The Margin at the Center: On *Testimonio*." In *De/Colonizing the Subject: The Politics of Gender in Women's Autobiography*, ed. Sidonie Smith and Julia Watson. Minneapolis: University of Minnesota Press, 1992. 91–114.

Beyene, Yewoubdar. *From Menarche to Menopause: Reproductive Lives of Peasant Women in Two Cultures*. Albany: State University of New York Press, 1989.

Birchfield, James D., Albert Boime, and William J. Hennessey. *Noble, Thomas 1835–1907*. Lexington: University of Kentucky Art Museum, 1988.

Blanchard, Peter. *Slavery and Abolition in Early Republican Peru*. Wilmington, Delaware: Scholarly Resources, 1992.

Bleser, Carol, ed. *The Diaries of James Henry Hammond, a Southern Slaveholder*. New York: Oxford University Press, 1988.

Blier, Suzanne Preston. "The Path of the Leopard: Motherhood and Majesty in Early Danhome." *The Journal of African History* 37 no. 3 (1995): 391–417.

Blouin, Andrée, in collaboration with Jean MacKellar. *My Country, Africa: Autobiography of the Black Pasionaria*. New York: Praeger, 1983.

Bohannan, Paul. "Theories of Homicide and Suicide." In *African Homicide and Suicide,* ed. Paul Bohannan. Princeton: Princeton University Press, 1980. 3–29.

———, ed. *African Homicide and Suicide.* Princeton: Princeton University Press, 1980.

Bohannan, Paul and Laura. "The Place of Swende in Relation to Other Matters." In *A Source Book on Tiv Religion.* Vol 3. New Haven, Conn.: Human Relations Area Files, c1969. 405.

Boilat, Abbé P. D. *Senegalese Sketches.* Human Relations Area Files. Paris: P. Bertrand, Libraire-Éditeur, 1853. n. p.

Boomert, Arie. "Island Carib Archaeology." In *Wolves from the Sea,* ed. Neil Whitehead. Leiden, Netherlands: KLITV Press, 1995. 23–35.

Bossis, Mireille. "Men/Women of Letters." *Yale French Studies* 71 (1986): 1–14.

———. "Methodological Journeys Through Correspondences." *Yale French Studies* 71 (1986): 63–75.

Botkin, B. A., ed. *Lay My Burden Down: A Folk History of Slavery.* Athens: University of Georgia Press, 1945.

Bouvard, Marguerite Guzman. *Revolutionizing Motherhood: The Mothers of the Plaza de Mayo.* Wilmington, Del.: Scholarly Resources, 1994.

Brand, Dionne. "Photograph." In *Her True-True Name: Anthology of Women's Writing from the Caribbean,* ed. Pamela Mordecai and Elizabeth Wilson. London: Heineman, 1989. 179–82.

Brathwaite, Edward Kamau. *The Arrivants: A New World Trilogy.* London: Oxford University Press, 1973.

———. *The Folk Culture of the Slaves in Jamaica.* London: New Beacon Books, 1971.

———. *Wars of Respect: Nanny and Sam Sharpe.* Kingston: Agency for Public Information, 1976.

Breinburg, Petronella. *Legends of Suriname.* London: New Beacon Books Ltd., 1971.

Brewer, Mason J. *American Negro Folklore.* Chicago: Quadrangle Books, 1968.

Brodzki, Bella. "Nomadism and the Textualization of Memory in André Schwarz-Bart's *La Mulâtresse Solitude.*" *Yale French Studies* 83 (1993): 213–30.

Brontë, Charlotte. *Jane Eyre.* London: Oxford University Press, 1848.

Brown, Judith K. "Cross-cultural Perspectives on Middle-Aged Women." *Current Anthropology* 23 no. 2 (1982): 143–56.

———. "Lives of Middle-Aged Women." In *In Her Prime,* ed. Virginia Kerns and Judith K. Brown. 17–30.

Brown, Sterling A. "Negro Characters As Seen by White Authors." *Journal of Negro Education* 2 (1933): 179–203.

Bruner, Charlotte H., ed. *Unwinding Threads: Writing by Women in Africa.* London: Heinemann, 1983.

Buchner, J. H. *The Moravians in Jamaica: History of the Mission of the United Brethren's Church to the Negroes in the Island of Jamaica, from the Year 1754–1854.* London: Longman & Co., 1854.

Bueno, Salvador, ed. *Introducción a la cultura africana en América Latina.* Paris: UNESCO, 1979.

Bugul, Ken. *The Abandoned Baobab: The Autobiography of a Senegalese Woman.* Trans. Marjoliyn de Jager. New York: Lawrence Hill Books, 1991. Originally published as *Le baobab fou* (Dakar: NEA, 1983).

Bush, Barbara. *Slave Women in Caribbean Society, 1650–1838.* London: James Curry Ltd., 1990.

Caminero-Santangelo, Marta. *The Madwoman Can't Speak, or Why Insanity Is Not Subversive.* Ithaca: Cornell University Press, 1998.

Campbell, Mavis. "Marronage in Jamaica: Its Origins in the Seventeenth Century." *Annals New York Academy of Sciences* 292 (1977): 389–419.

Casey, Ethan. "Remembering Haiti." *Callaloo* 18 no. 2 (1995): 524–26.

Castillo Bueno, Maria de los Reyes. *Reyita: The Life of a Black Cuban Woman in the Twentieth Century.* As told to Daisy Rubiera Castillo. Intro. Elizabeth Dore. Trans. Anne McLean. Durham, N.C.: Duke University Press, 2000.

Cattell, Maria G. "African Widows, Culture and Social Change: Case Studies from Kenya." In *The Cultural Context of Aging: Worldwide Perspectives,* ed. Jay Sokolovsky. Westport, Conn.: Bergin & Garvey, 1997. 71–98.

Césaire, Aimé. *Cahier d'un retour au pays natal.* 1939. Paris: Présence Africaine, 1971.

Chamoiseau, Patrick, and Raphaël Confiant. *Lettres créoles: tracées antillaises et continentales de la littérature: Haiti, Guadeloupe, Martinique, Guyane, 1635–1975.* Paris: Hatier, 1991.

Chancy, Myriam J. A. *Framing Silence: Revolutionary Novels by Haitian Women.* New Brunswick, N.J.: Rutgers University Press, 1997.

Charles, Jeannette. "Leh We Talk See." In *Caribbean Women Writers,* ed. Selwyn Cudjoe. Wellesly, Mass.: Calaloux Publications, 1990. 269–72.

Charlier, Ghislaine. *Mémoire d'une affranchie.* Montréal: Lemeac, 1989.

Chase, S. P. Letter to E. L. Pierce, 24 January 1864. Samuel Chase Papers. Library Company of Philadelphia, Pennsylvania.

Chinosole. "Audre Lorde and Matrilineal Diaspora: 'Moving history beyond nightmare into structures for the future...'" In *Wild Women in the Whirlwind: Afra-American Culture and the Contemporary Literary Renaissance,* ed. Joanne M. Braxton and Andrée Nicola McLaughlin. New Brunswick, N.J.: Rutgers University Press, 1990. 379–94.

Chodorow, Nancy. *The Reproduction of Mothering: Psychoanalysis and the Sociology of Gender.* Berkeley: University of California Press, 1978.

Chopin, Kate. *The Awakening.* New York: Putnam, 1964.

Chronicle of Higher Education. (10 May 1998): 10. "Letter Reveals Jefferson's Views on Slavery."

Clark, Edith. *My Mother Who Fathered Me: A Study of the Family in Three Selected Communities in Jamaica.* London: Allen & Unwin, 1957.

Clemons, Walter. "A Gravestone of Memories." *Newsweek.* 28 September 1987: 74–75.

Cliff, Michelle. *Abeng.* New York: The Crossing Press/Trumansburg, 1984.

———. "Clare Savage as a Crossroads Character." In *Caribbean Women Writers: Essays From the First International Conference,* ed. Selwyn Cudjoe, 263–68. Wellesly, Mass.: Calaloux Publications, 1990.

———. "Women Warriors: Black Writers Load the Canon." *Voice Literary Supplement.* May 1990: 20–23.

Coffin, Levi. *Reminiscences of Levi Coffin.* 1898. New York: Arno Press, 1968.

Cohen, Ronald. *Dominance and Defiance: A Study of Marital Instability in an Islamic African Society.* Washington, D.C.: American Anthropological Society, 1971.

Cole, Johnnetta B. "Preface." In *Double Stitch: Black Women Write About Mothers and Daughters,* ed. Patricia Bell-Scott et al. New York: HarperPerennial, 1993. xiii–xv.

Collins, Patricia Hill. *Black Feminist Thought: Knowledge, Consciousness, and the Politics of Empowerment.* New York: Routledge, 1991.

————. "The Meaning of Motherhood in Black Culture and Black Mother-Daughter Relationships." In *Double-Stitch: Black Women Write About Mothers and Daughters*, ed. Patricia Bell-Scott et al. 42–60.

Condé, Maryse. "Chercher nos vérités." In *Penser la créolité*, ed. Maryse Condé and Madeleine Cottenet-Hage. Paris: Éditions Karthala, 1995. 305–10.

————. *La parole des femmes: essai sur des romancières des Antilles de langue fran-çaise*. Paris: Editions L'harmattan, 1979.

————. *The Last of the African Kings*. Trans. Richard Philcox. Lincoln: University of Nebraska Press, 1997.

————. *Les derniers rois mages*. Paris: Éditions Mércure de France, 1992.

————. "Three Women in Manhattan." In *Green Cane and Juicy Flotsam: Short Stories by Caribbean Women*, ed. Lizabeth Paravisini-Gebert and Carmen Esteves. New Brunswick, N.J.: Rutgers University Press, 1991. 56–67.

Condé, Maryse, and Madeleine Cottenet-Hage, eds. *Penser la créolité*. Paris: Éditions Karthala, 1995.

Conrad, Robert Edgar. *Children of God's Fire: A Documentary History of Black Slavery in Brazil*. Princeton: Princeton University Press, 1983.

Cooper, J. California. *A Piece of Mine*. Navarro, Calif.: Wild Trees Press, 1984.

Cowley, Malcolm, ed. *Being A True Account of the Life of Captain Theodore Canot, Trader in Gold, Ivory, and Slaves on the Coast of Guinea: His Own Story as Told in the Year 1854 to Brantz Mayer*. 1854. New York: Albert & Charles Boni, 1928.

Craton, Michael. *Searching for the Invisible Man: Slaves and Plantation Life in Jamaica*. Cambridge: Harvard University Press, 1978.

Cudjoe, Selwyn. *Resistance and Caribbean Literature*. Athens: Ohio University Press, 1980.

————, ed. *Caribbean Women Writers: Essays From the First International Conference*. Wellesley, Mass.: Calaloux Publications, 1990.

Cunard, Nancy. *Negro Anthology*. 1934. New York: Negro Universities Press, 1969.

Cunningham, Lawrence S. "Women and Spirituality." *Commonweal* 121 no. 19 (4 November 1994): 38–41.

Dadzie, Stella. "Searching for the Invisible Woman: Slavery and Resistance in Jamaica." *Race and Class* 32 no. 2 (1990): 21–38.

Dallas, R. C. *The History of the Maroons*. London: T. N. Longman and O. Rees, 1803.

d'Almeida, Irène Assiba. "The Concept of Choice in Mariama Bâ's Fiction." In *Ngambika: Studies of Women in African Literature*, ed. Carol Boyce Davies and Anne Adams Graves. Trenton, N.J.: Africa World Press, 1986. 161–71.

————. *Francophone African Women Writers: Destroying the Emptiness of Silence*. Gainesville: University Press of Florida, 1994.

Dance, Daryl C. *Folklore from Contemporary Jamaicans*. Knoxville: University of Tennessee Press, 1985.

Danticat, Edwidge. *Breath, Eyes, Memory*. New York: Soho Press, 1994.

Dash, Julie. *Daughters of the Dust*. New York: Kino Video, 1992.

Davies, Carole Boyce. *Black Women, Writing, and Identity: Migrations of the Subject*. London: Routledge, 1994.

————. "Collaboration and the Ordering Imperative in Life Story." In *De/Colonizing the Subject: The Politics of Gender in Women's Autobiography*, ed. Sidonie Smith and Julia Watson. Minneapolis: University of Minnesota Press, 1992. 3–19.

Davies, Carole Boyce, and Anne Adams Graves, eds. *Ngambika: Studies of Women in African Literature.* Trenton, N.J.: Africa World Press, 1986.

Davies, Carole Boyce, and Elaine Savory Fido, eds. *Out of the Kumbla: Caribbean Women and Literature.* Trenton, N.J.: Africa World Press, 1990.

Davis, Angela. "Reflections on the Black Woman's Role in the Community of Slaves." *The Black Scholar.* 3:4 (1971): 2–15.

Davis, Darién J., ed. *Slavery and Beyond: The African Impact on Latin America and the Caribbean.* Wilmington, N.C.: Scholarly Resources, 1995.

Dayan, Joan. "Codes of Law and Bodies of Color." In *Penser la créolité,* ed. Maryse Condé and Madeleine Cottenet-Hage. Paris: Éditions Karthala, 1992. 41–67.

D'Costa, Jean. "Jean Rhys 1890–1979." In *Fifty Caribbean Writers,* ed. Daryl Dance. New York: Greenwood Press, 1986. 390–404.

D'Costa, Jean, and Barbara Lalla, eds. *Voices in Exile: Jamaican Texts of the 18th and 19th Centuries.* Tuscaloosa: University of Alabama Press, 1989.

de Abruna, Laura Niesen. "Twentieth-Century Women Writers from the English-Speaking Caribbean." In *Caribbean Women Writers: Essays From the First International Conference,* ed. Selwyn Cudjoe 1990. 86–97.

de Barros Mott, Maria Lucia. *Submissão e Resistência: A Mulher na luta contra a escravidão.* São Paulo, Brazil: Editora Pinsky Ltda, 1988.

Debbash, Yvan. "Le marronage: Essai sur la désertion de l'esclave antillais." *L'Année Sociologique* (1961): 1–112.

de Beaumont, Gustave. *Marie, or Slavery in the United States.* 1835. Trans. Barbara Chapman. Stanford: Stanford University Press, 1958.

Debien, G. "Le marronage aux Antilles Françaises au XVIII° siecle." *Caribbean Studies* 6 no. 3 (1966): 3–43.

de Groot, Silvia W. "Maroon Women as Ancestors, Priests, and Mediums in Surinam." *Slavery and Abolition* 7 no. 2 (1986): 160–74.

De Jesus, Carolina Maria. *Child of the Dark: The Diary of Carolina Maria De Jesus.* Trans. David St. Clair. New York: E. P. Dutton, 1962.

Depestre, René. "Réponse à Aimé Césaire." *Présence Africaine* 4 Octobre/Novembre (1955): 42–62.

DeShazer, Mary K. *Inspiring Women: Reimagining the Muse.* New York: Pergamon Press, 1986.

DeVeaux, Alexis. "Paule Marshall: In Celebration of Our Triumph." *Essence.* May 1971: 96.

Dia, Alioune Touré. "Succès littéraire de Mariama Bâ pour son livre *Une si longue lettre.*" *Amina.* November 1979: 12–14.

Diallo, Nafissatou. *A Dakar Childhood.* Trans. Dorothy S. Blair. Essex: Longman, 1982.

———. *De Tilène au Plateau: une enfance dakaroise.* Dakar: Nouvelles Éditions Africaines, 1975.

Diop, Abdoulaye Bara. *La famille wolof: tradition et changement.* Paris: Éditions Karthala, 1985.

Dominey, Craig. "Ibo Landing." *The Moonlit Road* http://www.themoonlitroad.com/ibo/ibo_cbg001.html (1998): 1–6.

Donnan, Elizabeth. *Documents Illustrative of the History of the Slave Trade to America.* Vol. II. Washington, D.C.: Carnegie Institution of Washington, 1931.

Dorson, Richard, ed. *American Negro Folktales.* Greenwich, Conn.: Fawcett, 1956.

Douglas, Marcia. *Madame Fate*. New York: Soho Press, 1999.

Douglass, Frederick. *The Narrative of the Life of Frederick Douglass*. 1845. Cambridge, Mass.: Belknap Press, 1960.

DuCille, Ann. "Postcolonialism and Afrocentricity: Discourse and Dat Course." In *The Black Columbiad: Defining Moments in African American Literature and Culture*, ed. Werner Sollors and Maria Diedrich. Cambridge, Mass.: Harvard University Press, 1994. 28–41.

Duchêne, Roger. *Madame de Sévigné ou la chance d'être femme*. Paris: Fayard, 1982.

Durkheim, Émile. *Suicide: A Study in Sociology*, ed. George Simpson. Glencoe, Ill.: Free Press, 1951.

Ega, Françoise. *Lettres à une Noire*. Paris: L'Harmattan, 1978.

Eichinger Ferro-Luzzi, Gabriella. "More on Salt Taboos." *Current Anthropology* 19 no. 2 (1978): 412–13.

Eliade, Mircea. *The Sacred and the Profane*. Trans. William R. Trask. New York: Harcourt, Brace & World, 1959.

Emecheta, Buchi. *The Joys of Motherhood*. New York: George Braziller, 1979.

Emery, Mary Lou. *Jean Rhys at "World's End": Novels of Colonial and Sexual Exile*. Austin: University of Texas Press, 1990.

Estés, Clarissa Pinkola. *Women Who Run with the Wolves: Myths and Stories of the Wild Woman Archetype*. New York: Ballantine Books, 1992.

Etter-Lewis, Gwendolyn, and Michele Foster, eds. *Unrelated Kin: Race and Gender in Women's Personal Narratives*. New York: Routledge, 1995.

Evans-Pritchard, E. E. *Witchcraft, Oracles, and Magic among the Azande*. Oxford: The Clarendon Press, 1937.

Fall, Aminata Sow. *La grève des bàttu, ou Les déchets humains*. Dakar: Nouvelles Éditions Africaines, 1979.

Farberow, Norman, ed. *Suicide in Different Cultures*. Baltimore: University Park Press, 1975.

Faull, Katherin Eze. "Self-Encounters: Two Eighteenth-Century African Memoirs from Moravian Bethlehem." In *Crosscurrents: African Americans, Africa and Germany in the Modern World*, ed. David McBride, Leroy Hopkins, et al. Columbia, S.C.: Camden House, 1998.

Faull, Katherine M. *Moravian Women's Memoirs: Their Related Lives, 1750–1820*. New York: Syracuse University Press, 1997.

Felman, Shoshana, and Dori Laub, M.D. *Testimony: Crises of Witnessing in Literature, Psychoanalysis, and History*. New York: Routledge, 1992.

Ferguson, Moira, ed. *The Hart Sisters: Early African Caribbean Writers, Evangelicals, and Radicals*. Lincoln: University of Nebraska Press, 1993.

Fields, Karen. "What One Cannot Remember Mistakenly." In *History and Memory in African-American Culture*, ed. Geneviève Fabre and Robert O'Meally. New York: Oxford University Press, 1994. 150–163.

Forster, Margaret. *Elizabeth Barrett Browning: A Biography*. London: Chatto & Windus, 1988.

Fouchard, Jean. *Les marrons de la liberté*. Paris: L'École, 1972.

Fox-Genovese, Elizabeth. *Unspeakable Things Unspoken: Ghosts and Memories in the Narratives of African American Women*. Elsa Goveia Memorial Lecture. Mona, Jamaica: Department of History, University of the West Indies, 1992.

Frank, Katherine. "Women without Men: The Feminist Novel in Africa." In *Women in African Literature Today,* ed. Eldred Durosimi Jones and Eustace Palmer et al. Trenton, N.J.: Africa World Press, 1987. 14–34.

Gadsby, Meredith. "'I Suck Coarse Salt': Caribbean Women Writers in Canada and the Politics of Transcendence." *Modern Fiction Studies* 44, no. 1 (1998): 144–63.

Galeano, Eduardo. *Las venas abiertas de américa latina.* Madrid: Siglo Veintiuno Editores, 1979.

———. *Open Veins of Latin America: Five Centuries of the Pillage of a Continent.* Trans. Cedric Belfrage. New York: Monthly Review Press, 1973.

Gates, Henry Louis, Jr., ed. *"Race," Writing, and Difference.* Chicago: University of Chicago Press, 1986.

Genovese, Eugene D. *Roll, Jordan, Roll: The World the Slaves Made.* New York: Vintage Books, 1976.

Georgia Writers' Project. *Drums and Shadows: Survival Studies among the Georgia Coastal Negroes.* 1940. New York: Anchor Books, 1972.

Giddens, Anthony. *The Sociology of Suicide: A Selection of Readings.* London: Cass, 1971.

Gilbert, Sandra M., and Susan Gubar. *The Madwoman in the Attic: The Woman Writer and the Nineteenth-Century Literary Imagination.* New Haven: Yale University Press, 1979.

Gilroy, Paul. *Against Race: Imagining Political Culture beyond the Color Line.* Cambridge, Mass.: Harvard University Press, 2000.

Gisler, Antoine. *L'Esclavage aux Antilles Françaises (XVII–XIX siécle): Contribution au problème de l'esclavage.* Paris: Karthala, 1981.

Goodison, Lorna. "For My Mother (May I Inherit Half Her Strength)." In *Jamaica Woman,* ed. Pamela Mordecai and Mervyn Morris. Kingston, Jamaica: Heinemann Educational Books (Caribbean) Ltd., 1980. 34–39.

———. *I Am Becoming My Mother.* London: New Beacon Books, 1986.

Goodwine, Marquetta L., ed. *The Legacy of Ibo Landing: Gullah Roots of African American Culture.* Atlanta: Clarity Press, Inc., 1998.

Gornick, Vivian. "The World and Our Mothers." *New York Times Book Review* 19 November 1987: 52+.

Gosden, R. G. *Biology of Menopause: The Causes and Consequences of Ovarian Aging.* London: Academic Press, 1985.

Goulart, José Alipio. *Da fuga ao suicidio.* Rio de Janeiro: Conquista, 1972.

Graves, Joseph L. *The Emperor's New Clothes: Biological Theories of Race at the Millennium.* New Brunswick, N.J.: Rutgers University Press, 2001.

Gregg, Veronica Marie. *Jean Rhys's Historical Imagination: Reading and Writing the Creole.* Chapel Hill: University of North Carolina Press, 1995.

Griaule, Marcel. *Conversations With Ogotemmêli: An Introduction to Dogon Religious Ideas.* London: Oxford University Press, 1975.

Griffin, Farah Jasmine. "Textual Healing: Claiming Black Women's Bodies: the Erotic and Resistance in Contemporary Novels of Slavery." *Callaloo* 19, no. 2 (1996): 519–36.

Guimarães, Carlos Magno. *Uma Negacão da ordem escravista: Quilombos em Minas Gerais no Século XVIII.* São Paulo: Icone Editora Ltda, 1988.

Gullick, Charles J. M. R. C. "Communicating Caribness." In *Wolves from the Sea,* ed. Neil Whitehead. Leiden, Netherlands: KITLV Press, 1995. 157–70.

Gutiérrez Alea, Tomás. *La Última Cena.* New York: New Yorker Video, 1976.

Gutman, Herbert G. "Slave Culture and Slave Family and Kin Network: The Importance of Time." *South Atlantic Urban Studies* 2 (1978): 73–88.

Gyssels, Kathleen. "Dans la toile d'araignée: conversations entre maître et esclave dans *Pluie et vent sur Télumée Miracle.*" In *Elles écrivent des Antilles,* ed. Suzanne Rinne and Joëlle Vitiello. 145–59.

Hafez, E. S. E. *Human Reproductive Physiology.* Ann Arbor, Mich.: Ann Arbor Science Publishers, 1978.

Hall, Neville A. T. *Slave Society in the Danish West Indies: St. Thomas, St. John, and St. Croix.* Mona, Jamaica: University of the West Indies Press, 1992.

Hamilton, J. Taylor, and Kenneth G. Hamilton. *History of the Moravian Church: Renewed Unitas Fratrum, 1722–1957.* Bethlehem, Pa.: Moravian Church in America, 1967.

Hamilton, Virginia. *The People Could Fly: American Black Folktales.* New York: Alfred A. Knopf, 1985.

Harrell-Bond, Barbara. "Interview: Mariama Bâ." *The African Book Publishing Record* 6 (1980): 209–14.

Harris, Wilson. *The Womb of Space: The Cross-Cultural Imagination.* In *Contributions in Afro-American and African Studies* 73. Westport, Conn.: Greenwood Press, 1983.

Haskell, Francis. *History and Its Images.* New Haven: Yale University Press, 1993.

Head, Bessie. "The Collector of Treasures." In *The Collector of Treasures and Other Botswana Village Tales.* London: Heinemann, 1977. 87–103.

Henderson, Mae. "Speaking in Tongues: Dialogics, Dialectics, and the Black Woman Writer's Literary Tradition." In *Changing Our Own Words,* ed. Cheryl A. Wall. New Brunswick, N.J.: Rutgers University Press, 1989. 16–37.

Henderson, Robert. "The Destiny of America." 36th Annual Green Lake Bahá'í Conference. Green Lake, Wisc.: 1995.

Herskovits, Melville J. *Dahomey: An Ancient Kingdom.* Evanston: Northwestern University Press, 1976.

———. "A Footnote to the History of Negro Slaving." In *The New World Negro,* ed. Frances S. Herskovits. Bloomington: Indiana University Press, 1966. 83–89.

Hoff, Berend J. "Language Contact, War, and Amerindian Historical Tradition: The Special Case of the Island Carib." In *Wolves from the Sea,* ed. Neil L. Whitehead. Leiden, Netherlands: KITLV Press, 1995. 37–59.

Hoffer, Peter C., and N. E. H. Hull. *Murdering Mothers: Infanticide in England and New England 1558–1803.* Linden Studies in Anglo-American Legal History. New York: New York University Press, 1981.

Holmes, John. *Historical Sketches of the Missions of the United Brethren for Propagating the Gospel among the Heathen: From Their Commencement to the Present Time.* Dublin: R. Napper, 1818.

Holy, Ladislav. "Gender and Ritual in an Islamic Society: The Berti of Darfur." *Man* 23, no. 3 (1988): 469–87.

hooks, bell. *Sisters of the Yam: Black Women and Self-Recovery.* Boston: South End Press, 1993.

Horn, Miriam. "Five Years of Terror." *U.S. News and World Report* (103) 1987: 75.

Horvitz, Deborah. "Nameless Ghosts: Possession and Dispossession in *Beloved.*" *Studies in American Fiction* 17, no. 2 (1989): 157–67.

Hughes, Langston, and Arna Bontemps, eds. *The Book of Negro Folklore*. New York: Dodd, Mead, 1958.

Hurston, Zora Neale. *Their Eyes Were Watching God*. 1937. Greenwich, Conn.: Fawcett, 1965.

Iga, Mamoru, and Kichinosuke Tatai. "Characteristics of Suicides and Attitudes toward Suicide in Japan." In *Suicide in Different Cultures*, ed. Norman L. Farberow. Baltimore: University Park Press, 1975. 255–80.

Jacobs, Harriet A. *Incidents in the Life of a Slave Girl: Written by Herself*. 1861. Ed. L. Maria Child. Introduction by Jean Fagan Yellin. Cambridge, Mass.: Harvard University Press, 1987.

Jamaica Archives. "Nanny Land Patent." Land Patent Office, vol. 22, folio 15B, 1741. Spanish Town, Jamaica.

Jara, René, and Hernán Vidal. *Testimonio y literatura*. Edina, Minn.: Society for the Study of Contemporary Hispanic and Lusophone Revolutionary Literatures, 1986.

Johnson, Lemuel. "A-beng: (Re)Calling the Body In(to) Question." In *Out of the Kumbla: Caribbean Women and Literature*, ed. Carole Boyce Davies and Elaine Savory Fido. Trenton, N.J.: Africa World Press, 1990. 111–42.

Johnson, Michael P. "Smothered Slave Infants: Were Slave Mothers at Fault?" *Journal of Southern History* 47 (1981): 493–520.

Jones, Adam. "Female Slave-Owners on the Gold Coast: Just a Matter of Money?" In *Slave Cultures and the Cultures of Slavery*, ed. Stephan Palmié. 100–111.

Jones, Eldred Durosimi, Eustace Palmer, et al. *Women in African Literature Today*. Trenton, N.J.: Africa World Press, 1987.

Jones, Jacqueline. "My Mother Was Much of a Woman: Black Women, Work, and the Family under Slavery." *Feminist Studies* 8 (1982): 235–69.

Joseph, Gloria. "Black Mothers and Daughters: Their Roles and Functions in American Society." In *Common Differences: Conflicts in Black and White Feminist Perspectives*, ed. Gloria Joseph and Jill Lewis. New York: Anchor Press, 1981. 75–126.

Junker, Wilhelm. *Travels in Africa during the Years 1882–1886*. London: Chapman and Hall, 1892.

Kaggwa, Sir Apolo. *The Kings of Buganda*. Trans. Kiwanuka, M. S. M. Nairobi: East African Publishing House, 1971.

Karasch, Mary C. *Slave Life in Rio de Janeiro: 1808–1850*. Princeton: Princeton University Press, 1987.

Kassindja, Fauziya, and Layli Miller Bashir. *Do They Hear You When You Cry?* New York: Doubleday, 1998.

Kaufert, Patricia A., and Margaret Lock. "What Are Women For? Cultural Constructions of Menopausal Women in Japan and Canada." In *In Her Prime*, ed. Virginia Kerns and Judith K. Brown. Chicago: University of Illinois Press, 1992. 201–20.

Kerns, Virginia, and Judith K. Brown, eds. *In Her Prime: New Views of Middle-Aged Women*. Urbana: University of Illinois Press, 1992.

Kincaid, Jamaica. *Annie John*. New York: Farrar, Straus, & Giroux, 1985.

———. *The Autobiography of My Mother*. New York: Farrar, Straus, & Giroux, 1996.

Kolodziej, E., ed. *Histoire de l'esclavage*. Paris: Édition et diffusion de la Culture antillaise, 1984.

Kom, Ambroise, and Lucienne Ngoué, eds. *Le code noir et l'afrique*. Ivry, France: Nouvelles du Sud, 1991.

Kubayanda, Josaphat B. "Minority Discourse and the African Collective: Some Examples from Latin American and Caribbean Literature." *Cultural Critique* 6 (1987): 113–30.

Kupperman, Karen Ordahl. *Providence Island 1630–1641: The Other Puritan Colony.* Cambridge: Cambridge University Press, 1993.

Lacour, M. A. *Histoire de La Guadeloupe.* Vol. III. 1858. Paris: Maisonneuve, 1960.

Lacrosil, Michèle. *Cajou.* Paris: Gallimard, 1961.

Lancaster, Jane B., and Barbara J. King. "An Evolutionary Perspective on Menopause." In *In Her Prime,* ed. Virginia Kerns and Judith K. Brown. Urbana: University of Illinois Press, 1992. 7–16.

Leaming, Hugo Prosper. *Hidden Americans: Maroons of Virginia and the Carolinas.* New York: Garland Publishing, 1995.

Lebsock, Suzanne. "Free Black Women and the Question of Matriarchy: Petersburg, Virginia, 1784–1820." *Feminist Studies* 8 (1982): 271–92.

Lee, Kathy. *Prelude to the Lesser Peace.* Massanetta, Va.: New Era Productions, 26–28 August 1988.

Leigh, Nancy J. "Mirror, Mirror: The Development of Female Identity in Jean Rhys's Fiction." *World Literature Written in English* 25 (1985): 270–85.

Lerner, Gerda. "Women and Slavery." *Slavery and Abolition* 4, no. 3 (1983): 173–98.

Lester, Julius. "People Who Could Fly." *Black Folktales.* New York: Grove Press, 1969. 147–52.

Lionnet, Françoise. *Autobiographical Voices: Race, Gender, Self-Portraiture.* Ithaca: Cornell University Press, 1989.

———. *Postcolonial Representations: Women, Literature, Identity.* Ithaca: Cornell University Press, 1995.

Lipsitz, George. *Time Passages: Collective Memory and American Popular Culture.* Minneapolis: University of Minnesota Press, 1990.

Livermore, Mary. "The Slave Tragedy at Cincinnati." *National Anti-Slavery Standard* 16 February (1856): n.p.

Lovelace, Earl. *Salt.* London: Faber & Faber, 1996.

MacGaffey, Wyatt. "The West in Congolese Experience." In *Africa and the West: Intellectual Responses to European Culture,* ed. Philip D. Curtin. Madison: University of Wisconsin Press, 1972. 49–74.

Madison, D. Soyini, ed. *The Woman That I Am: The Literature and Culture of Contemporary Women of Color.* New York: St. Martin's Press, 1994.

Mair, Lucille Mathurin. "Recollections of a Journey into a Rebel Past." In *Caribbean Women Writers,* ed. Selwyn Cudjoe. 51–60.

Mandeleau, Tita. *Signare Anna, ou Le voyage aux escales.* Dakar: Les Nouvelles Éditions Africaines du Sénégal, 1991.

Manigat, Leslie F. "The Relationship between Marronage and Slave Revolts and Revolution in St. Domingue-Hati." *Annals of the New York Academy of Sciences* 292 (1977): 420–38.

Markus, Julia. *Dared and Done: The Marriage of Elizabeth Barrett and Robert Browning.* New York: Alfred Knopf, 1995.

Marshall, Paule. *Brown Girl, Brownstones.* Chatham, N.J.: Chatham Bookseller, 1959.

———. *The Chosen Place, the Timeless People.* New York: Avon Books, 1969.

———. *Daughters.* New York: Atheneum, 1991.

————. "From the Poets in the Kitchen." *New York Times Book Review* 9 January 1983. 31+.

————. *Praisesong for the Widow.* New York: Putnam & Sons, 1983.

————. "Shaping the World of My Art." *New Letters* 40 (1973): 97–107.

Martin, Emily. *The Woman in the Body: A Cultural Analysis of Reproduction.* Boston: Beacon Press, 1987.

Martinez-Alier, Verena. *Marriage, Class, and Colour in Nineteenth-Century Cuba: A Study of Racial Attitudes and Sexual Values in a Slave Society.* Ann Arbor: University of Michigan Press, 1989.

Mattoso, Katia M. De Queiros. *To Be a Slave in Brazil.* New Brunswick, N.J.: Rutgers University Press, 1986.

May, Samuel. *The Fugitive Slave Law and Its Victims.* New York: American Anti-Slavery Society, 1861.

Mbiti, John S. *African Religions and Philosophy.* New York: Doubleday, 1970.

McDaniel, Lorna. *The Big Drum Ritual of Carriacou: Praisesongs in Rememory of Flight.* Gainesville: University Press of Florida, 1998.

McKay, Nellie. "'Crayon Enlargements of Life': Zora Neale Hurston's *Their Eyes Were Watching God* as Autobiography." In *New Essays on "Their Eyes Were Watching God,"* ed. Michael Awkward. Cambridge: Cambridge University Press, 1990. 51–70.

McKinney, Kitzie. "Memory, Voice, and Metaphor in the Works of Simone Schwarz-Bart." In *Postcolonial Subjects: Francophone Women Writers,* ed. Mary Jean Green et al. Minneapolis: University of Minnesota Press, 1996. 22–41.

McLaurin, Melton A. *Celia, a Slave.* Athens: University of Georgia Press, 1991.

McMaster, John, Marian Pitts, Glenrose Poyah. "The Menopausal Experiences of Women in a Developing Country—'There Is a Time for Everything—To Be a Teenager, a Mother, and a Granny.'" *Women & Health* 26, no. 4 (1997): n.p.

Montejo, Esteban. *The Autobiography of a Runaway Slave.* Ed. Miguel Barnet. Trans. Jocasta Innes. New York: Pantheon Books, 1968.

————. *Biografía de un cimarrón.* Buenos Aires: Editorial Galerna, 1968.

Moon, Bucklin, ed. *Primer for White Folks.* New York: Doubleday, 1945.

Mordecai, Pamela, and Betty Wilson, eds. *Her True-True Name: Anthology of Women's Writing from the Caribbean.* London: Heinemann, 1989.

Moreno Fraginals, Manuel. *El Ingenio: complejo económico social cubano del azúcar.* La Habana: Editorial de ciencias sociales, 1978.

Morgan, Winifred. "Gender-Related Difference in the Slave Narratives of Harriet Jacobs and Frederick Douglass." *American Studies* 35, no. 2 (1994): 73–94.

Morrison, Toni. *Beloved.* New York: Knopf, 1987.

————. *Playing in the Dark: Whiteness and the Literary Imagination.* Cambridge, Mass.: Harvard University Press, 1990.

————. "Rootedness: The Ancestor as Foundation." In *Black Women Writers (1950–1980),* ed. Mari Evans. New York: Anchor Books, 1984. 339–45.

————. "The Site of Memory." In *Inventing the Truth: The Art and Craft of Memoir,* ed. William Zinsser. Boston: Houghton Mifflin, 1987. 103–24.

————. *Song of Solomon.* New York: Knopf, 1977.

————. *Sula.* New York: Knopf, 1974.

————. *Tar Baby.* New York: Knopf, 1981.

Moura, Clóvis. *Quilombos: Resistência ao escravismo.* São Paulo: Editora Atica, 1987.

Munford, Clarence. *The Black Ordeal of Slavery and Slave Trading in the French West Indies: 1625–1715.* Vol. 2. New York: Edwin Mellen Press, 1991.

Murphy, Joseph M. *Santería: An African Religion in America.* Boston: Beacon Press, 1988.

Myerhoff, Barbara G., and Andrei Simic, eds. *Life's Career—Aging: Cultural Variations on Growing Old.* Beverly Hills: Sage Publications, 1978.

Ndiaye, Christiane. *Danses de la parole: Études sur les littératures Africaines et Antillaises.* Yaoundé, Cameroon: Nouvelles du Sud, 1996.

Newman, Judie. *The Ballistic Bard: Postcolonial Fictions.* London: Arnold, 1995.

Nichols, Grace. "I Is a Long Memoried Woman." In *The Fat Black Woman's Poems.* London: Virago Press, 1984. 53–64.

Nora, Pierre. "Between Memory and History: *Les Lieux de Mémoire.*" *Representations* 29 (spring 1989): 7–25.

Nuland, Sherwin B. *How We Die: Reflections on Life's Final Chapter.* New York: Knopf, 1994.

Nunley, John, and Judith Bettelheim. *Caribbean Festival Arts: Each and Every Bit of Difference.* Seattle: University of Washington Press, 1988.

O'Connor, Teresa F. *Jean Rhys: The West Indian Novels.* New York: New York University Press, 1986.

Oldendorp, C. G. A. *History of the Mission of the Evangelical Brethren on the Caribbean Islands of St. Thomas, St. Croix, and St. John.* Ed. Johann Jakob Bossard. Ann Arbor: Karoma, 1987.

Orr, William. "An Escape from Slavery in America." *Chambers' Edinburgh Journal* 15 March 1851: 174–75.

Palmer, Colin A. *Human Cargoes: The British Slave Trade in Spanish America, 1700–1739.* Urbana: University of Illinois Press, 1981.

Palmié, Stephan, ed. *Slave Cultures and the Cultures of Slavery.* Knoxville: University of Tennessee Press, 1995.

Parker, Bettye J. "Complexity: Toni Morrison's Women—An Interview Essay." In *Sturdy Black Bridges: Visions of Women in Literature,* ed. Roseann P. Bell et al. New York: Anchor Books, 1979. 250–57.

Parrinder, Geoffrey. *African Mythology.* New York: Peter Bedrick Books, 1987.

Patterson, Orlando. *Freedom.* Vol. 1, *Freedom in the Making of Western Culture.* New York: Basic Books, 1991.

———. "Slavery and Slave Revolts: A Socio-Historical Analysis of the First Maroon War, 1655–1740." *Social and Economic Studies* 19 (1970): 289–25.

Paul, Norman. *Dark Puritan: The Life and Work of Norman Paul.* Trans. by M. G. Smith. Kingston, Jamaica: University of the West Indies, 1963.

Perret, Delphine. "Dialogue with the Ancestors." *Callaloo* 18, no. 3 (1995): 661–62.

———. "Lire Chamoiseau." *Penser la créolité,* ed. Maryse Condé and Madeleine Cottenet-Hage. Paris: Éditions Karthala, 1995. 153–72.

Perry, Donna. "Initiation in Jamaica Kincaid's *Annie John.*" *Caribbean Women Writers,* ed. Selwyn Cudjoe. 245–53.

Perry, Ruth. *Women, Letters, and the Novel.* New York: AMS Press, 1980.

Perry, Ruth, and Martine Watson Brownley, eds. *Mothering the Mind: Twelve Studies of Writers and Their Silent Partners.* New York: Holmes & Meier, 1984.

Philip, Marlene Nourbese. "Managing the Unmanageable." In *Caribbean Women Writers.* Ed. Selwyn Cudjoe. 295–300.

Philip, Nourbese M. *Frontiers*. Stratford, Ontario: Mercury Press, 1992.

Piercy, Marge. "For Strong Women." In *The Moon Is Always Female*. New York: Alfred A. Knopf, 1981. 56–57.

Piersen, William D. "White Cannibals, Black Martyrs: Fear, Depression, and Religious Faith as Causes of Suicide among New Slaves." *The Journal of Negro History*. vol. LXII no. 2 (1977): 147–59.

Plante, David. "Jean Rhys: A Remembrance." *Paris Review* 76 (1979): 238–84.

Porter, Charles A. "Foreword: Men/Women of Letters." *Yale French Studies* 71 (1986): 1–14.

Porter, Dennis. "Of Heroines and Victims: Jean Rhys and *Jane Eyre*." *Massachusetts Review* 17, no. 3 (1976): 540–52.

Porter, Kenneth. "The Flying Africans." In *Primer for White Folks*, ed. Bucklin Moon. Garden City, N.Y.: Doubleday, Doran, and Co, 1945. 171–76.

"Possess Your Bird of Passage: The Flying Africans." http://www.oxy.edu/~tigger/fly.htm. (Accessed 2001).

Poumier Taquechel, María. "El suicido esclavo en Cuba en los años 1840." *Anuario de Estudios Americanos XLIII*. Sevilla, 1986. 69–86.

Price, Richard, ed. *Maroon Societies: Rebel Slave Communities in the Americas*. Baltimore: Johns Hopkins University Press, 1979.

Price, Richard, and Sally Price. "Shadowboxing in the Mangrove." *Cultural Anthropology* 12, no. 1 (1997): 3–36.

Prince, Mary. *The History of Mary Prince, a West Indian Slave, Related by Herself.* 1831. Ed. Moira Ferguson. London: Pandora, 1987.

Rainwater, Lee, and William L. Yancey, eds. *The Moynihan Report and the Politics of Controversy: A Transaction of Social Science and Public Policy Report*. Cambridge, Mass.: MIT Press, 1967.

Ramos, Juanita. "Latin American Lesbians Speak on Black Identity—Violeta Garro, Minerva Rose Perez, Digna, Magdalena C, Juanita." In *Moving beyond Boundaries: Black Women's Diasporas*, ed. Carole Boyce Davies. New York: New York University Press, 1995. 57–93.

Randall, Margaret. *Cuban Women Now: Interviews with Cuban Women*. Toronto: Women's Press, 1974.

———. *Sandino's Daughters: Testimonies of Nicaraguan Women in Struggle*. New Brunswick, N.J.: Rutgers University Press, 1995.

Randolph, Laura. "The Magic of Toni Morrison." *Ebony* 43 (July 1998): 100–106.

Rea, Annabelle. "Les femmes au travail dans *Lettres á une noire*." In *Elles écrivent des Antilles*, ed. Suzanne Rinne and Joëlle Vitiello. Paris: Éditions L'Harmattan, 1997. 297–306.

Reis, João José, and Eduardo Silva. *Negociação e conflito: A resistência negra no Brasil escravista*. São Paulo: Editora Schwarcz Ltda, 1989.

Renault, François. *L'abolition de l'esclavage au Sénégal*. Paris: Société Française d'Histoire d'Outre-Mer, 1972.

Research Department of the Universal House of Justice. compil. *Women*. Wilmette, Ill.: Bahá'i Publishing Trust, 1986.

Reyes, Angelita. "Christophine, Nanny, and Creole Difference: Reconsidering Jean Rhys's West Indian Landscape and *Wide Sargasso Sea*." In *On the Road to Guinea: Essays in Black Comparative Literature*, ed. Edward Ako. Yaoundé, Cameroon: Yaoundé University Press, 1993. 143–75.

————. Editorial to *Signs: Journal of Women in Culture and Society* 20 no. 4 (1995): 787–98.

————. "Rereading a Nineteenth-Century Fugitive Slave Incident: From Toni Morrison's *Beloved* to Margaret Garner's Dearly Beloved." In *Annals of Scholarship: Studies of the Humanities and Social Sciences* 7 no. 4. (1990). 464–86.

Rhys, Jean. "The Day They Burned the Books." In *The Collected Stories of Jean Rhys.* New York: Norton, 1987. 151–56.

————. *Good Morning, Midnight.* 1939. London: Penguin, 1969.

————. *Smile Please: An Unfinished Autobiography.* 1979. London: Deutsch, 1984.

————. *Voyage in the Dark.* 1934. London: Penguin Harmondsworth, 1969.

————. *Wide Sargasso Sea.* Introduction by Francis Wyndham. New York: W. W. Norton & Company, 1966.

Rich, Adrienne. *Of Woman Born: Motherhood as Experience and Institution.* New York: Norton, 1976.

Rinne, Suzanne, and Joëlle Vitiello, ed. *Elles écrivent des Antilles (Haïti, Guadeloupe, Martinique).* Paris: Éditions L'Harmattan, 1997.

Ripley, C. Peter, ed. *The Black Abolitionist Papers.* Chapel Hill: University of North Carolina Press, 1985.

Robinson, Randall. *The Debt: What America Owes to Blacks.* New York: Dutton, 2000.

Rochmann, Marie-Christine. *L'esclave fugitif dans la littérature antillaise.* Paris: Éditions Karthala, 2000.

Rose, Lionel. *The Massacre of the Innocents: Infanticide in Britain, 1800–1939.* London: Routledge & Kegan Paul, 1986.

Rosenberg, Harriet G. "Complaint Discourse, Aging, and Caregiving among the Ju/'hoansi of Botswana." In *The Cultural Context of Aging: Worldwide Perspectives,* ed. Jay Sokolovsky. Westport, Conn.: Bergin & Garvey, 1997. 33–55.

Rushdy, Ashraf H. A. "'Rememory': Primal Scenes and Constructions in Toni Morrison's Novels." *Contemporary Literature* 31 (1990): 300–323.

Sacks, Karen Brodkin. "Introduction: New Views of Middle-Aged Women." In *In Her Prime,* ed. Virginia Kerns and Judith K. Brown. Urbana: University of Illinois Press, 1992. 1–6.

Sadoff, Dianne F. "Black Matrilineage: The Case of Alice Walker and Zora Neale Hurston." *Signs* 11 no. 1 (1985): 4–26.

Said, Edward W. *Orientalism.* New York: Pantheon Books, 1978.

————. "Representing the Colonized: Anthropology's Interlocutors." *Critical Inquiry* 15, no. 2 (1989): 205–25.

Sala-Molins, Louis. *Le Code Noir.* Paris: Presses Universitaires de France, 1987.

Sanchez-Eppler, Karen. *Touching Liberty: Abolition, Feminism, and the Politics of the Body.* Berkeley: University of California Press, 1993.

Savitt, Todd L. "Smothering and Overlaying of Virginia Slave Children." *Bulletin of the History of Medicine.* 49, no. 9 (1975): 400–404.

Schattschneider, D. "The Missionary Theologies of Zinzendorf and Spangenberg." *Transactions of the Moravian Historical Society* 22 (1975): 213–33.

Schoelcher, Victor. *Des colonies françaises: abolition immédiate de l'esclavage.* 1842. Vol. 4. Basse-Terre: Société d'histoire de la Guadeloupe, 1976.

Schoepf, Johann David. *Travels in the Confederacy, 1783–1784.* Philadelphia: Campbell, 1911.

Schuckers, J. W. *The Life and Public Services of Salmon Portland Chase*. 1874. New York: DaCapo, 1970.

Schuler, Monica. *"Alas, Alas, Kongo" A Social History of Indentured African Immigration into Jamaica, 1841–1865*. Baltimore: Johns Hopkins University Press, 1980.

Schwarz-Bart, André. *La mulâtresse Solitude*. Paris: Éditions du Seuil, 1972.

Schwarz-Bart, Simone. *Between Two Worlds*. Trans. Barbara Bray. Portsmouth, N.H.: Heinemann, 1992.

———. *The Bridge of Beyond*. Caribbean Writers Series. London: Heinemann, 1982.

———. *Pluie et vent sur Télumée Miracle*. Paris: Éditions du Seuil, 1972.

———. *Ti Jean L'horizon*. Paris: Éditions du Seuil, 1979.

Schwarz-Bart, Simone, in collaboration with André Schwarz-Bart. *Hommage à la femme noire*. 6 vols. Belgium: Éditions Consulaires, 1989.

———. *Un plat de porc aux bananes vertes*. Paris: Éditions du Seuil, 1967.

Scisinio, Alaôr Eduardo. *Escravidāo & A saga de Manoel Congo*. Rio de Janeiro: Achiamé, 1988.

Scott, James C. *Domination and the Arts of Resistance: Hidden Transcripts*. New Haven: Yale University Press, 1990.

Scottron, S. R., and Henry Highland Garnet. *Cuban Anti-Slavery Committee. Slavery in Cuba: A Report of the Proceedings of the Meeting*. Cooper Institute, New York: Powers, Macgowan & Slipper, 1872.

Sears, William. *Release the Sun*. Wilmette, Ill.: Bahá'í Publishing Trust, 1995.

Segal, Ronald. *The Black Diaspora*. London: Faber and Faber, 1995.

Sells, William. *Remarks on the Condition of the Slaves in the Island of Jamaica*. 1823. Shannon, Ireland: Irish University Press, 1972.

Sensbach, Jon J. *A Separate Canaan: The Making of an Afro-Moravian World in North Carolina, 1763–1840*. Chapel Hill: University of North Carolina Press, 1998.

Sierra, Maestra. *¡dundunbanza!* London: World Circuit, 1994. WCD041AM. Compact disc recording.

Smith, Amanda. "PW Interviews: Toni Morrison." *Publishers Weekly*. 21 August 1987: 50–51.

Smith, Honor Ford, ed. *Lionheart Gal: Life Stories of Jamaican Women*. London: The Women's Press, 1986.

Smith, John David. *Black Slavery in the Americas: An Interdisciplinary Bibliography, 1865–1980*. Vol. 2. Westport, Conn.: Greenword Press, 1949.

Smith-Rosenberg, Carroll. "The Hysterical Woman: Sex Roles and Role Conflict in Nineteenth-Century America." *Social Research* 39 no. 4 (1972): 652–78.

Société Africaine de Culture, *La civilisation de la femme dans la tradition africaine*. Paris: Présence Africaine, 1975.

Sokolovsky, Jay, ed. *The Cultural Context of Aging: Worldwide Perspectives*. 2d ed. Westport, Conn.: Bergin & Garvey, 1997.

Solway, Jacqueline S. "Middle-Aged Women in Bakgalagadi Society (Botswana)." In *In Her Prime: New Views of Middle-Aged Women*, ed. Virginia Kerns and Judith K. Brown. Urbana: University of Illinois Press, 1992. 49–60.

Sourieau, Marie-Agnès. "La vie scélérate de Maryse Condé: Métissage narratif et héritage métis," In *Penser la créolité*, ed. Maryse and Madeleine Cottenet-Hage. Paris: Éditions Karthala, 1995. 113–23.

Spector, Janet D. *What This Awl Means: Feminist Archaeology at a Wahpeton Dakota Village*. St. Paul: Minnesota Historical Society Press, 1993.

Spillers, Hortense. "Mama's Baby, Papa's Maybe: An American Grammar Book." *Diacritics* 17 no. 2 (summer 1987): 65–81.

Spivak, Gayatri Chakravorty. "Three Women's Texts and a Critique of Imperialism." In *"Race," Writing, and Difference*. Chicago: University of Chicago Press, 1986. 262–80.

Stanislavsky, Konstantin. *An Actor Prepares*. 1948. Trans. Elizabeth Reynolds Hapgood. New York: Theatre Arts Book, 1965.

Stavans, Ilan. *Imagining Columbus: The Literary Voyage*. New York: Twayne Publishers, 1993.

Steady, Filomina Chioma, ed. *The Black Woman Cross-Culturally*. Cambridge: Schenkman, 1981.

Suggs, J. D. "The Flying Man." In *American Negro Folktales*, ed. Richard Dorson. Greenwich, Conn.: Fawcett, 1956.

Taylor, Susan. *In the Spirit*. New York: HarperCollins, 1994.

Thiam, Awa. *La parole aux négresse*. Paris: Denoel/Gonthier, 1978.

Thoby-Marcelin, Philippe, and Pierre Marcelin. *Contes et légendes d'Haïti*. Paris: Fernand Nathan, 1967.

Thompson, Robert Farris. *Flash of the Spirit: African & Afro-American Art & Philosophy*. New York: Vintage Books, 1984.

Thurer, Shari, L. *The Myths of Motherhood: How Culture Reinvents the Good Mother*. New York: Penguin Books, 1995.

Timothy, Helen Pyne. "About Our Name." *MaComère*. 2 (1999): i.

Tobin, Jacqueline, and Raymond G. Dobard. *Hidden in Plain View: The Secret Story of Quilts and the Underground Railroad*. New York: Bantam Books, 1999.

Toumson, Roger. "Avec Simone et André Schwarz-Bart sur les pas de Fanotte." *Textes Études et Documents*. Fort-de-France, Martinique: Éditions Caribéennes, 1979. 13–23.

Trinh T. Minh-ha. *Woman, Native, Other: Writing Postcoloniality and Feminism*. Bloomington: Indiana University Press, 1989.

Turner, Victor. *The Ritual Process*. Chicago: Aldine Publishing, 1969.

United Brethren. *Periodical Accounts Relating to the Missions of the Church of the United Brethren Established Among the Heathen*. Vols. 1–25. 1790–1865.

Universal House of Justice. *The Promise of World Peace*. Haifa: Universal House of Justice, 1985.

van Hooff, Anton J. L. *From Autothanasia to Suicide: Self-killing in the Ancient World*. London: Routledge, 1990.

Vanony-Frisch, Nicole. *Les esclaves de la Guadeloupe à la fin de l'ancien régime d'après les sources notariales (1770–1789)*. Vol. 63–64 of Basse-Terre: Bulletin de la Société d'Histoire de la Guadeloupe, 1985.

Vanzant, Iyanla. *Tapping the Power Within: A Path to Self-Empowerment for Black Women*. New York: Writers & Readers Publishing, 1992.

Vatuk, Sylvia. "Sexuality and the Middle-Aged Woman in South Asia." In *In Her Prime: New Views of Middle-Aged Women*, ed. Virginia Kerns and Judith K. Brown. Urbana: University of Illinois Press, 1992. 155–72.

Vento, Saul A. *Las Rebeldias de Esclavos en Matanzas*. La Habana: Filial de Instituto de Historia del Partido Comunista de Cuba, 1976.

Voorhoeve, Jan, and Ursy M. Lichtveld, eds. *Creole Drum: An Anthology of Creole Literature in Surinam*. New Haven: Yale University Press, 1975.

Walker, Alice. *The Color Purple.* New York: Harcourt Brace Jovanovich, 1982.

———. "A Definition of A Womanist." In *Making Face, Making Soul, Haciendo Caras: Creative and Critical Perspectives by Women of Color,* ed. Gloria Anzaldúa. San Francisco: Aunt Lute Foundation, 1990.

———. "A Letter of the Times, or Should This Sado-Masochism Be Saved?" In *The Complete Stories.* London: Women's Press, 1994. 242–47.

———. *Possessing the Secret of Joy.* New York: Harcourt Brace Jovanovich, 1992.

Walker, Keith L. "Postscripts: Mariama Bâ, Epistolarity, Menopause, and Postcoloniality." In *Postcolonial Subjects: Francophone Women Writers,* ed. Mary Jean Green et al. Minneapolis: University of Minnesota Press, 1996. 246–64.

Walters, Wendy W. "'One of Dese Mornings, Bright and Fair/Take My Wings and Cleave de Air': The Legend of the Flying Africans and Diasporic Consciousness." *MELUS* 22 no. 3 (fall 1997): 3–29.

Warner-Lewis, Maureen. "The Nkuyu: Spirit Messengers of the Kumina." *Savacou* 3 (1977): 57–82.

Warner-Vierya, Myriam. *Juletane.* Paris: Présence Africaine. 1982.

———. *Juletane.* Trans. Betty Wilson. London: Heinemann, 1987.

———. *Le quimboiseur l'avait dit.* Paris: Présence Africaine. 1980.

Warrior Marks. Directed by Pratibha Parma. Presented by Alice Walker. New York: Women Make Movies, 1993.

Washington, Mary Helen. "Paule Marshall Talking with Mary Helen Washington." In *Writing Lives,* ed. Mary Chamberlain. London: Virago Press, 1988. 161–68.

Washington Bâ, Sylvia. "Mariama Bâ and Toni Morrison: Voices Unveiled, Unhushed, and Otherwise Underground." Presentation, 22 September 1999. University of Minnesota.

Weathers, Diane. "Jamaica Kincaid: Her Small Place." *Essence.* (March 1996): 96.

Webster, Donovan. "Journey to the Heart of the Sahara." *National Geographic.* 195 no. 3 (March 1999): 2–33.

Wheeler, Leslie, ed. *Loving Warriors: Selected Letters of Lucy Stone and Henry B. Blackwell 1853–1893.* New York: Dial Press, 1981.

White, Deborah Gray. *Ar'n't I a Woman? Female Slaves in the Plantation South.* New York: Norton, 1985.

Whitehead, Neil, ed. *Wolves from the Sea: Readings in the Anthropology of the Native Caribbean.* Caribbean Series 14. Leiden, Netherlands: KITLV Press, 1995.

Wide Sargasso Sea. Directed by John Duigan. 100 mins. Fine Line Features. 1993.

Wilkinson, James. "A Choice of Fictions: Historians, Memory, and Evidence." *PMLA* 111 no. 1 (1996): 80–92.

Williams, Lorna Valerie. *The Representation of Slavery in Cuban Fiction.* Columbia: University of Missouri Press, 1994.

Williams, Sherley Anne. *Dessa Rose.* 1986. New York: Berkley Books, 1987.

Wilson, Lucy. "'Women Must Have Spunks': Jean Rhys's West Indian Outcasts." In *Critical Perspectives on Jean Rhys,* ed. Pierette Frickey. Washington, D.C.: Three Continents Press, 1990. 67–74.

Wood, Betty. "Some Aspects of Female Resistance to Chattel Slavery in Low Country Georgia, 1763–1815." *The Historical Journal* 30 (1987): 603–22.

Woolf, Virginia. *A Room of One's Own.* New York: Harcourt Brace, 1929.

Wyndham, Francis, and Diana Melly. *Jean Rhys Letters, 1931–1966.* London: Andre Deutsch, 1984.

Yadin, Yigael. *Masada: Herod's Fortress and the Zealot's Last Stand.* London: Weidfeld and Nicolson, 1966.

Yanuck, Julius. "The Garner Fugitive Slave Case." *Mississippi Valley Historical Review* 40 (1953): 47–66.

Yellin, Jean Fagan. "Text and Contexts of Harriet Jacobs' *Incidents in the Life of a Slave Girl.*" In *The Slave's Narrative,* ed. Charles T. Davis and Henry Louis Gates Jr. New York: Oxford University Press, 1985. 262–82.

Young, Sir William. *An Account of the Black Charaibs in the Island of St. Vincent's with the Charaib Treaty of 1773, and other original documents.* 1795. London: Frank Cass & Co., 1971.

Yuscaran, Guillermo (William Lewis). *Conociendo a la Gente Garífuna.* Tegucigalpa, Honduras: Nuevo Sol Publicaciónes, 1990.

Zahno, Kamila. "Ethnic Monitoring or a Geography Lesson." In *Black Women, Writing, and Identity: Migrations of the Subject,* ed. Carole Boyce Davies. New York: Routledge, 1994.

Archival Sources

The American Baptist
Anti-Slavery Bugle
Archives départmentales de la Guadeloupe
The British Friend
Cincinnati Commercial
Cincinnati Daily Enquirer
Cincinnati Daily Gazette
Cincinnati Times
Glasgow Chronicle
Edinburgh University Library
The Glasgow Courier
Glasgow Emancipation Society Minute Books
Harper's Weekly
Jamaica Archives, Spanish Town
Journals of the Assembly of Jamaica
The Liberator
Library Company of Philadelphia
Louisville Courier
National Anti-Slavery Standard
Ohio Historical Society
The Pacific Appeal
Periodical Accounts Relating to the Missions of the Church of the United Brethren Established among the Heathen
The Provincial Freeman
Rigsarkivet (Danish National Archives)
Samuel Chase Papers
Shields Family Papers
West India Collection, University of the West Indies, Mona
Yale University Libraries

Index

Cliff, Michelle: girl friendship, 42, 100, 101; grandmother image, 17, 18, 29; marronage, 2, 29, 79, 105; white Creole identity 79. *See also Abeng*
Cockpits, 80, 81, 105
Coffin, Levi, 59
Cole, Johnnetta, 14
Collective memory, 130. *See also* Memory-telling
"Collector of Treasures, The" (Head), 161
Collins, Patricia Hill, 19
Color Purple, The (Walker), 159
Comadre, 14
Condé, Maryse, 124, 130 133
Craft, Ellen and William, 57
"Crazy saints," 28, 30, 176
Creole: *Abeng* 100, 101; color prejudice, 104; consciousness: 94–96, 104; definitions of, 92–94; miscegenation in the Caribbean, 93, 94, 104. *See also* Creole Danish; *Créolité;* Jean Rhys
Creole Danish, 26, 114, 117
Créolité, 123, 124
Cuffee Ned, 106

Danticat, Edwidge, 130, 133, 181
Dash, Julie, 34
Daughters (Marshall), 55
Daughters of the Dust (Dash), 34
"Day They Burned the Books, The" (Rhys), 95
Death agony, 109; *See also* Agonal phase
de Casa Bayona, Count, 51
Decolonizing representations, 6, 8
Delgrès, Louis, 46, 126
De Tilène au Plateau ((Diallo), 17
Diallo, Nafissatou, 17
Door of no return, 144, 145. *See also* Gorée Island
Do They Hear You When You Cry? (Kassindja), 155
Douglas, Marcia, 190, 191
Douglass, Frederick, 17
Dunbar Creek, 34, 36
Durkheim, Émile, 46. *See also* Suicide

Eliade, Mircea, 71
Éloge de la créolité (In Praise of Creoleness) (Bernabé et al.), 123, 124
Emecheta, Buchi, 167
Endorphins: physiological medication, as, 109–10; purpose, 108–9
Epistolary fiction, 152, 153, 158, 159
Escape. *See* Taking flight
Estrada Hill, Apolonia, 13
Evidence in history, 21

Fancy girls, 67
Female genital cutting, 155
First educators, women as, 4, 12. *See also* First teachers
First Maroon War, 79
First mothers, 121
First teachers, 4, 11, 12
Flying Africans: defense mechanism, 46–48, 49; discussion of 37–54; euphemism for suicide, 23, 24, 38, 39; honored, 144; in marronage, 53; methods of suicide (during slavery) 41, 49; motif, in *Wide Sargasso Sea*, 78, 107, 111, 112; mystery of, 37; myth of, 44, 36, 37, 38, 41–45, 76; Nanny legends of, 78; oral story, as 40; in "The People Who Could Fly," 37; as a signifier, 54, 58; in *Song of Solomon*, 54. *See also* Return to Africa; Salt avoidance
"For strong women" (Piercy), 74
Fugitive Slave Law, 59, 62–64, 79
Fugitive slaves, 61, 62, 120, 126. *See also* Marronage

Garífuna, 14, 81
Garner, Margaret, 21, 22; death of, 64; as historical reference, 22; infanticide case, 59–70; journey of escape, 58–59; role of suicide, 23. *See also Beloved*
Gender and slavery, 21. *See also* Margaret Garner; Sarah Remond
Gender warmth, 55, 56
Gentry, Minnie, 136, 137
Gilbert, Sandra, 87
Global feminisms, 5, 147, 148, 150
Goodison, Lorna, 9, 13, 172

Angelita Reyes is associate professor and Morse Alumni Professor of Distinguished Teaching of African American and African studies at the University of Minnesota. She is the coeditor of *Global Voices: Literatures of the Non-Western World* and *African Research in Its Political and Social Dimensions*. Her areas of teaching and research encompass multicultural, African diaspora, and postcolonial studies with a focus on women and culture in Africa, the Caribbean, and the United States.